GEORGE ELIOT AND MONEY

Unlike other Victorian novelists, George Eliot rarely incorporated stock market speculation and fraud into her plots, but meditations on money, finance and economics, in relation both to individual ethics and to wider social implications, infuse her novels. This volume examines Eliot's understanding of money and economics, its bearing on her moral and political thought, and the ways in which she incorporated that thought into her novels. It offers a detailed account of Eliot's intellectual engagements with political economy, Utilitarianism, and the new liberalism of the 1870s, and also her practical dealings with money through her management of household and business finances and, in later years, her considerable investments in stocks and shares. In a wider context, it presents a detailed study of the ethics of economics in nineteenth-century England, tracing the often uncomfortable relationship between morality and economic utility experienced by intellectuals of the period.

DERMOT COLEMAN gained his doctorate at Exeter University and is a Founding Partner of SISU Capital, a London-based investment management company. He is a contributor to *George Eliot in Context* (Cambridge, 2013) and acts as a reviewer for the journal *Nineteenth-Century Literature*.

GEORGE ELIOT
AND MONEY

Economics, Ethics and Literature

DERMOT COLEMAN

CAMBRIDGE
UNIVERSITY PRESS

University Printing House, Cambridge CB2 8BS, United Kingdom

Cambridge University Press is part of the University of Cambridge.

It furthers the University's mission by disseminating knowledge in the pursuit of
education, learning and research at the highest international levels of excellence.

www.cambridge.org
Information on this title: www.cambridge.org/9781107057210

First published 2014

Printed in the United Kingdom by Clays, St Ives plc

A catalogue record for this publication is available from the British Library

Library of Congress Cataloguing in Publication data
Coleman, Dermot.
George Eliot and Money : Economics, Ethics and Literature / Dermot Coleman.
pages cm. – (Cambridge Studies in Nineteenth-Century Literature and Culture; 90)
Includes bibliographical references and index.
ISBN 978-1-107-05721-0 (hardback)
1. Eliot, George, 1819–1880 – Knowledge – Economics.
2. Money in literature. 3. Ethics in literature. I. Title.
PR4692.E25C65 2013
823'.8–dc23
2013039529

ISBN 978-1-107-05721-0 Hardback

Contents

Acknowledgements

I wrote my first essay on George Eliot in my entrance examination for University College, Oxford and spelled her name (consistently) wrong throughout. Despite this, Helen Cooper and Roy Park let me in and I thank them both for helping to inspire a passion for the subject of this book that has endured since those undergraduate years. I am also very grateful for Helen's advice and support when I first contemplated a return to academic study after many years in the investment world. Having made that decision, the late Sally Ledger and Ella Dzelzainis encouraged me not only to advance those studies but also to do so under the inspirational guidance of Regenia Gagnier. I could not have hoped for a better mentor and I thank her with all my heart. Regenia stands in the vanguard of a veritable army of nineteenth-century literary scholars whose words, spoken and written, have informed and inspired me in this project. But I would like to record particular thanks to Nancy Henry, Claire Pettit, Helen Small and Paul Young for the time, guidance and encouragement they have so generously given me and for the kindness and humour with which those gifts were delivered. Janette Rutterford has been an invaluable source of economic and financial historical information. I am also indebted to Grant Jones and Andrew Spink QC for their opinions on Victorian bankruptcy and insolvency law.

Part of this book considers character and virtue in specific relation to economic action and it would be remiss of me to pass over the opportunity to thank the many friends and colleagues in the financial industry who, individually and collectively, embody those very virtues. My business partner, Joy Seppala, has been unfailingly supportive of my decision to follow this path, a characteristic generosity of spirit for which I will always be grateful. She, along with other present and past colleagues, has helped me form and develop many financially related ideas. In particular, I thank David Mills and Justin Fitzsimmons for their economic and historical insights respectively. Beyond our own firm, John Cummins also illustrates well the value of a wide-ranging historical perspective now sadly lacking in the senior management of many major financial institutions. John Smith and Stephen Phipps have imparted most useful specifically economic historical wisdom. A perusal of the latter's extensive library in this field was more often than not followed by a most convivial and enlightening lunch. Convivial lunches and dinners have long been the sites of regular meetings with three friends, all of whom started within a year or two of me at the venerable stockbroking firm of de Zoete and Bevan. Having survived the many financial crises of the nineteenth century, de Zoete is now sadly departed but our friendship and laughter survive. Nick Collier, Martin Daws and Nick Gregory may be a little surprised to hear that they have contributed to this book but I can assure them they have helped me in ways beyond telling.

I would like to thank those staff who patiently assisted me in my research at the University of Exeter Library, the British Library, the London Library, the Guildhall Library, the Beinecke Library, Yale, and the Berg Collection at the New York Public Library. Individual thanks go to Simon Blundell, librarian at the Reform Club, Alice-Ford Smith at the Dr Williams's Library and Ms L. J. Pilkington, librarian at Marlborough College. Linda Bree, Anna Bond and Jonathan Ratcliffe at Cambridge University Press have been patient and expert guides through the complexities of the modern-day 'commerce of literature', while Katherine Fender's late assistance was invaluable.

My final thanks go to my extended and immediate family, all of whom have been wonderfully supportive of my decision to undertake this project and extraordinarily indulgent of its demands on my time and attention. I thank them all and apologise for the many times I seemed to drift out of this world, alternatively known as 'doing a George'. My greatest debts are to Tilda, Oonagh, Gabriel and Bede and, especially, to Tessa who has lived for so long with another, albeit long-dead woman in our lives.

Introduction

Starting with some simple definitions, I will refer to 'money' as both a measurable store of material value and a commonly accepted (and to some extent guaranteed) medium of exchange; by 'finance' I mean that which pertains to money, including the institutions and instruments by which it is held, traded and dispersed; and 'the economic' I take to be that which, theoretically or practically, relates to the personal or communal management of money or finance. Considering our understanding of each concept today relative to the Victorian period, it appears the first has become globally accepted and, via currency convertibility, homogenised; the second and third are much more complex. Which should at least cause us to consider exactly why we care about what any nineteenth-century writer, let alone the author of provincial, largely historical novels, has to say on the subject.

History, as Mark Twain reminds us, if not exactly repeating itself, tends to rhyme and the economic historical lessons of the Victorian period certainly continue to resonate powerfully. Several years ago I largely withdrew from the investment management business I had co-founded at the end of the last century. My departure coincided with precipitous falls in the value of many financial assets, as problems stemming from the over-expansion of lending in the 'sub-prime' mortgage market in the United States escalated into a full-blown banking crisis, the economic aftershocks of which are still being felt. A number of investors in my company's hedge funds credited me with a quite unwarranted level of prescience. Like most people in the industry, I did not see it coming, even though my relative knowledge of Victorian history and literature should have given me a distinct prophetic edge. Had I, for example, paid a little more attention to David Morier Evans's description of the causes of the 1857 banking crisis, I might have deduced an uncanny relevance to events exactly 150 years later:

> In the lenders there was utter recklessness in making advances; in the borrowers unparalleled avidity in profiting by the occasion; and thus an unwieldy edifice

of borrowed capital was erected ready to topple down on the first shock given to that confidence which was, in fact, its sole foundation. Such a shock was given by the American failures – this was the result of the same system, carried to a still more mischievous excess – and then the panic began.[1]

What follows is neither an economic history nor a presentist reflection on the financial landscape and events during the second and third quarters of the nineteenth century. But it is a useful starting point to remember that financial crises and attendant economic disruption recurred frequently throughout the period this book will cover. This pattern created an uncertainty that framed Victorian debates on the nature of wealth as surely as the current economic turmoil has brought into increasing prominence questions of individual, social and corporate financial responsibility. Recent calls from religious leaders and secular politicians of all shades for the formulation of 'moral capitalism' represent the economic counterpart of the revived concept of the 'two nations' which has been appropriated by both major parties in the British political arena.

History does indeed seem to be rhyming, but returning to my opening question, what should be the focus of our specific study of money and the Victorian novel? Terry Eagleton's comment concerning the recently published correspondence of two prominent modern-day novelists is certainly worth bearing in mind as we address that question: 'It is a Romantic delusion to suppose that writers are likely to have something of interest to say about race relations, nuclear weapons or economic crisis simply by virtue of being writers.'[2] Much of *George Eliot and Money* will argue that Eliot had many things of interest to say about money and the economic; if not historical crises per se, then certainly the psychological and moral conditions that, underlying all individual financial actions, give rise to wider economic outcomes. My specific work on Eliot, however, is predicated on a more general thesis that the realist novel in the mid- to late nineteenth century had a unique and central role as a critical interrogator of the developing money economy. Indeed, the novel genre itself was a rapidly expanding product of that economy, its cost of production falling as its market penetration (supply- and demand-led) increased. Tamara Wagner, in a wide-ranging analysis of both canonical and now barely read nineteenth-century novels, has shown that the incorporation of financial speculation plots, the sheer proliferation of which undoubtedly reflected the fascination and insatiable demand of the readership, was much more than a 'monolithic' fictional restatement of either actual economic events or the moral debates they ignited. If this was a unique period in the development of market-driven financial capitalism, it was an equally formative and transformative period for the novel. While financial instability was both a symptom and an effect of the former, the latter embraced the motifs and metaphors of uncertainty in a pervasively speculative world and reshaped them at each stage of the novel's evolution and across its various sub-genres. As Wagner nicely summarises the complex interrelationship:

> There is much more to literature's use of the stock market than a mere reflection of contemporary financial crises alone. It formed a new cultural imaginary that expressed changing ideas of moral probity and indeterminate identity, creditworthiness and the management of financial risks, the experience of instability and the contesting strategies to consider its repercussions at home and abroad.[3]

Economic historians too have noted the importance of the 'crossovers' between the various written forms, factual and fictional, which 'brought the seemingly unrelated worlds of finance and literary culture together, normalizing and naturalizing the operations of the financial world within the minds of the British public'.[4]

The period's greatest financially related novels are those that explore the interconnections of ethics and economics in psychologically satisfying ways. It was notable that the uncovering of elaborate fraudulent schemes during our own recent financial crisis brought detailed comparisons between their perpetrators and those fictional characters that have retained a particularly vivid existence in the cultural imagination, Merdle and Melmotte. The authority with which Dickens and Trollope incorporated financial plots and used them to explore the ambiguities of economic ethics in part reflected their personal acquaintance not only with finance and the theories of political economy but also with the relatively small group of individuals both developing and contesting those theories. George Eliot also met these intellectual and personal criteria, yet her novels have largely stood outside this critical tradition, even though money undoubtedly pervades her fiction on many layers. This may partly be because stock market speculation features little in her work, but also, I suspect, because critical orthodoxy associates women novelists either with the 'silver fork' sub-genre or, even in the case of more canonical figures, outside the masculine orbit of money and economic knowledge. The error of such an omission is compounded by the fact that Eliot became wealthy through sales of her books and successfully invested most of those proceeds into the stock market. An absence of a wide-ranging study on Eliot and money seemed to me, as I started my research, anomalous.

Early in that process I came across two interesting quotations from George Eliot scholars. The first is from the editors of *The Journals of George Eliot*, explaining in their introduction to the 1879 diary: 'While information about her investment income and various expenditures has a certain interest, these extensive financial memoranda have not been reproduced in the text of this journal.'[5] The second is William Baker's assertion that the fact that specifically economic texts comprise only 1 per cent of the Eliot–Lewes collection at the Dr Williams's Library 'seems to attest to [their] lack of interest in the subject'.[6] Harris and Johnston's omission, I believed, was significant and Baker's conclusion somewhat misleading. Both encouraged me that my broad, though somewhat unformed, project held promise.

In fact it was the reaction to the unfurling of our own century's financial crisis, as much as my growing understanding of Eliot's own writings in their cultural, intellectual and economic context, that brought a clearer focus and structure to my work. In particular, there was universal agreement in the main opinion-forming media that events were, at least in part, the result of the practically flawed theoretical assumptions and methodology of hegemonic neoclassical economics and its somewhat exclusive academic trajectory. The *Financial Times* newspaper ran a major series entitled 'The Future of Capitalism', which included contributions from a range of prominent academic and business figures from within finance and much further afield, including moral philosophy.[7] Tellingly, it was the *FT*'s highly respected and veteran economic commentator Samuel Brittan who concluded his contribution to that series (1 May, 2009): 'I know that some financial types hate their subject being mixed up with alien topics such as the study of English literature. Yet more is to be learnt from the novelist Jane Austen ... than from modern tomes on business ethics.'

Brittan is making the case for the novel as a powerful ethical medium, but, more specifically, the novel from a period when that form lay at the centre of cultural transfer. Twenty-first-century novelists did indeed respond to the financial crisis, but their sales and impact on public understanding paled against reportage and analysis from financial journalists, economists, sociologists and even anthropologists.[8] In fact, the events of 2008, served to accelerate and fortify an emerging trend in the cultural understanding of economics that had already seen the enormous popular success of books including *Freakonomics* and *The Undercover Economist*.[9] From a different perspective, Diane Coyle's *The Soulful Science: What Economists Really Do and Why it Matters* is a robust defence of the discipline, describing a 'hidden humanization' of creative and socially focused economics.[10] In short, an increasingly accepted need to overlay theoretical assumptions with behavioural understanding and empirical observation was accompanied by a growing call for economics to reconnect with the moral philosophical roots from which its modern form sprang in the late eighteenth century. And practitioners from both disciplines have indeed taken up the call. Since 2010, the following self-explanatory titles have appeared from eminent scholars across the moral and social sciences: *The Price of Civilization: Economics and Ethics After the Fall*; *What Money Can't Buy: The Moral Limits of Markets*; *How Much is Enough? The Love of Money, and the Case for the Good Life*; and *Finance and the Good Society*.[11] They leave little doubt as to the direction of one of the most pressing topics in contemporary academic, political and wider social debate.

Such a reconnection would also seem to open the way for literary studies to contribute significantly as a cultural prism through which psychology and ethics, as they relate to economic motivation and action, can be better understood. Again, recent work by economists including Richard Bronk, George Akerlof and Robert Shiller would suggest that the profession itself, or at least a growing number of its participants, is responsive to such a trend.[12] Bronk's call for a more overt infusion of creativity and imagination into neoclassical economics builds on the earlier work of Philip Mirowski and Deidre McCloskey in recognising the metaphorical and rhetorical underpinnings of all economic exchange.[13]

These various calls for economically focused interdisciplinarity are effectively seeking ways to reassess how value, in both an individual and a social context, is theorised, located and promoted. The strapline of the long-running advertising campaign from the high-net-worth, private banking division of Barclays asks: 'Wealth. What's it to you?' The range of answers provided by the advertisers largely deal in non-material, even intangible concepts: time, travel, giving choice to one's children, seclusion, reverting to a state of childlike enjoyment. Very few actually mention money, and even then only to suggest transcendence of the material: 'Going to places where money ceases to matter.' In summation, the copywriters have added very little to John Ruskin's conclusion back in 1862 that 'There is no wealth but life.' Eliot respected Ruskin but was dismissive of his economics; the link prompted me to turn the question in Eliot's direction and ask: 'Wealth. What was it to her?' I became increasingly confident that answering (or at least attempting to answer) that question would provide greater insight into her thought and a richer understanding of the complex ways money and the economic are treated within the novels.

Nineteenth-century political economy sought to answer the question posed by Barclays definitively, but, as I will discuss throughout this book, the question kept recurring, in progressively complex and urgent formulations, throughout the period of Eliot's writing life. In so doing, it crucially

informed the development of the novel genre. This may partially explain why
the literary scholarship of that period has developed in directions that are
particularly relevant for my work. Martha Woodmansee and Mark Osteen's
important collection, *The New Economic Criticism: Studies at the Intersection of
Literature and Economics* appeared in 1999, with contributions from many
scholars active in nineteenth-century studies. The collection was the outcome
of mounting interest in a topic that spanned a number of academic departments over the previous decade, marking an interdisciplinarity that has
continued to thrive.[14] Donald Winch, in his work on the intellectual history
of British political economy in the nineteenth century, signals economic
criticism's enduring influence in his welcome acknowledgement 'that the
engagement of literary historians with the serious economic literature of the
past is moving beyond the old stereotypes, making rapprochement with
intellectual histories of economic debate possible'.[15]

Patrick Brantlinger, Regenia Gagnier, Catherine Gallagher and Mary
Poovey are prominent among a large and widening group of predominantly
nineteenth-century literary scholars who have incorporated the economic
into aesthetic, ethical and epistemological meditations on literature that go
far beyond the more narrow, ideologically driven interpretations that characterised the previous generation of critics in this field. As a group, they are
methodologically diverse and each comes to different conclusions as to
exactly how literary writers engaged with and incorporated political economic writing, and how those connections influenced the wider cultural
imagination. However, their knowledge and understanding of how crucial
economic transitions – from the evolution of paper money at one end of the
century to the emergence of a demand-led, marginal utility theory of value
at the other – infuse literature and underpin cultural formation have added
greatly to study in this field. More recent works by Deanna Kreisel and
Eleanor Courtemanche exemplify how the analysis of literary and economic
interconnections continues to develop in interesting directions.[16] Kreisel's
readings of the themes and narrative structures of two novels each by
George Eliot and Thomas Hardy illuminate an anxiety linked to contemporary demand theories of value and their implications for the creation of
surpluses and economic stagnation. One of Kreisel's starting points is an
analysis of the language and metaphors employed by the political economists. Courtemanche drills down into the most famous image of the whole
economic canon: Adam Smith's 'invisible hand' metaphor which, she
argues, is more fully worked-out through the narratorial shifts and multiple
perspectives of the best Victorian novels. 'Realist fiction', she concludes,
'both draws on and improves Smith's understanding of social complexity'.[17]

The development of industrial capitalism in nineteenth-century Britain gave rise to a rapid expansion of financial forms and institutions. Contextual literary studies of the period, including by those writers mentioned above, have illuminated the multiple connections between these products of capitalism and Victorian literature. Literature itself became immersed in the process of production, sales and marketing and thereby gave rise to a new form of capital, intellectual property, whose value and duration were uncertain and shifting, and whose very ownership was contested. Under these changing external conditions, which fundamentally affected George Eliot's career and art, the economies of authorship and the book took on layers of meaning that have been perceptively unravelled in recent critical works.[18] Important deliberations on genre by, among others, John Guillory and, more recently, Mary Poovey have considered the historical process whereby literary and non-literary writing become differentiated and ranked.[19] Aesthetic value and, ultimately, canonicity are interrogated against the sometimes conflicting forces of the market. Within that market, the physical object of the book enters the realm of the commodity, and Victorian materiality, in its constant, if continually shifting dialogue with literary fiction has been a further rich source of critical debate.[20] In this context, Simon R. Frost's recent work offers a detailed 'commodity reading' of *Middlemarch*, focusing on how the novel was received by its early readers from an explicitly economic perspective.[21]

This condensed snapshot of the various intersections of literature and economics in nineteenth-century criticism pre-empts the more specific consideration of where George Eliot scholarship stands within this broad area. Many important historicist and contextual studies have greatly enriched our understanding of the intellectual, artistic and cultural background within which she wrote: factors that crucially shaped Eliot's thought and art. Science, sociology, religion, history, music and the visual arts have been particularly well served in this regard. Kreisel is unusual in explicitly recognising Eliot's economic literacy and relates her theoretical understanding to the early novels, but, with the exception of Alexander Welsh's *George Eliot and Blackmail* – which extends to a wider consideration of the price and value of information in a modernising society – there has been no single major Eliot study with an explicitly economic theme.[22] While this is somewhat surprising, critics have increasingly incorporated economic considerations into their wider thematic studies of Eliot. Her life and work often feature prominently in more general works of theory, genre and contextual analysis exploring the complex interrelationships between economics and Victorian culture and literature.

Neither have her biographers, from Gordon Haight to Rosemary Ashton and, most recently, Nancy Henry, ignored the detailed financial information that record and measure her expanding wealth.[23] Feminist and Marxist critics have extracted this information to reach varied interpretations of Eliot's position in the patriarchal hierarchy of Victorian publishing. Gillian Beer and Deirdre David have each contributed perceptive and, for me, invaluable analyses of how gender shaped Eliot's particular character as an independent economic agent and a public intellectual.[24] And more recently, critics including Rosemary Boddenheimer and Clare Pettitt have presented nuanced considerations of how she attempted to reconcile values in her private and public lives.[25] While details of her literary earnings and the publishing deals that produced them have been discussed by biographers and critics, it was not until Nancy Henry's *George Eliot and the British Empire* (2002) that Eliot's stock market investments were discussed in any meaningful detail.[26] Like Henry, I have pored over the Eliot–Lewes portfolios and dividend receipts with, however, a little more focus on how these developed after John Cross began to advise the couple in the early 1870s. I share what I believe to be Henry's opinion – that an understanding of how Eliot valued her financial capital has bearing not only on her concepts of wider forms of human and social capital. I also believe it helps support my central thesis that, for her, the economic was essentially constitutive of a comprehensive ethical understanding.

Well before the 'turn to ethics' in literature that the work of Martha Nussbaum and others helped direct some twenty years ago,[27] there had been a long tradition of Eliot criticism that centrally located her moral philosophic questioning, if not vision, at the heart of the novels and her literary art. Moral philosophy in the nineteenth century was, as Alasdair MacIntyre reminds us, much more directly influential on social and political formation than is the case today, so its incorporation into Eliot's work is seminal to the main thesis of this book.[28] Building on F. R. Leavis's work, Bernard Paris's *Experiments in Life* (1965) is a study of 'her intellectual development and of the ways in which she employed her novels in her quest for values in a Godless universe'.[29] William Myres, Valerie Dodd, Elizabeth Deeds Ermath and K. M. Newton all fall broadly within this tradition, which reads the novels as 'work[ing] out in concrete and dramatic terms problems of a broadly philosophical and moral nature'.[30] Barbara Hardy's assessment is that: 'She could have been, and nearly was, a Victorian sage, like John Stuart Mill, Carlyle or Spencer, but she became an artist who extended and re-imagined her emotional experience, which, as her characters insist, is not separable from the intellectual life.'[31] The most recent addition to this particular field is Avrom Fleishman's impressively wide-ranging intellectual history of Eliot, which focuses particularly on her extensive reading.[32]

The extent to which she directly or implicitly incorporates the theories of the many moral philosophers with whose work she was intimately acquainted has always been, and remains, a source of critical debate. Largely absent from the moral philosophical line of Eliot scholarship, however, is any detailed consideration of what I will call economic ethics. Again, given the Smithean origins of nineteenth-century political economy and the fact that many of its greatest practitioners, including Mill and Henry Sidgwick, were equally celebrated as moral philosophers, the omission is puzzling.

Against this critical background, I attempt to pull a number of divergent threads together to address two primary questions: 'How did Eliot conceptualise economic value within her broader individual and social ethics?' and 'How was the integration of economic and wider "good" tested and measured within the novels?' The structure within which I address these questions is contained within three distinct yet related sections. The largely biographical first section leads onto three central chapters which contain close readings of several of the novels. The final section returns to a more general consideration of the economic bearings in Eliot's sociology and political thought.

Framing and addressing my questions demands some chronological structure in order to track Eliot's progression from the years ahead of the novels all the way to her final written statements; a long period which saw remarkable changes in how economics was theorised and dramatic developments in her own life and material circumstances. The fact that by the beginning of the 1860s she was wealthy and becoming wealthier each year served to bring a particular focus to all questions of valuation, not least concerning her own work. My first three chapters, therefore, have a strong biographical element, although I attempt in each to lay foundations for themes I develop, by way of reference to the essays and novels, in later chapters.

The opening chapter looks at George Eliot in relation to the 'science' of political economy as it developed over her lifetime and argues that she was much better theoretically informed and engaged than most criticism acknowledges. I establish some of the roots of her domestically forged economic ethics, which were in part shaped by the tales and popular instruction of writers including Harriet Martineau and Jane Marcet. As she matured, I trace seminal and lifelong intellectual connections with Adam Smith and John Stuart Mill. Her position as a figure that bridged the older (female) genre of the moral fable of political economy with the new (male) increasingly professionalised social science was cemented when, later in her life, she became acquainted with a number of influential theorists, including Walter Bagehot, Henry Sidgwick, Henry Fawcett, Sir Henry Maine and William Stanley Jevons. She was, I argue, familiar with the growing rifts in the emerging profession during the third quarter of the century. The economic content I present is not technically difficult and it is made relevant to her life and works; for example, I illustrate how she incorporated (and effectively critiqued) some core elements of Ricardian deductive theory into the novels.

Chapter 2 extends Eliot's economic understanding into the application of that knowledge in her private life, largely by reference to her letters and essays. Her rapidly gained wealth in the early 1860s and its diversion into the stock market (at a much greater level than, for example, either Dickens or Trollope, despite their higher earnings) influenced how she perceived various interconnected forms of capital and their attendant risks which, I will argue, progressively influenced the production and content of the novels. As an unmarried woman, the independence she achieved through her professional earnings was extended by her ability to legally own and manage her invested assets in her own name. I describe the evolution and development of her unusually well-balanced and diversified investment portfolio, a process in which, despite the influence of Lewes and subsequently John Cross, I believe she played a very active role. The chapter describes a lifelong abhorrence of debt and financial imprudence and traces how her questioning of the adequacy and limits of economic liberalism, to which I return in Chapter 8, was becoming informed by a new and illuminating personal perspective.

Eliot's shifting and developing quest for values changes location in Chapter 3 to 'the commerce of literature' and her attempts to reconcile her art with the high financial rewards it was generating. Eliot died just two years before the year in which George Gissing set *New Grub Street*, by which time 'your successful man of letters … thinks first and foremost of the markets; when one kind of goods begins to go off slackly, he is ready with something new and appetizing'.[33] I describe how her particular career progression gave her a somewhat unique perspective on the debates and crucial developments around book pricing, copyright and intellectual property in the third quarter of the century. Eliot's personal development in this context is considered by focusing on a pivotal point in her relationship with her publisher and a negotiation that transformed her financial situation: the publication terms for *The Mill on the Floss* in 1859. Clare Pettitt believes that

Eliot hereafter 'lost no time in disengaging herself from the economic world of publishing, choosing rather to represent her own fiction as a moral form of "good work"'.[34] My conclusion is less clear-cut: I believe an inability fully to reconcile these elements personally gave the economic ethics she tested in the novels an extraordinary urgency and complexity.

The central chapters primarily comprise readings of the three final major novels, with backward- and forward-looking glances to *The Mill on the Floss* and *Impressions of Theophrastus Such*. The latter, her final completed work, contains many fragmented meditations on various ways of how best to be rich and live life well. This includes 'A Half Breed', which plots the evaporation of Mixtus's 'old ideal of a worthy life', leaving him 'indistinguishable from the ordinary run of moneyed and money-getting men'.[35] The collision of often uncontrollable economic forces and personal ideals lies at the heart of all the novels I discuss in this section. My contention, which defines the structure of these three chapters, is that the motivations and actions by which her characters attempt to manage economic choice simultaneously parallels and is contained within competing contemporary ethical systems. Each chapter begins by establishing Eliot's understanding of and level of intellectual alignment to each of these systems (broadly Utilitarianism, Kantianism, Aristotelianism), which I then illustrate and expand through readings of individual novels.

Chapters 4 and 5, therefore consider Eliot's testing of the nature and limitations of economic ethics as they relate first to Utilitarianism and then to a deontological alternative, informed by Kant but tracing an English line to T. H. Green. Green is an interesting and somewhat problematic figure who reappears in Chapter 8 in relation to Eliot's political thought. He and Eliot are unlikely allies in the fields of either moral or political philosophy, but I trace various sympathetic intellectual connections in both, which serve to illustrate the difficulties and dangers of attempting to neatly categorise Eliot's thought. My reading of *Felix Holt* in Chapter 4 explicitly links Utilitarianism with classical economics and contextualises Eliot's critique of both against significant developments in the intellectual history of both schools, as most notably articulated by Mill. I argue that during the 1860s and 1870s she recognised the emergence of a tendency in economic thought towards greater system and mathematical quantification which, both independently and in its appropriation of Utilitarian ethics, ultimately threatened the line of morally informed political economy which connects Smith and the post-Benthamite Mill. It is this recognition that informs her depiction of the 'calculating agents' that pervade *Felix Holt*, threatening individual and social moral erosion.

While deontological ethics has no such closely linked economic relation, my reading of *Middlemarch* in Chapter 5 attempts to measure the actions and development of a number of the novel's characters against Kantian principles and, thereby, give an insight into Eliot's weighing of specifically economic ethics. I trace a somewhat ambivalent attitude to Kant, but argue that Eliot's search for 'the moral motive', a concept at the heart of Kant's deontology and notably absent from ends-based Utilitarianism, was central and critical to her own ethical theory. As in Chapter 4, my subsequent reading of the novel (here *Middlemarch*) focuses closely on particular characters (most substantively Dorothea and Lydgate) thinking and making decisions about money in both neutral and more morally charged situations. It thereby reinforces my claim for Eliot's brand of psychologically insightful realist novel as an enlightening ethical medium.

My conclusion in Chapter 5 is that Eliot's criticism of Kant lies not in what his ethics teaches, but in what it leaves out. What Ladislaw describes as Dorothea's 'fanaticism of sympathy' is a flaw that precludes the attainment of a wider personal thriving or flourishing. The required corrective is in the direction of classical concepts of eudaimonism, which I believe informed Eliot's ethics as surely as they were rejected within Kant's. In Chapter 6 I consider how she came to prioritise an essentially Aristotelian ethics of virtue above any rule-based system of either duty or outcome. I show how in *The Mill on the Floss* and *Daniel Deronda* (works at either end of her career as a novelist) economic, or what McCloskey calls the bourgeois virtues, are incorporated to varying degrees by characters striving, sometimes unwittingly, for a wider concept of the good life. I include at the end of the book an appendix describing Edward Tulliver's descent into and emergence from financial insolvency, details of which are somewhat obscure in the text. I conclude that the long-standing assumption that Tulliver became bankrupt is technically incorrect.

My final two chapters – the most speculative – look out beyond individual ethical choice to consider how Eliot's social and political vision accommodated the economic and its attendant institutions. Chapter 7 breaks the largely chronological series of the previous section by stepping back to an earlier work, *Romola*, the only one of her novels set in the distant past. Eliot's analysis of an essentially proto-capitalist society to illustrate interconnections between social networks and economic behaviour – both individual and collective – embodies one of her later stated aims as a novelist, to imaginatively work out 'how institutions arose'.[36] It also supports Bruce Mazlish's ambitious assertion that Eliot was an important link bridging the emerging field of late nineteenth-century British sociology and its leading European practitioners, Durkheim and Weber, at the beginning of the twentieth.[37] The link is underpinned by Eliot's close acquaintance with the main intellectual foundations of British and European sociology through her readings of Auguste Comte, Herbert Spencer, Mill and Wilhelm von Riehl, which I consider here.

Chapter 8 returns to some of the themes introduced in Chapter 1 and attempts to, as it were, extract the 'political' from political economy. Largely by reference to contemporary economic theory and policy, I posit a connection between Eliot and the new liberalism which was starting to emerge in the final years of her life. A connection with one of that movement's most important theorists, T. H. Green, is again made here. I argue that her moral and sociological concerns were informed by essentially political questions around the role of the state in the governance of individual citizens and that, moreover, these questions fundamentally hinged on aspects of economic duty and responsibility. The arguments are supported by reference to the essays and short fiction, particularly 'Brother Jacob', as well as the novels. A complete political characterisation remains elusive, but I firmly conclude that her conception of individual self-realisation is contingent on its reconciliation with the promotion of the common good, supported, if necessary, by state intervention.

CHAPTER I

'A subject of which I know so little': George Eliot and political economy

> Among the delusions which at different periods have possessed themselves of the minds of large masses of the human race, perhaps the most curious – certainly the least creditable – is the modern *soi-distant* science of political economy, based on the idea that an advantageous code of social action may be determined irrespective of the influence of social affection.[1]
>
> – John Ruskin, 1860

> We shall then find that our political economy is not a questionable thing of unlimited extent, but a most certain and useful thing of limited extent. By marking the frontier of our property we shall learn its use, and we shall have a positive and reliable basis for estimating its value.[2]
>
> – Walter Bagehot, 1876

The years in which George Eliot wrote her novels – broadly circumscribed by the quotations above – coincided with heightened and increasingly diverse challenges to both the methodology and the practical scope of political economy. The spirit of Ruskin's criticism was not unique but, as a theoretical economic challenge, it still, in 1860, had the air of a voice in the wilderness. Indeed, the loud and widespread opposition that greeted *Unto this Last* gave little indication of the fractures that were about to emerge, as principles which had come to saturate political and wider social thought through the middle half of the century were called into question. An 1862 review of Ruskin's work in the *Westminster Review* offers a representative reassertion of the definitive and overarching claims of classical economics. The role of the economist, the reviewer argues, is limited to the investigation and deduction of 'the laws which have regulated and do regulate' the production of wealth. The process is described in overtly scientific terms, with any socially grounded, normative complications firmly proscribed: 'Economists have no direct concern with what ought to regulate either consumption or production.'[3]

While the economic theories of Ruskin remained, at least in Eliot's lifetime, largely isolated from the mainstream, by the time Bagehot began what was to be his last and unfinished major work on political economy in 1876, the terms of the debate had changed markedly. In a preface to a later edition of 'The Postulates', Alfred Marshall wrote that Bagehot's work 'promised to make a landmark in the history of economics, by separating the use of the older, or Ricardian, economic reasonings from their abuse, and freeing them from the discredit into which they had fallen through being often misapplied'.[4] In the final years of George Eliot's life, Bagehot was one of a number of eminent political economists attempting to reformulate a 'science', which, he believed, '[lay] dead in the public mind'.[5] As Donald Winch argues in his analysis of what he describes (referencing Ruskin's famous maxim) as 'the conflict between wealth and life', the debate was no longer limited to those either in favour of or opposed to the material precepts of classical economics: 'it also took place *within* political economy'.[6]

In tracing some elements of this external and internal conflict, this chapter will argue, largely by reference to her letters and essays, that George Eliot was more knowledgeable of the emerging theoretical battle lines than has been acknowledged by most critics and biographers. The first economic writings of Ruskin in the early 1860s and the later reactions of the emerging profession itself to the mathematical and historical methodological challenges to mainstream Ricardianism, largely as reinterpreted by John Stuart Mill, neatly bookend Eliot's career as a novelist. Subsequent chapters will relate contemporary developments in economic thought to Eliot's morally and intellectually informed responses in readings of the novels. These readings locate attempts to test the ethical implications and complications of money-related attitudes, choices and actions.

This approach is informed by what David Carroll has described as the 'crisis of interpretation' which characterised the mid- to late Victorian period and which he believes Eliot's novels exploit and uniquely investigate. As political economy sought to shed, or at least refashion its deductive heritage amid competing theoretical and policy-led factions, it faced its own 'crisis of interpretation' which mirrors Carroll's wider hypothesis. Eliot's novels, he argues, show that 'strict deduction is not possible in human affairs, and it is in the inevitable discrepancy between the desire for a comprehensive explanatory scheme and particular, recalcitrant circumstances that the energy and challenge of George Eliot's fiction are to be found'.[7] The contention here – and it is one that is central to this whole work – is that the economic was a complex, yet integral component of Eliot's conception of 'human affairs' and a focus of her exploratory art.

In the last decade of her life, as her sphere of intellectual influence widened, Eliot and Lewes's personal acquaintance with men including

Bagehot, Henry Sidgwick, Henry Fawcett, Sir Henry Maine and William Stanley Jevons – all of whom influenced, through their various fields, the development of economic thought during the period – contributed to her understanding of that process. Later discussion will consider how the critiques of contemporary culture that appear in her post-1870 writings attempt to mediate value in the realms of non-financial capital (social, cultural, human and intellectual) in terms directly related to, if not always directly compatible with, contemporary neoclassical theories of supply and demand. However, political economy pervaded Eliot's thought well before her own wealth and increasing intellectual capital brought a more personal focus to questions of valuation. Her life spanned a period of extraordinary developments in economic theory. She was born just two years after David Ricardo's *On the Principles of Political Economy and Taxation* (1817) formalised the teachings of Adam Smith for a new post-war generation. Within ten years of her death, Marshall's *Principles of Economics* had taken the discipline to such a recognisably modern form that John Maynard Keynes could look back on its author as: 'the first great economist pur sang that there ever was; the first who devoted his life to building up the subject as a separate science, standing on its own foundations with as high standards of scientific accuracy as the physical or biological sciences'.

Keynes goes on to compare this newly professionalised and singularly male world of economic science with those who popularised a simplified version of political economy earlier in the century:

> It was Marshall who finally saw to it that 'never again will a Mrs Trimmer, a Mrs Marcet, or a Miss Martineau earn a goodly reputation by throwing economic principles into the form of a catechism or of simple tales, by aid of which any intelligent governess might make clear to the children nestling round her where lies economic truth.'[8]

The dismissal of the work of Martineau and Marcet is patronising and unfair, but by pointing to the schematic limitations of the moral-fabular genre, Keynes unwittingly hints at the possibilities of a different type of fiction opening up a richer understanding of 'economic truth'. This was one of the achievements of Eliot the novelist who, by the time she turned to fiction, was already bridging the gap between her early economic understanding and the developing social science with whose theories and main practitioners she was becoming progressively acquainted. Whether that youthful understanding was formed by the secular female populisers or the religiously inspired proponents of political economy, it is notable that economically informed language and concepts occasionally infuse even her earliest surviving writings. A letter to her childhood friend Maria Lewis in 1840 describing her current reading programme contains an unexpected metaphor for a young provincial woman:

> Have you not alternating seasons of mental stagnation and activity? Just such as the political economists say there must be in a nation's pecuniary condition – all one's precious specie, time, going out to procure a stock of commodities while one's own manufactures are too paltry to be worth vending.[9]

The following year, Eliot records her excitement on receiving a six-volume edition of the sermons of Thomas Chalmers, whose 'Bridgewater Treatise' (1833), an influential text in the promotion of Christian political economy, made an explicit and direct connection between moral value and, under the guidance of providence, the accumulation of money.[10]

Whatever the extent of her early theoretical grounding, her knowledge and understanding of its application in the real world of business was extended over the next decade by her close association with the Bray family and the Coventry commercial classes they introduced her to. Her practical, business-like approach to the organisation of the Prospectus and relaunch of the *Westminster Review* and prescient observations on Chapman's catastrophic financial mismanagement of the magazine is indicative of the commercial maturity she had already developed when she reached London in the early 1850s. Her economic education accelerated in the years that followed, as her position at the *Review* exposed her to many of the leading lights of economic liberalism. She seemed more than able to hold her own in technical discussion. The formidable George Combe, the magazine's main financial backer and a man of forthright liberal views, recorded his first meeting with Eliot in 1851, in which he notes 'the great strength of her intellect': 'We had a great deal of conversation on religion, political economy, and political events, and altogether . . . she appeared to me the ablest woman whom I have seen.'[11] With Combe's approval, Eliot was installed by Chapman as the magazine's de facto editor, a role in which she was instrumental in commissioning articles from 'the ablest and most liberal thinkers of the time'.[12] Robust defences of the principles of classical economics, including the increasingly hegemonic pillars of free trade and competition, were a feature of the *Westminster Review* both during and long after Eliot's editorial involvement.

By the late 1850s, these intellectual and social experiences had taken her to a new level of economic understanding. In December 1857, the year in which *Scenes of Clerical Life* appeared in *Blackwood's Magazine*, she wrote to

Charles Bray. Her letter was a response to a pamphlet Bray had sent her, the central argument of which was incorporated in his open letter which appeared in the *Leader* on 19 December of that year, entitled 'Our Monetary System'. Before discussing the economic background which gave rise to Bray's pamphlet and his particular monetary position, let us consider Eliot's reply. One of the admittedly few surviving letters in which economic theory and debate feature quite so prominently marks a clear elevation from any domestically grounded concept of economics:

> [S]o far as I am capable of judging, your views are the 'sound' ones. But it has often appeared to me – and your letter is, I think, open to similar criticism – that the opponents of the 'gold standard' do not make it sufficiently clear to their readers that they presuppose, as a necessity, some guarantee such as a government security, as a basis for confidence; so that the holder of a bag of courries for example, where courries are the circulating medium, should not be liable, some fine morning, to discover that his courries will purchase him nothing. That contingency, so far as I am able to see, is the one stronghold of those who maintain that the circulating medium should have an intrinsic value, and therefore all the emphasis of argument and illustration should storm them at that point. But whether I am talking 'sanity or insanity', as Carlyle says of himself, is a perfectly equal chance, on a subject of which I know so little.[13]

Bray's apparently direct canvassing of her opinion on his pamphlet in itself signifies the relative shift in the intellectual relationship and standing between Bray and Eliot in the twenty years since they first met. He may not have expected expert advice, but he clearly respects her opinion on a contentious monetary matter. In fact, her interest in and engagement with the debate at issue are suggested not only by the fact that she had pre-emptively read Bray's letter in the *Leader* but also by the succinct argument she presents. Her response displays a clear understanding of Bray's central contention and is given authority by the sure employment of the technical vocabulary of political economy.

Bray's wealth derived from a family business engaged in the manufacture of ribbons, an enterprise he took over on his father's death in 1835. In common with all branches of the textile industry, the scale and profitability of Bray's company had been transformed by technological advances, most notably the development of the power loom. The business had continued to prosper during the war years when high prices had been maintained as a result of the inflationary monetary expansion that had followed the suspension of the requirement that all bank note issuance be backed by (and be convertible into) gold. Between 1797 and 1819 an inconvertible paper currency operated before cash payments were finally resumed after the war. It was against this return to the gold standard that, almost forty years later and against prevailing mainstream economic thought, Bray continued to argue.

The gold standard backed the British currency throughout George Eliot's life and, despite fragmented anti-bullionist opposition, serious debate over its endurance tended to surface only during periodic financial crises, including the severe panic of autumn 1857. It was in response to this crisis that Bray was writing.[14] With intense liquidity pressures threatening the survival of some leading discount houses, the government had succumbed to pressure from the City to suspend the Bank Charter Act of 1844 – which had enshrined the principle of linking notes in issue strictly to gold reserves – by instructing the Bank of England to issue emergency funding. This was not the first and by no means the last time the bank would intervene to correct market excesses. Why, Bray asked, maintain what is effectively an illusory asset-backed standard when, as a result of the actions of 'people [who] over-trade and over-speculate' the bank is forced to issue 'fourteen millions of notes on Government security, and these are as valuable as those that are readily convertible'? It is notable that, while his promotion of fiat money at the expense of gold ran counter to Ricardian teaching and the ascendant Currency School, his letter is emphatic in its assertion of the theoretical cornerstone that links him with the mainstream of classical economists from Smith to Mill and beyond: 'Labour, or the cost of production, is the only real and natural standard or measure of value, and production is the first thing we have to care for.'[15]

It is unclear from Eliot's response where she stood on convertibility, despite her loyal opening assertion of Bray's 'sound' views. By basing her opinions on an implicitly imperfect knowledge ('so far as I am capable of judging') and then proceeding further to undermine her position ('a subject of which I know so little'), her effective criticism of the logical flaw in Bray's position is softened. Her modesty, however, fails to disguise her essentially perfect understanding of the arguments propounded on both sides of the monetary debate. The case for maintaining a currency with 'intrinsic value' was a key concept, along with 'exchange value', of classical economics. Eliot recognises the potential for that value to be undermined when the rules linking money to precious metal are forcibly suspended, as happened in 1857. Against this, however, she theoretically accepts Bray's case for inconvertible paper money, but rightly concludes that the credibility of fiat money rests on the support of an equal or greater guarantee than gold can give: a 'government security'. She is, in effect, recognising that money has value and meaning because society grants it: the social meaning of money thus transcends any purely theoretical valuation. In this, Eliot is articulating a shift that Mary Poovey identifies around the middle of the century which saw a social acceptance of paper currencies and the writing they contained. These, as much as metallic currency and writings 'about' money came to be accepted as representations of fact. Poovey describes this process as one of 'naturalization' which, as the century progressed, embraced increasingly abstract financial instruments, as they 'passed beneath the horizon of cultural visibility'.[16]

Overall, Eliot appears unconvinced by the arguments of Bray, whose own business was being adversely affected by tighter monetary conditions and was, a few years later, to be even worse hit by the abolition of import duties on ribbon. Ironically, the liberal Bray was undone by free trade and laissez-faire economics. It seems unlikely that Eliot was immune from the general sense that – financial crises and economic cycles notwithstanding – gold and, therefore, the pound sterling continued to represent security and 'intrinsic value'. Up until 1870, the interest coupon on UK government consols was paid in gold in an almost ceremonial linking of the great social and material embodiments of security: the state and the precious metal. As Martin Daunton explains the metal's symbolic and psychological hold: 'To question gold was tantamount to an attack on the queen whose head appeared on the newly designed gold sovereigns ... The gold standard and gold sovereign were not technical issues, but were embedded in personal culture.'[17] Something of this ordering of value is hinted at in Eliot's essays. In 'The Life of John Sterling' (1852), she writes of a man 'of whom poetry and philosophy were not merely a form of paper currency or a ladder to fame but an end in themselves'.[18] Four years later an alchemic image again establishes a link between the highest art and the precious metal: Heinrich Heine, she writes, 'touches leaden folly with the magic wand of his fancy, and transmutes it into the fine gold of art.'[19]

Gold may have remained the ultimate store of value, but new money forms were becoming increasingly pervasive. Most of Eliot's novels are set in the first third of the nineteenth century, at an important stage of transition from an early industrial to a full market and cash economy: the years just ahead of Poovey's 'vanishing point'. The period saw great changes in both the representational forms of money and the institutions in which it was stored and exchanged. In her most fabular tales, *Silas Marner* and 'Brother Jacob', gold coinage takes on mysterious, non-material meaning. Its talismanic status allows Eliot to explore concepts of money-related pathology (hoarding in the former, stealing in the latter) and transformation in richly allegorical ways that rely on the period settings. Reflecting on the success of *Silas Marner* in

May 1861, she tells Blackwood: 'There can be no great painting of misers under the present system of paper money – cheques bills scrip and the like: nobody can handle that dull property as men handled the glittering gold.'[20] Throughout the novels, money-forms explore the tension between intrinsic and exchange value. Precious stones and gold; metal coins and paper notes; cheques, exchangeable mortgages and gambling chips: all are charged with rich symbolism and anthropological meaning. In Eliot's hands, they establish individual and social frameworks of power and control.

Eliot's occasional and diffident professions of ignorance, of both economic theory and commercial practice, therefore, seem somewhat at odds with her experience and revealed understanding. William Baker, in his analysis of the sparsely represented Economics section of the George Eliot–George Henry Lewes Collection in the Dr Williams's Library, takes her at face value, concluding that his data evidence a lack of interest in the subject.[21] However, this opinion should be put in the context both of the remarkable size of the couple's recorded and dispersed libraries and of the significance of those works that did survive, including important texts by Adam Smith, Mill, Fawcett and John Elliot Cairnes.[22] Baker's conclusion also ignores the much wider sphere with which nineteenth-century political economy connected. The couple's extensive collection of moral philosophical, political, sociological and scientific books reveal many insights into a much broader definition of economics and provide clues as to how Eliot came to frame her considerations of the wider ethical and sociological implications of the study of material wealth.

Baker specifically notes the absence of Ricardo's works in the collection. However, there is evidence that Eliot was fully conversant with his central theory in the *Principles*, which reciprocally linked wages and capital within an interdependent scheme, at the centre of which lay the labour theory of value. His central incorporation of land and rent would have had particular resonance for Eliot, whose father was agent to a large country estate in the post-war years, when the memory of high food prices and inflated land values was fresh. Ricardo's core theory of diminishing returns was cast in agricultural terms and relates directly to Thomas Malthus's work on population. As the population grows, Ricardo argued, increasingly unproductive marginal land is cultivated, driving up both the price of rent and the capital value of land while reducing profits. Eliot has Mr Poyser in *Adam Bede* articulate the value of his marginal land in distinctly Ricardian terms: '[it] isna worth ten shillings an acre, rent and profits'. In *Felix Holt*, she goes on to undermine the limitations of Ricardo's theory of rent, by illustrating its vulnerability to capricious human behaviour:

> Mr Goffe ... had never had it explained to him that, according to the true
> theory of rent, land must inevitably be given up when it would not yield a
> profit equal to the ordinary rate of interest; so that for want of knowing what
> was impossible ... he kept his land.[23]

Ricardo went on to theorise a direct and quantifiable link between wages,
profit and rent. From a social perspective, this determination was particularly significant as it inevitably pitted the landowner against the farmer;
the landlord against the manufacturer providing the industrial capital.[24]
The theory found empirical evidence in the support of landowners for the
maintenance of the Corn Laws, which, by inflating the price and demand
for home-grown corn, invariably raised rents. Conversely, those same landowners, in accordance with Ricardo's model, were disincentivised to make
any improvements to their land as the benefits of higher productivity and a
lower cost of production would accrue not to them but to their tenant
farmers. The typically less enlightened landowners in George Eliot's novels
often fit the Ricardian bill closely. In *Silas Marner*, Squire Cass is the specific
target of the narrator's criticism, but the wider critique is of the thought and
morals of a particular generation and class:

> It was still that glorious war-time which was felt to be a peculiar favour of
> Providence towards the landed interest, and the fall of prices had not yet
> come to carry the race of small squires and yeomen down that road to ruin
> for which extravagant habits and bad husbandry were plentifully anointing
> their wheels.[25]

In spite of his other failings of character, by the end of the novel Godfrey
Cass is at least implementing land improvement schemes. He thereby
joins a line of new-generation estate modernisers stretching from Arthur
Donnithorne, another substantially imperfect heir out to correct the selfish mismanagement of the previous generation, to Sir James Chettam in
Middlemarch. Like Donnithorne, Chettam is contrasted to a representative of 'old' landed attitudes, although here somewhat incongruously
espousing radical politics, Mr Brooke. Brooke claims the authority of
both Adam Smith and Humphry Davy in his opposition to 'fancy-
farming' and reveals again the Ricardian opposition of technology-
resistant landlord and tenant:

> 'A great mistake, Chettam,' interposed Mr Brooke, 'going into electrifying
> your land and that kind of thing, and making a parlour of your cow-house. It
> won't do. I went into science a great deal myself at one time; but I saw it
> would not do. It leads to everything; you can let nothing alone. No, no – see
> that your tenants don't sell their straw and that kind of thing; and give them

draining-tiles, you know. But your fancy-farming will not do – the most expensive sort of whistle you can buy; you may as well keep a pack of hounds.'[26]

The influence on Eliot of Ricardo's most prominent successor, John Stuart Mill, is even more apparent and pervasive. In a letter of 1875 to Elizabeth Stuart Phelps, while denying both a personal acquaintance with Mill and that his works represented 'any marked epoch in my life', Eliot nevertheless admits that she has 'studied his books, especially his Logic and Political Economy, with much benefit'.[27] Ten years earlier, while writing *Felix Holt*, and following publication of popular editions of a number of Mill's major works, she reflects that 'some of his works have been frequently my companions of late, and I have been going through many *actions de grace* towards him'.[28] Her diary reveals that her specific 'companions' at this time were *The Principles of Political Economy*, which she was rereading, and *On Liberty*. In view of the socio-political and religious themes central to *Felix Holt*, it is instructive that Mill's great texts of classical economic and social liberalism feature on Eliot's reading list alongside Auguste Comte's *Social Science*, David Friedrich Strauss's *Life of Jesus* and Aristotle's *Poetics* – writers whose influence on Eliot's thought are well documented – together with Fawcett's *Economic Condition of the Working Classes*.[29] In fact, it is not at all surprising that any interest Eliot might have had in the study of political economy in the 1850s and 1860s should have been largely shaped by Mill. Since it was first published in 1848, the *Principles* had exerted an extraordinarily wide and enduring influence on economic thought. Leslie Stephen, writing more than fifty years after its original publication, summarised the impact of the work, which 'became popular in a sense in which no work upon the same topic had been popular since the *Wealth of Nations*'.[30]

It became Eliot's primary work of economic reference. In an 1852 letter to the Brays describing her varied and hectic workload at the *Westminster Review*, she explains that her research for a review of a recent periodical piece by W. R. Greg on 'Principles of Taxation' largely comprised reading 'all that J. S. Mill says on the same subject'.[31] Mill, in the *Principles*, essentially held with Smith's four great maxims on the requirements of taxation: equality, certainty, convenience (i.e. at a time convenient to the payer) and minimum cost of collection.[32] He did not object to contemporary levels of income tax and believed capital should not be exempt from levy. He was, however, opposed to an increased rate for higher earners: echoing modern-day debate, his desire to mitigate 'the inequalities of wealth' was outweighed by an objection 'to impose a penalty on people for having worked harder and saved more than their neighbours'. Like Gladstone, Mill did not believe that income tax should be a redistributive tool. Where he did believe the wealthy should be liable to increased taxation, however, was on 'large fortunes acquired by gift or inheritance'.[33] Eliot herself did not appear to have a problem paying out part of her profits of production, writing in 1852: 'So the budget is come out – and I am to pay Income Tax. All very right.'[34] At the same time, she writes of attending meetings of the Association for the Repeal of the Taxes on Knowledge in support of the abolition of the Newspaper Stamp Tax, indicating a wider questioning of the extent and proper balance of the state's power to tax its citizens.[35]

Mill's views on taxation were part of a much wider theorising of wealth distribution, a process, he argued, that must remain subject to human will and adjustment rather than to unalterable deductive laws.[36] In this important distinction, Mill's *Principles* marked a significant advance both on Smith's 'invisible hand' and Ricardo's unified theory of production and distribution. His theory finds an imaginative parallel in Eliot's novelistic explorations of the co-existence of classical economic principles and altruism. Sir James Chettam allows his largely practical and economically driven land improvements to take a more altruistic colouring under Dorothea's enthusiasm to assist him. Her formulation of detailed plans for new workmen's cottages, however, is taken by Brooke as evidence that 'young women don't understand political economy'. Brooke represents a patriarchal view of political economy and its applications in which the overlaying of human sympathy represents a feminising of classical principles. Ironically, his creator's understanding of that science, in this very context, may well have been advanced by her long-standing acquaintance, Harriet Martineau, whom Eliot had visited in 1852 in the midst of Martineau's cooperative scheme for building working men's cottages in Cumbria.[37] Eliot's observation of the great admirer of Malthus – and the era's pre-eminent populiser and policy lobbyist for classical political economy – dedicating herself to such a scheme would suggest that she is pointing to Dorothea's unworldly naïvety, rather than the incompatibility of emotion and reason in the application of Martineau's 'science'. While Eliot's fictional heroine may bemoan the constraints of 'political economy, that never-explained science which was thrust as an extinguisher over all her lights', this is hardly a complaint her reforming, real-life friend would be likely to make.[38]

Martineau's proposed solutions to address the economic condition of the working classes combine old-fashioned paternalism with the doctrine of self-help. The latter, given its most extensive and popular charter in Samuel

Smiles's work of that name in 1859, was most closely in step with the hegemonic economic and social liberalism of the third quarter of the century.[39] Against this swell, however, divergent socialist interpretations of the theoretical investigations into the creation and distribution of wealth were already being voiced, some years ahead of the radical formulations of Marx and Engels. As early as the 1820s, the first generation of so-called Ricardian socialists tried, in the words of Maurice Dobb, 'to carry Ricardian theory . . . into a critique of capitalism itself' by calling for the right of labour, as the sole creator of wealth, to the whole produce.[40] Eliot was undoubtedly aware of the aims and progress of the Owenite movement, although her caustic assessment of its founder and leading light as early as 1843 indicates that she was little swayed by its ideology: 'I saw Robert Owen yesterday . . . and I think if his system prospers it will be in *spite* of its founder, and not because of his advocacy; but I dare say one should even begin to like him if he were known long enough to erase the first impression.'[41] More direct ideological criticism is found in her important review essay 'The Natural History of German Life' (1856), in which she observes the essential self-interest with which the peasants greet plans for the communal partition of the land. Any emotional attraction she may have felt towards socialism in theory was offset by a recognition of its practical limitations.[42]

This work's final chapter will return to Eliot's thoughts in the final years of her life concerning the role and limitation of the state in the economy, including private ownership rights to land and property. However, it is notable that these issues already figured prominently at the outset of her career. She was an early reader of Herbert Spencer's *Social Statics* (1851), in which the author argues that 'it is manifest that exclusive possession of the soil necessitates an infringement of the law of equal freedom'. Spencer consequently calls for a nationalisation of land, with rents passing to the state rather than individual landlords. Although he attempts to distinguish his proposal from 'Messrs. Fourier, Owen, Louis Blanc, and Co' and, in his later writings, increasingly distanced himself from practical advocacy of land nationalisation, Spencer was to become an unlikely champion of socialist land-reformers by the end of the century.[43] It is unclear what Eliot thought of his thesis. She sent a copy of the book to Charles Bray, not 'because I thought you would admire the book – far from it'.[44] Mill's re-statement of the benefits and necessity of private property ownership was probably a better reflection of Eliot's own position. In the *Principles*, he gives serious consideration to the theoretical basis and attractions of communism and its small-scale historical application. His conclusion is essentially pragmatic: that 'for a considerable time to come', the political economist will be chiefly concerned with the conditions of existence and progress belonging to a society founded on private property and individual competition; and that the object to be principally aimed at in the present stage of human improvement, is not the subversion of the system of individual property, but the improvement of it, and the full participation of every member of the community in its benefits.[45]

While Mill continued wholeheartedly to defend property rights and competition, his proposals for redistributive inheritance tax and lengthy consideration of the position of the working classes in the *Principles* revealed socialist bearings with which even his staunchest followers struggled.[46] Eliot, together with Lewes, was also greatly concerned with the position of the 'Labouring Classes'. While her own vision of how a more mobile and egalitarian society might emerge was more gradualist than Mill's, his main socio-economic position, which included a forceful rejection of paternalism, is certainly traceable in Eliot.[47] His objection to welfare dependency was both practical – it is an idealised state that 'has never been historically realised' – and philosophical, in that it contravened his concept of individual liberty. Eliot shared the latter objection, although its expression occasionally carries a hard liberal edge, as when she writes to Mrs Nassau John Senior in 1874 on the inadequacy of the Poor Laws: 'Do what one will with a pauper system it remains a huge system of vitiation, introducing the principle of communistic provision instead of provision through individual, personal responsibility and action.'[48]

What Mill looked forward to for the working classes was 'their own mental cultivation', a goal achievable primarily through education and greater cooperation both within and across classes.[49] From this foundation he envisaged the eventual creation of partnerships and even joint-ownership between the sharply divided camps of employers and workers. In *Felix Holt*, Eliot is emphatic that education of the working classes must precede electoral enfranchisement.[50] She directs the oratory of Felix, both in the novel and later in the 'Address to Working Men', to argue that 'votes would never give you political power worth having while things are as they are now'.[51] In this context, the strength and essential virtue of her two principal working-class heroes – Felix Holt and Adam Bede – as well as that of more minor characters such as Caleb Garth, establish them as model representatives of their class and fitting participants in the cooperative schemes Mill envisaged. It is notable that, while all three characters are united in the skill and diligent commitment they bring to their respective crafts, their individual positioning within the market economies in which they work varies significantly. Felix Holt actively chooses to stand outside the market; Caleb

Garth operates within it yet is hampered by a naïve and over-trusting nature; and Adam Bede attempts to practise a kind of moral capitalism: insisting on a fair mark-up for his handiwork and aspiring to a small-scale business ownership. To some extent, and somewhat counter-intuitively, it is possible to read Adam's character in terms of both Spencerian social evolutionary theory and laissez-faire economics. His superior character and mathematical ability allow him to 'evolve' to a higher economic state, while the rest of Bartle Massey's night-school class remain in a steady (and lowly) position.

Yet it is not only on the *exceptional* representatives of the working class that Eliot bestows status and value. The conclusion of Chapter 19 of *Adam Bede* celebrates the value of labour in a tone reminiscent of Ruskin's idealisation of the medieval stonemasons. The narrator concedes that Adam while 'not an average man' was also not wholly uncommon of many 'trained in skilful courageous labour':

> they make their way upward, rarely as geniuses, most commonly as painstaking honest men, with the skill and conscience to do well the tasks that lie before them. Their lives have no discernible echo beyond the neighbourhood where they dwelt, but you are almost sure to find there some good piece of road, some building, some application of mineral produce, some improvement in farming practice, some reform of parish abuses, with which their names are associated by one or two generations after them . . . They have not had the art of getting rich, but they are men of trust, and when they die before the work is all out of them, it is as if some main screw had got loose in a machine; the master who employed them says, 'Where shall I find their like?'[52]

Does such a passage place Eliot in that long line of thought running counter to the main tenet of political economy in its distrust or outright criticism of those whose ruling passion is 'the art of getting rich'? Up to a point. The mechanised image of the industrial worker as a 'screw . . . in a machine' is certainly in tune with the language of Dickens and the mid-century Condition of England novelists. Their chief inspiration, Thomas Carlyle, famously denounced 'the Mechanical Age' in all its manifestations: 'Not the external and physical alone is now managed by machinery, but the internal and spiritual also.'[53] Eliot came to intellectual and creative maturity at a time of economic growth and stability which had dulled the fear of Carlyle's calamitous projections and bred an acquiescent acceptance of the nexus of cash exchange. Yet his influence on her should not be underestimated. She maintained, writing in 1855, that 'there is hardly a superior or active mind of this generation that has not been modified by Carlyle's writings' and his ideas continued to reverberate in the work of Ruskin and indeed Mill.[54]

Carlyle's idealisation of mediaeval hierarchical social and economic structures is founded on a direct exemplary link to the Church of the Middle Ages, most prominently in the portrayal of Abbot Samson and his monastic community in *Past and Present*. Biblical and Christian teaching on money were obviously intimately known to Eliot but the particular tradition Carlyle describes here belongs more to the Catholic Church than to the Evangelical Protestantism so central to her early life. Interpreting Riehl, she draws a distinction between the impact of religion in Britain and continental Europe that was to form the basis of Max Weber's influential sociological theory more than fifty years later: 'for though our English life is in its core intensely traditional, Protestantism and commerce have modernized the face of the land and the aspects of society in a far greater degree than in any continental country'.[55] Medieval Catholic teaching on the dangers of following mammon and, in particular, the evil of usury marks an opposition between commerce and morals that links this critical tradition even further back to Greek philosophy and, in particular, Aristotle. The favourite classical philosopher of Lewes and Eliot (to whom she turned 'to find out what is the chief good'[56]) draws, in *The Politics*, a sharp distinction between 'natural' and 'unnatural' money: the former, what is required for the necessities of the good life; the latter, the creation and pursuit of money for its own sake.[57]

John Ruskin, here at least, sits along Carlyle in this Aristotelian line of opposition against money as an intrinsic good. It is therefore worth recalling Eliot's complaint that Ruskin's work, whatever its other qualities, contained 'stupendous specimens of arrogant absurdity on some economical points'.[58] Ruskin, in turn, identifies Eliot as a proponent of the commercially contaminated 'English Cockney school' of literature, in which 'the personages are picked up from behind the counter and out of the gutter; and the landscape, by excursion train to Gravesend, with return ticket for the City-road'.[59] Both quotations overstate the differences between two writers, whose wider perceptions of value have a similar foundation. Eliot greatly admired Ruskin's writing on art and his attempts to converge aesthetics and economics were mirrored, to some extent, by her own struggles to reconcile artistic creativity and ever-rising sales of what was becoming increasingly a commodity item.[60]

Her novels avoid reductive attacks on commerce and those enriched by it, but contain complex investigations of the moral psychology of choices concerning the acquisition and distribution of money and the ethics of the consumption its possession facilitates. Few of her wealthy characters (either of old or new money) possess the human sympathy required of the properly enlightened individual and, in accordance with the main lines of attack of both Ruskin and Carlyle, the theoretical application of the calculus of Benthamite Utilitarianism to unravel the mysteries of human nature is frequently brought under attack. In Eliot's first published fiction, the narrator of 'Janet's Repentance' satirises 'certain ingenious philosophers of our own day', whose reaction to the greater joy in heaven over the one repentant sinner than of the other ninety-nine not in need of repentance is to 'take offence at a joy so entirely out of correspondence with arithmetical proportion'. The satire takes on a harder edge when the inadequacy of a purely arithmetical approach is exposed in the face of individual human loss:

> the mother, when her sweet lisping little ones have all been taken from her one after another, and she is hanging over her last dead babe, finds small consolation in the fact that the tiny dimpled corpse is but one of a necessary average, and that a thousand other babes brought into the world at the same time are doing well, and are likely to live; and if you stood beside that mother – if you knew her pang and shared it – it is probable you would be equally unable to see a ground of complacency in statistics.[61]

It was a criticism she had voiced in more general terms the previous year in 'The Natural History of German Life', when she described the folly 'of modern generalization, to believe that all social questions are merged in economic science, and that the relations of men to their neighbours may be settled by algebraic equations'.[62]

The reading of *Felix Holt* in Chapter 4 argues that, by the late 1860s, Eliot's critique of Utilitarianism had become both pervasive and more nuanced. This shift was partly in response not only to developments in political economic debate including Mill's modifications to Jeremy Bentham's hedonistic scheme in 'Utilitarianism' (1861), but also to gradually widening fault lines in the theoretical foundations of classical economics, which was finally starting to undermine Mill's dominance. Returning to Baker's catalogue of part of the surviving Eliot–Lewes library, two of the contemporary works of economics listed are Henry Fawcett's *Manual of Political Economy* and John Elliott Cairnes's *Some Leading Principles of Political Economy Newly Expounded*, first published in 1863 and 1874 respectively.[63]

Reflecting the changing political, social and economic preoccupations of the mid-1870s, the fourth edition of Fawcett's *Manual* (1874) in the Dr Williams's collection included a new chapter on 'the Nationalisation of the Land'. This contains references to what Fawcett describes as 'modern socialism', including considerations of the need for 'state intervention'. His reflections point to 'the important economic advantages which would

result, if the entire people were brought under the influence of a comprehensive system of national education'.[64] Eliot's annotated copy of Cairnes's
Principles, meanwhile, was used for reference during the writing of *Daniel
Deronda* and his 'Preface' gives some indication of the disputes flaring
within contemporary political economics. While defending the core methodology of the classical school (which 'combined deduction and verifica-
tion'), he proposes to update the 'intermediate principles' against what he
sees as 'no small proportion of faulty material' prevalent in the early 1870s.

The inclusion of Cairnes and Fawcett in the surviving library is significant. Both men were personal acquaintances of Eliot and Lewes and, as
academic economists, both belonged to the loosely described School of
Mill. As such, and in opposition to the newly developed theories of value
that were starting to take hold by the early 1870s, both resolutely defended
the core Ricardian value theory, including the concept of the wages-fund –
that is, the population-dependent 'fixed' amount of capital in the system
required to fund the wages of the labourer. Fawcett, in later editions of the
Manual, opens his chapter 'On Wages' with a summary of the theory, its
challenge (partially acknowledged by Mill) by W. T. Thornton and the
subsequent response from Cairnes, 'justly regarded as the leading advocate
of the wages fund theory'.[65] Cairnes became the leading guardian of Mill's
legacy, and remained staunchly resistant to the innovations of Jevons and
the other marginal utility theorists.[66]

However, even Cairnes recognised that some of the pillars of classical
economic orthodoxy were becoming untenable. In his inaugural lecture as
professor of Political Economy at University College London in 1870, he
argued for 'positive and reconstructive' reforms within his discipline, urging, in particular, that its historically intimate association with the dogma of
laissez-faire should be broken.[67] Alternative schools of economic thought
were arguing for much more radical reinterpretations. Even Bagehot, who
continued to support the main abstract principles of Ricardo and regarded
Cairnes's modified version of Mill as the best way forward for political
economy, ceased to regard the science as absolutely and universally applicable. Rather, he argued, it had full relevance only in 'a society of grown-up
competitive commerce such as we have in England'.[68] In this expression of
relativism, Bagehot reveals some alignment with the historical or comparative method that Sir Henry Maine had spearheaded in the field of jurisprudence and which was rapidly gaining traction in other disciplines,
including economics.[69] As later chapters will discuss, it was an intellectual
methodology that was to influence Eliot's work, most notably in the socio-
economic themes she explored in *Romola* and *Middlemarch*.

These various debates and fractures around the scope and proper methodology of political economy were reaching a climax just around the centenary, in 1876, of the publication of *The Wealth of Nations*. It is significant that all the competing factions tried to claim Smith's inheritance for their own cause. For, as Bagehot described the enduring legacy of Smith's work:

> The life of almost everyone in England – perhaps of everyone – is different and better in consequence of it. The whole commercial policy of the country is not so much founded on it as instinct with it ... its teachings have settled down into the common sense of the nation and have become irreversible.[70]

Almost forty years earlier, in his Preface to the *Principles*, Mill had pointed to a similarly enduring debt that goes beyond the economic:

> The design of this book is different from that of any treatise on Political Economy which has been produced in England since the work of Adam Smith ... And it is because Adam Smith never loses sight of this truth; because, in his applications of Political Economy, he perpetually appeals to other and often far larger considerations than pure Political Economy affords.[71]

In his reaching back to Smith, Mill here sets a central course of practical, 'human economics'[72] resistant to the branches of 'abstract speculation' – both classical and neoclassical – that sought to impose restrictive, theoretical confines on the subject. My locating of George Eliot in that same tradition rests not on the scant evidence that foremost among Baker's twelve recorded works of economics in her surviving library is an edition of *The Wealth of Nations*.[73] The connection is more fundamental. Just as Smith's economics 'perpetually appeals to other and far larger considerations', so too does Eliot's investigation of humanity's 'larger considerations' embody the economic. As she writes in *Adam Bede*, using the abstraction of impersonal economic theory for very different ends:

> the existence of insignificant people has very important consequences in the world. It can be shown to affect the price of bread and the rate of wages, to call forth many evil tempers from the selfish, and many heroisms from the sympathetic, and, in other ways, to play no small part in the tragedy of life.[74]

To quote Mill again, this time from the *Autobiography*, 'Political Economy, in truth, has never pretended to give advice to mankind with no lights but its own; though people who knew nothing but political economy (and therefore knew that ill) have taken upon themselves to advise, and could only do so by such lights as they had.'[75] Although the neoclassical economists admitted the limitations of their science (Alfred Marshall, for example, recognises the partial dependence of great questions of economic distribution 'on the moral and political capabilities of human nature'[76]), the mathematical basis of the marginal utility theorists tended to quantify, redefine or simply ignore Smith's 'larger considerations'. Jevons, in his 'Preface' to the first edition of *The Theory of Political Economy* (1871), explains his treatment of economics 'as a calculus of pleasure and pain . . . The nature of wealth and value is explained by the consideration of indefinitely small amounts of pleasure and pain, just as the theory of statics is made to rest upon the equality of indefinitely small amounts of energy.'[77]

As classical theories of growth gave way to equilibrium and optimisation, value came to reside with the consumer, which, as will be discussed in the following chapters, proved problematic for a morally informed artist growing rich from her ever greater sales. Only *Daniel Deronda* and *Theophrastus Such*, of George Eliot's finished novels, were written after the publication of Jevons's *Theory*, whose main impact, in any case, was felt several years later. However, the growing acceptance of subjective, demand-led theories at a time when her own wealth and material accumulation was, in part, being fuelled by the development of her books as consumer items changed, confused and even upset the basis of value on which most of her personal and professional life rested.

Following the receipt of a cheque from Blackwood for sales of *The Mill on the Floss* in April 1861, she writes: 'I prize the money fruit of my labour very highly as the means of saving us dependence [*sic*] or the degradation of writing when we are no longer able to write well or write what we have not written before.'[78] It is one instance of many in which she writes to her publisher and friend of the value and product of her labour, but, in its prudential basis, its temporal dimension and its distinction between money and real value it reveals a debt to Adam Smith, from whom she secured both the foundation of her theoretical economic understanding and a means of incorporating that understanding into a wider normative framework.[79]

CHAPTER 2

'Intentions of stern thrift': the formation of a vernacular economics

I thank you also for your offer about the money for Adam, but I have intentions of stern thrift, and mean to want as little as possible.[1]   – George Eliot to John Blackwood, July 1859

That science [political economy], although it considers wealth as an object of desire, and inquires what circumstances are favourable to its increase, lays down no doctrine whatever with regard to the moral propriety of devoting our energies to making money.[2]   – *Westminster Review*, July 1865

By the time the *Westminster Review* issued yet another in its long series of staunch defences of the principles of political economy in 1865 (the article referenced above was, ostensibly, a review of the latest edition of Mill's great work), George Eliot's direct connection with the magazine had long since ceased. However, the explosion of her career in the six years that followed her professed intention sternly to conserve her literary earnings had propelled her into the ranks of high earners for whom the wider moral issues raised by the *Review*'s article were most pertinent. In the three years prior to the publication of *Adam Bede* in 1859, her annual earnings averaged around £300. By 1864, advances and sales on her first four full novels (*Adam Bede*, *The Mill on the Floss*, *Silas Marner* and *Romola*) alone had earned her around £15,000. To put those earnings in context, an 1868 analysis of income distribution in England and Wales shows that a family earning in excess of £1,000 per year fell within the top 0.5 per cent of the total population. Within ten years of this survey, Eliot was earning more than £1,000 in annual stock dividend income alone.[3]

This chapter and the next will extend the consideration of Eliot's theoretical understanding of economic matters to their application in her private and professional lives. Chapter 3 will deal specifically with George Eliot as a professional writer against the background of the changing economics of the publishing industry over her working life, including considerations of the value of literature in an increasingly commoditised market for the printed

33

word. The current chapter, while referential to those literary earnings, will focus on her attitudes towards spending, investing and distributing money. The intention in both is not simply to retrace well-documented biographical details, but also to consider her recorded thought and actions as she became wealthier within the context of contemporary debate surrounding the benefits, dangers and limitations of the market economy and the formation of her own 'applied economics'. This chapter will argue that monetary and economic elements are inextricably entwined in her understanding of practical ethics; a relationship that is subject to broad and complex treatment in the novels, as subsequent readings will show. The more immediate contention is that, beyond the intellectual influences of religious, moral philosophical and economic writers, the economic ethics explored in the novels are informed by her personal experiences of having first little and subsequently significant material wealth and the choices for action its possession imposed. Crucially, considerations of selfishness and altruism that were to become central to her moral philosophy find a testing-ground in her own personal situations. The chapter will conclude with a description of Eliot's stock market investments and consideration of her attitude to risk in relation to her financial capital.

In the same year that George Eliot was professing her 'intentions of stern thrift' to Blackwood, Samuel Smiles's newly published *Self Help* was urging the absolute necessity of that same virtue to all working men seeking to elevate their character and material condition 'by means of individual action, economy, and self-denial'.[4] Thrift, in fact, constituted an essential individual requirement that underlay both secular and religious manifestations of classical political economy and was central to its populisers of varying ideological persuasions from Martineau to Smiles. It was to remain a central tenet of both individualistic and more communitarian forms of liberalism throughout the century.[5] Eliot's own thrift is similarly traceable to a variety of sources.

Chapter 1 argued that by 1859 Eliot's intellectual grasp of economics owed much to the work of Mill and those other *Westminster Review* contributors swimming in the secular stream of the Philosophic Radicals. However, while Mill, following Bentham, held that Christianity and political economy were incompatible, for much of Eliot's childhood and formative years such a linkage was central to a deeply influential Evangelical ideology. Boyd Hilton's now well-accepted contention is that this ideology was a strong and unifying factor among policy-makers during the 1820s and 1830s. He concludes that it 'contributed more than "classical economics" or utilitarianism to the formation of that public morality (or doctrine) in the context of which the new economic policy emerged and by which it was sanctioned'.[6] Within the framework of this Christian political economy, thrift, together with other financial and materially related characteristics, was elevated so as to create, in the words of Thomas Chalmers, an 'inseparable connection between the moral worth and the economic comfort of a people'. Chalmers's influential 'Bridgewater Treatise', first published in 1833, but successfully reissued some twenty years later, makes this theological link yet more explicit when it describes political economy as 'but one grand exemplification of the alliance, which a God of righteousness hath established, between prudence and moral principle on the one hand, and physical comfort on the other'.[7] As A. C. M. Waterman concludes, Chalmers and leading academic theologians such as John Sumner, Edward Copleston and Richard Whately succeeded in persuading the intellectual establishment that Christianity could be consistent with a number of political principles (both Whig and liberal Tory) which were being sharpened by political economy: 'private property rights, free and competitive markets ... and a high degree of social and economic inequality'.[8]

This was the ideological background against which the teenage George Eliot observed the passing of the Reform Act of 1832 and the enactment by a Whig-led coalition government of a series of social and economic reforms that were to test the relationship between individual economies and state support. The most controversial of these, the 1834 Poor Law Amendment Act, was – as even Eliot's own letters show – to continue to prick the liberal social conscience for most of the century.[9]

Eliot's reading of Chalmers is indicative of the somewhat stern Evangelicalism she adopted as a teenager in the mid-1830s. Her father's religious tastes, together with his politics, were much more conventional, but the main tenets of Christian political economy would have found fertile soil in his sober, hard-working and thrifty household from his daughter's earliest years. Robert Evans emerges from her own descriptions as a kind of Smilsean ideal: 'he raised himself from being an artisan to be a man whose extensive knowledge in very varied practical departments made his services valued through several counties. He had a large knowledge of buildings, of mines, of plantation, of various branches of valuation and measurement'.[10] His accomplishments clearly match those of the fictional Caleb Garth with the very significant exception that Robert Evans (and, I think his daughter) would never have been so imprudent as to secure a debt for the likes of Fred Vincy – an imbalance between personal affection and economic calculation that we learn had earlier cost Garth his building business.

Evans was a traditional Anglican and a lifelong Tory; like the tenant farmers of Treby in *Felix Holt*, his allegiance was unquestionably towards the party of his squire. Nevertheless, he recognised the shortcomings of the Old Poor Law and consequently approved of the 1834 Amendment, hoping it would better distinguish between an 'industrious good man' and 'an idle bad man' in the distribution of parish relief.[11] Eliot must have considered the implications of the distinction between worthy 'poverty' and self-induced 'pauperism' even as she assisted her new wealthy Coventry Evangelical friends in distributing aid to the city's poor.[12] At home, her assumption of the role of mistress of the house at the age of seventeen (following her mother's death) necessitated careful household management and a habit of meticulous bookkeeping that she maintained throughout her life: 'I like to be able to calculate with precision my incomings', she wrote in 1860 and the later diaries are notable for the frequency with which well-ordered columns of income, expenditure and investment holdings are interspersed among her writing.[13] The contrast between the author and the fictional Rosamond Vincy in the domestic economic sphere is particularly striking. In her final years, accounting duties were largely passed on to John Cross but she maintained an attention to carefully ordered detail, noting with satisfaction that he 'brought me a register with all my investments neatly written out'.[14]

Eliot's individual personal and professional progression is exceptional but in the way she thought about money, initially in a domestic context, she is, to some extent, representative of her particular generation. As Hilton has observed, it was not Ricardo and Mill but Martineau and other women writers 'who mediated political economy for the masses by placing it in the current of domestic household management'.[15] In her carefully documented records of earnings and outgoings, portfolio valuations and dividend receipts she testifies to the increasing pervasiveness of the money economy, supported by both secular and religious ideologies, as industrial capitalism matured in Britain during the nineteenth century.

The application of an intuitive and domestically honed financial prudence into a wider and lifelong money ethic is most evident in Eliot's attitude to debt. In a letter to Blackwood in 1859 – when the success of *Adam Bede* had laid the ground for what was to be a financially transformative next book contract – she tries to explain the value of money to her by reference to the consequences of its absence:

> I certainly care a great deal for the money, as I suppose all anxious minds do that love independence and have been brought up to think debt and begging the two deepest dishonours short of crime.[16]

The link between money and independence is one that recurs in her letters and journals. Celebrating her physical removal from the Chapman household in 1854, she writes: 'I like my independent life in lodgings better and better and want nothing but a little more money.'[17] Three years later, the break from her family following the admission of her attachment to Lewes provokes a determined statement of her financial independence:

> I am not dependent on anyone, the larger part of my income for several years having been derived from my own constant labour as a writer. You will perceive, therefore, that in my conduct towards my own family I have not been guided by any motives of self-interest, since I have been neither in the reception nor the expectation of the slightest favour from them.[18]

By this stage, Eliot had established herself as a translator, essayist, reviewer and, effectively, editor of a leading national periodical; collectively an almost unheard of portfolio of work for a woman. She had not yet accumulated capital but when, with the advances and royalties on the novels, she did so, the cash, securities and other assets would remain in her own name rather than being transferred to that of her husband, as the law required of all married women.[19] Thus, the heroines of her novels, unlike their creator, are only allowed to make meaningful money choices when their husbands die. The loss of financial independence – to be dependent on anybody, including in Eliot's mind, one's own family – constitutes a form of beggary and thereby dishonour. This causal relationship is central to liberal economic theory and policy, supporting, for example, the enforcement of less eligibility in Poor Law administration and minimal state interference in the economy. In its more populist manifestations it was at the heart of the doctrine of self-help. For Smiles, the accumulation of wealth, beyond the attainment of physical comfort, was not an end in itself, but a means of securing independence, respectability and moral enlargement.

If Eliot's deep-rooted abhorrence of financial dependency aligns her with all shades of mid-century liberal economic thought, her characterisation of debt as an almost criminal source of dishonour, while again culturally orthodox, goes somewhat against the grain of the rapidly developing credit economy.[20] *The Mill on the Floss*, as later analysis will show, explores financial and wider notions of risk at a temporal inflection point, as a wider acceptance of debt and institutional credit was starting to gain traction. Eliot's critical observation of the sympathetic limitations of the affluent Dodson sisters is checked by a recognition of the probity of their 'old fashioned' and 'narrow notions about debt'. The implicit criticism turns on the casuistry of moral justifications of debt prevalent in the mid-century:

in these days of wide commercial views and wide philosophy, according to which everything rights itself without any trouble of ours: the fact that my tradesman is out of pocket by me, is to be looked at through the serene certainty that somebody else's tradesman is in pocket by somebody else; and since there must be bad debts in the world, why, it is mere egoism not to like that we in particular should make them instead of our fellow-citizens.[21]

The passage is a reminder that, whatever the supposed sophistication of credit arrangements, debt is not an abstract concept that relates only to states, banks or the corporate world, but is a threat to the 'personal integrity and honour' of every individual who takes it on. Eliot was never in debt and was careful never to assume overly restrictive financial commitments. In 1860, even as her success as a high-selling novelist was becoming apparent, she resisted the idea of buying her first house, 'dreading a step that might fetter us to town, or a more expensive mode of living than might ultimately be desirable'.[22] A corresponding situation is most notably dramatised in *Middlemarch*, where the imprudence of Lydgate and Rosamond's domestic-economic choices has destructive consequences.[23]

As a couple they are equally complicit in the financial mismanagement that brings Lydgate perilously close to the terrifying extreme fate of the debtor: bankruptcy. Barbara Weiss has traced the incidence, legal history and the artistic and literary representations of a process that assumed a grimly fascinating ascendancy in the Victorian cultural imagination.[24] While identifying certain contradictions between the rhetoric of the public perception of bankruptcy and the pragmatic legislative response thereto, two significant points in relation to Eliot's imaginative treatment of bankruptcy and financial distress emerge from her study. First, social judgement on those afflicted went beyond the financial and legal to wider issues of character and morality: as Weiss concludes, 'there is no denying the sincerity of the Victorians' moral outrage toward bankruptcy'.[25] Second, although the extent of its novelistic treatment may tend to exaggerate its actual frequency, the incidence of bankruptcy and insolvency rose significantly over the century and embraced not only those engaged in entrepreneurial commercial activities, but also individuals imprudently exposed to the period's recurrent financial speculative frenzies as well as the simply financially inept.[26]

Consequently, in her personal and professional life, Eliot was not unusual in coming into direct contact with those touched by bankruptcy. She records, somewhat dispassionately, the failed china clay speculation and bankruptcy of Arthur Helps, an acquaintance and collateral victim of market excesses: 'In the panic last year all turned out badly for him and he has had to part with everything – even to his library.'[27] Her shrewd business eye also quickly alerted her to the implications of John Chapman's financial mismanagement and inability either to quantify or control his growing indebtedness: 'The way he is behaving is, between ourselves, generally the prelude to bankruptcy.'[28] Her main experience, however, was rather more intimate. Her sister Chrissy married a country doctor, Edward Clarke, whose gradual descent into debt was finally accompanied by illness and early death in 1852. The revelation that his property was already mortgaged left Chrissy and her children reliant on the generosity of her family, including her still far from financially secure sister.

This incident clearly informed Eliot's treatment of Mr Tulliver's insolvency in *Mill on the Floss* both in its effects on his dependents and in the psychological impact on Tulliver himself. His perception of self, both intrinsically and socially, is rooted in his ownership of Dorlcote Mill and the continuity and social position it embodies. In insolvency, he is diminished in every sense, declaring that 'I'm nought but a bankrupt – it's no use standing up for anything now' (350). The analysis of his financial collapse provided in Appendix B concludes that Eliot knowingly reveals that Tulliver inaccurately describes his legal status. Rather, he agrees a composition arrangement out of bankruptcy with his creditors before eventually repaying them in full. Within his family, however, the inability to discharge debts, even after the forced sale of intimate personal belongings, represents a state of diminishment that is indifferent to strict legal definition. Mrs Tulliver in particular largely defines herself by the possessions she has brought to the marriage and, failing fully to understand the reality of the situation, appeals first to her family then to Wakem to try to keep possession of them. Her sisters and their husbands deplore the affront to their bourgeois virtues – thrift, prudence, temperance – which Tulliver's character and actions represent and which have undermined their all-important family honour and reputation. Tom initially shares their resentment of his father's imprudence – 'Why should people give away their money plentifully to those who had not taken care of their own money?' (308) he asks – and emerges as a model of entrepreneurial self-help and independence. Conversely, Maggie, until her need to earn an independent income late in the novel, remains largely outside the market economy and love and sympathy for her father transcend any financially based judgement during the downfall. Her perception of what she wrongly perceives as her father's bankruptcy immediately attains the wider meaning: '"Why . . . what . . . have they made me a *bankrupt?*" "O father, dear father!" said Maggie, who thought that terrible word really represented the fact' (347). His financial collapse triggers a kind of personal disintegration which undermines the very continuity of his character over time.

Eliot reacted to the reality of Chrissy's financial distress with a mixture of Maggie's compassion and Tom's determined practicality.[29] In striving for this balance, she reveals an understanding of the necessity of combining the moral and the economic in the application of practical ethics in real-life crises. It is a synthesis that serves to distance her from the traditional economic dualism of market and non-market (domestic) activity and its gendered assumptions. There is evidence that, even in her youth, she was mentally linking the two domains by employing what Stefanie Markovits describes, in a different context, as her 'ethical cost-benefit analysis'.[30] In 1847, Eliot writes of the exchange of letters as a system of debits and credits; and an overly dramatic admonition to Sara Hennell for failing to remind her of a two shilling loan outstanding again extends the image of the balance sheet to wider commitments of duty and responsibility: 'save me from the pain of finding that I have neglected to pay even my money debts, when there are so many others which I am unable to defray'.[31]

Similar juxtapositions recur throughout the novels: Will Ladislaw, thinking with annoyance of his obligations to Mr Casaubon, wished 'that he could discharge them all by a cheque', an echo of Godfrey Cass's observation in an earlier novel that '"there's debts we can't pay like money debts"'. Even Savonarola presents Romola's sacramental and civic duties in explicitly financial terms: '"And you are flying from your debts: the debt of a Florentine woman; the debt of a wife"'.[32] When she became financially wealthy, Eliot continued to set appraisals of her material gains alongside higher stores of familial contentment, while, as already noted, her personal diaries freely intersperse financial tables and schedules. In the final years of her life, she turned to John Cross not only to provide dispassionate investment advice, but also to mediate on the repeated claims on her generosity. 'I am in dreadful need of your counsel' she writes, before presumably taking his advice to decline requests for loans to Vivian Lewes and Mde Beloc.[33]

The next chapter will describe how the reconciliation of high financial reward and the creation of art through literature was not always an easy or straightforward process for Eliot. However, this should not imply that she was wholly critical of the commercial system within which book publishing was increasingly becoming integrated. As with much of her thought, her reflections on commercial society are nuanced and her position difficult to categorise precisely. From her youth she was exposed to her father's business efficiency and careful financial management and, in her early adulthood, became well acquainted with the details of the Bray family manufacturing business. For them and the other prosperous Coventry Evangelicals, money-making, morality and philanthropy were not only compatible but also mutually dependent.[34]

The various, albeit partial influences of Mill, Comte and Spencer, supported a general perception that the age of industrial capitalism was an unevenly progressive historical stage, which would in turn give rise to a more elevated and enlightened social state. For Spencer, the progression was conceptualised as arising from the 'militant' to the 'industrial' state, the latter characterised by the triumph of consensually agreed contract underpinning legal, commercial and social systems.[35] Rather than attempting to undermine the status of contract Eliot, in her life and work, sought to find ways of either incorporating or overlaying higher moral considerations. In Spencerian terms, the novels illustrate how individual action – including money choices – is the foundation of collective progress towards the altruistic social stage. An illustration is Tom Tulliver's decision to destroy the loan note issued by his father to his Uncle Moss. His recognition that this is both an honourable and a dutiful act (it would be, he is convinced, his father's wish) transcends the strictly legal interpretation expressed by Mr Pullet, who is fearful that 'anybody could set the constable on you for it' (301).

The incident has an interesting real-life echo in the sad case of Edward Clarke. In 1842, Robert Evans rescued his son-in-law with a loan secured against a bond: 'and if he does not pay it to me in my life time it must be stoped [*sic*] out of my Daughters fortune after my Death'.[36] With Chrissy's family inheritance accordingly reduced and her husband's estate largely worthless, she became reliant on the support of her family. Eliot offered the little help she was able to afford and, significantly, her sense of duty becomes crystallised in the desire to help financially. This in turn focuses her motivation for her own work: 'the dear creatures here will be a constant motive for work and economy', she writes the week after Clarke's death.[37] Four months later her concern spills over into guilt that she 'dare not incur the *material* responsibility' of somehow housing and supporting Chrissy and her children. Her assessment speaks more to her wider philosophical concerns around motivation than the practicality of any alternative scheme:

> Yet how odious it seems that I, who preach self-devotion, should make myself comfortable here while there is a whole family to whom, by renunciation of my egotism I could give almost everything they want. And the work I can do in other directions is so trivial![38]

In the difficult choices surrounding the earning, accumulation and distribution of money, Eliot was starting to negotiate the shifting and sometimes overlapping boundaries of egoism and altruism.

The year before writing this letter, her first reference to the work of Auguste Comte appeared in a *Westminster Review* article.[39] Much has been written about the influence of Comte on Eliot's thought and the extent of that influence has long remained a subject of critical disagreement.[40] Comte's writing certainly helped her focus her own criticism of established forms of Christian observance, although Wright is correct to point to a combination of influences in her important later *Westminster Review* essays: 'Her attacks on the baptised egoism of Dr. Cumming and Edward Young owe as much to Feuerbach as Comte, but maintain a strong humanist position.'[41] Whatever Comte's precise influence, humanism gave a distinct edge to her thinking on money and moral choice. Her criticism of the controversial and hugely popular minister, Dr John Cumming, highlights aspects of self-interest and consequentialism that facilitated the ideological reconciliation of Evangelicalism with an unconstrained market economy and great social inequality in the second quarter of the century.[42] Her greatest fictional representation of the translation of this ethic into the actions and character of the businessman is *Middlemarch*'s Bulstrode, whose hypocrisy and moral relativity are supported by a selfish ends-based interpretation of Divine Will.

Bulstrode belongs, appropriately, to the 1830s, for by the time Eliot began her career as a novelist, the ascendancy of Christian Political Economy had passed. Historians including Hilton and Searle have analysed the changing relationship between churchmen and the market apologists during the 1850s and 1860s, the former tracing a shift he characterises as from Atonement to Incarnationalism.[43] While pointing to the growth of economics as a more independent and professional academic discipline, Searle too examines the opposition from both religious and secular humanist schools to what they each saw as the increasing prevalence in society of an unconstrained commercial moral code.[44] This criticism went beyond commentary on the periodic excesses of the stock market and financial world to question the ethical core of the whole market economy.

It was a criticism with which Eliot was largely in accord. The year in which she took up the editorship of the *Westminster Review*, 1852, saw the publication – incidentally, by John Chapman – of *Money and Morals: A Book for the Times*, written by the influential economic journalist and Unitarian John Lalor. While Lalor accepts the economic and, indeed, moral advantages that arise when men 'are perfectly free to exchange with each other the products of their industry', he unequivocally rejects what he sees as the partial and misguided conclusion of theoretical political economy: 'the doctrine that buying in the cheapest and selling in the dearest market is to be the supreme rule of human action'. Such doctrine, he argues, elevates the market above essential human values and leads to a sanctification of the market's single value measure – money.[45]

Lalor's book, whose themes chime strongly with twenty-first century debates on moral capitalism, had some impact. Interestingly, Mill, despite being praised by the author for his elevation of human welfare over the pursuit of wealth, was critical of the book and defended both Ricardo in particular and political economy in general against Lalor's criticism.[46] While many secular liberals would also have objected to Lalor's specifically Christian recommendations, his conclusions were starting to resonate with a widening body of opinion, including even Spencer. Spencer's article in the *Westminster Review* at the end of the decade, 'The Morals of Trade', is notable for its indictment of the motives and actions of all sectors of the commercial economy from manufacturing to retailing, wholesaling, banking and finance. Like Lalor, he characterises the age as being driven by an 'intense desire for wealth', which is a result of 'the indiscriminate respect paid to wealth'.[47] By implication, the manner in which wealth is created has abandoned any qualitative scale, which explains the paradoxical social acceptance of the abuses of trade. 'To a terrible extent' he continues, 'dishonesty is, not an exceptional or temporary, but a general and permanent element of our mercantile system.' Trade, he concludes, is essentially corrupt.[48]

Somewhat unconvincingly, Spencer ends the article by insisting that the age is still one of progress and development in which 'undue admiration for wealth seems to be the necessary accompaniment'.[49] Ironically, Adam Smith himself largely foresaw the attendant problems of creating an economy in which the self-interested capitalist was to play an increasingly influential role.[50] Hence, his well-known observation that men of the same trade can rarely meet without moving the conversation to price fixing. His conclusion, similar in essence to Spencer's, is that the commercial sector represents 'an order of men, whose interest is never exactly the same with that of the publick, who have generally an interest to deceive and even to oppress the publick'.[51]

It is also worth remembering that Smith recognised that the consequences of an increasing division of labour in the economy – the productivity benefits of which were, of course, central to the thesis of the early part of *The Wealth of Nations* – were not entirely favourable. George Eliot's most overt criticism of this cornerstone of political economy comes early in the second chapter of 'Brother Jacob', which is discussed more fully in my final chapter, by reference to Smith's work. There, Eliot's observations on the changing competitive dynamics of retailing and an emergent consumerism address individual moral and wider social issues. These changes had first been observed in the years preceding the novels. Her 1855 essay, 'Three Months in Weimar', describes a similarly undeveloped commercial society, in which retail distribution is unspecialised and competition barely existent. Abuses exist, but the 'peculiar Weimarian logic' nevertheless retains a value as part of a community, shaped organically by custom and history.[52]

In 'Brother Jacob', the exposure of Edward Freely reverses Smith's theory of stadial progression and Grimworth returns to the traditional retailing practices Eliot also describes in *The Mill on the Floss*, which was written in the same year. The town of St Ogg's had 'no plate-glass in shop windows . . . The shop windows were small and unpretending; for the farmers' wives and daughters who came to do their shopping on market-days were not to be withdrawn from their regular, well-known shops.'[53] This narrative thread of 'Brother Jacob' makes it somehow fitting that the publication of the story followed a path completely outside the mechanism of market pricing: Eliot simply gave it to George Smith for publication in the *Cornhill Magazine* as amends for the shortfall he suffered on *Romola*.

In her attitudes to credit and the limits of the marketplace in a commercial society, Eliot's singular synthesis of intuition, humanist sympathy, scientific analysis and metaphysical questioning make her economics, or, rather her moral economics difficult to align precisely. In turning to the management of the assets on her personal balance sheet, categorisation becomes no less problematic. An understanding of her motivation and action as a stock market investor over the bulk of the fiction-writing years gives valuable insights into her economic ethics, including important considerations of risk and capital forms, which are later tested in the novels. Relative to the depth of research and commentary that has attended most of Eliot's biographical history, her life as an investor has received little attention. Nancy Henry, who has done much to correct this oversight, concludes that both editorial decisions on primary documents and a lack of biographical focus on 'mundane' financial information have created a perception that 'Eliot appears less interested in her investments than she actually was.'[54]

Again, it is possible to trace this interest in the prudence and thrift that characterised her upbringing by a financially competent father, whose legacy was to provide Eliot's first modest, yet independent income. Financial assets with an ability to generate cash income were a tangible reality for her throughout her adult life. A letter of 1854 to Charles Bray expresses her concern at the prospect of a much-needed dividend flow being reduced:

circumstances render it desirable for the trustees to call in £1,500 of my money, which must consequently be found in the funds until a new investment can be found for it ... I only hope he [Isaac] will think it worthwhile to get another investment. For a considerable part of my sister's money he gets 5%.[55]

The yield on the benchmark consols in which her uninvested money sat varied over the period, but was typically around 3–4 per cent. She was therefore fully aware that any returns above that rate carried additional risk. Even before she became an active stock market investor, Eliot explored risk and investment returns in relation to character formation, most notably in *The Mill on the Floss*. The novel is set in a period when small-scale share investment was not yet open to the lower middle classes. Mr and Mrs Glegg are therefore representative of a practice, particularly in provincial communities of 'putting out' and 'calling in' money to match local funding opportunities. The riskiness of any particular venture is reflected in the required rate of return. Glegg tells his wife that 'You can't get more than five per cent with security' (416), explaining why the 'ten or twelve per cent' offered by Tom and Bob Jakin's scheme is inherently more risky than the secured loans and mortgages that comprise their typical investments. Indeed, 5 per cent appears to mark the vernacular boundary between secured investment and speculation: for her own money, Eliot regarded that level of income as representing an appropriate premium over consols with an acceptable level of risk. Thus her first stock market investment, a Guaranteed 5 per cent stock, made with the proceeds of the advance on *The Mill on the Floss*, is recorded both by Lewes (who arranged the transaction with a stockbroker) and Eliot herself, who again juxtaposes the material and the familial in her journal entry:

> my cup is full of blessings: my home is bright and warm with love and tenderness, and in more material vulgar matters we are very fortunate. I have invested £2000 in East Indies stock, and expect shortly to invest another £2000, so that with my other money, we have enough in any case to keep us from beggary.[56]

This was a good period in which to have capital available for investment in the stock market, with steady returns available in domestic and, increasingly, foreign and colonial securities.[57] Colonial stocks paid a significantly higher dividend yield than consols but had the same de facto backing of the UK government, which might explain the choice of Eliot's first investment. The substantial growth of large infrastructure projects, both in the empire and throughout the world, provided a steady supply of new issues to an expanding UK investor base. Over the next twenty years, Eliot achieved diversity in her steadily growing portfolio by adding similarly sized holdings. From the early 1870s, this process became a collaborative effort with John Cross, who came to assume progressively greater control of Eliot's financial affairs. In relation to how Cross might have influenced Eliot's perception of financial capital risk (which in turn related to how she viewed other forms of capital), it is notable that his own major career move represented a shift from the principal, proprietary risk-taking that his work for the family firm of Dennistoun Cross involved, to the advisory, fee-generating nature of the firm he set up with Robert Benson in 1875.[58] In his early career with the family business, Cross lived through what were likely to have been a traumatic series of financial events, including the transatlantic banking crisis of 1857 (his first year at work in New York), which temporarily brought Dennistoun Cross down.[59] By the time he came to advise Lewes and Eliot, Cross had developed into a cautious and diligent investor, as his own financial writings demonstrate.[60] Moreover, he was an unusually well-informed proponent of investment opportunities in the post-civil war United States, where he had lived and worked for fifteen years.

As a result, the Eliot–Lewes portfolio evolved to display great geographical and industry-sector diversification.[61] The highly speculative railway investments of the 1840s and 1850s had settled into a more mature, consolidated sector, which was easily the biggest group by value on the London market and was correspondingly well represented in Eliot's portfolio, which contained domestic, North American and Indian issues. The overall geographical profile is well diversified with a good representation of both foreign (mostly US) and colonial stocks. This feature is unusual for a contemporary private investor and is more typical of the portfolio of a City professional, reflecting Cross's expertise and Eliot's openness to a broad global exposure. Notably absent are the speculative mining ventures that are fictionalised in her only two contemporaneously set works: *Impressions of Theophrastus Such*, in which the rapacious Sir Gavial Mantrap devises ingenious mining speculations 'for the punishment of ignorance in people of small means' (129); and *Daniel Deronda*, where the demise of Grapnell & Co is attributed by Mrs Davilow to 'great speculations ... about mines and that sort of thing' (199). These, Eliot's final fictional works, include her only treatments of specifically stock market financial speculation. In *Daniel Deronda*, it is incorporated into a pervasive gambling trope that extends questions of chance and probability from the roulette table to both the stock and the marriage markets.

The triangulation of gambling, speculation and investment, the specific points of which were rarely securely fixed during the period, is here further complicated by the fact that the academic mathematical work which had long theorised odds in games of pure chance was starting to be adapted to the statistical modelling of stock portfolios. Eliot read up on probability theory in preparation for *Daniel Deronda* and Lewes was well acquainted both person-ally and with the work of many influential mathematicians, including John Venn, Jevons and Augustus de Morgan, some of whom were pioneering new work in the field.[62] De Morgan's 'An Essay on Probabilities and on Their Application to Life Contingencies and Insurance Offices' includes an intro-duction describing the history of probability theory from its gambling-related origins. Although by the end of the century an early breed of financial analysts was starting to recommend theories of investment diversification, it was not until some eighty years after her death that mathematical modelling enabled the formalisation of efficient portfolio theory.[63] Yet it is evident that Eliot and Cross managed an increasingly well-balanced and relatively low-risk portfolio, which, in its stock and industry weightings, shows signs of sophisticated qualitative and quantitative construction. What she certainly seems to have grasped is that this was a strategy that was less risky than simply leaving money in the bank at a time when no single institution, whether Grapnell & Co or its real-life counterpart Overund & Gurney, was 'too big to fail'.[64] In the last year of her life, when her portfolio was valued at over £30,000, fully three-quarters of her total estate value at death, Eliot never had more than about £1,000 in the Union Bank of London (ironically now part of the 'too big to fail' Royal Bank of Scotland).

However, while she remained fully invested throughout the decade, the 1870s did see some reduction in Eliot's investment risk appetite, partly facilitated by the growth in issuance of lower-risk debenture securities. By the early 1880s, debenture and fixed-return preference shares (both signifi-cantly less risky than ordinary shares) had grown to represent almost 40 per cent of the issues traded on the London Stock Exchange.[65] Eliot was clearly instrumental in the decision to reduce the equity component of her portfo-lio, at a time when Lewes's deteriorating health was prompting an increased desire for capital preservation. When Lewes writes to Cross in February 1877, instructing him to invest the second half of the payment for *Daniel Deronda*, he is explicit that Eliot wishes the £2,000 to be invested 'without any risk' in domestic debentures of Cross's choice.[66] By the time of her death, the yield on her portfolio had fallen close to 4 per cent, with US government bonds representing her largest single investment, at around 13 per cent of the portfolio.[67]

Less than three months before making her first investment in the Great Indian Peninsular Railway, Eliot replied to Charles Bray's letter seeking investment in his increasingly stretched business ventures:

> I know no capitalist to whom I could mention it ... At present I have no
> money that I could invest ... But I have a small sum in the Bank of Deposit,
> which we keep there to supply extra calls, and from this I could manage, on
> due notice, to lend you £100.[68]

Blackwood's substantial advance on *The Mill on the Floss* was promised, but
not yet in the bank and the prudent Eliot was not going to count on any
unhatched chickens even for such an old friend. Reckless lending, of the
type that undid the generous and otherwise estimable Caleb Garth in
trusting the creditworthiness of Fred Vincy, was not in her nature. What
is also interesting about this passage, however, is the distinguishing of
herself (about to become a woman of significant capital) from the 'capitalist'
Bray is seeking. The word had a narrower and more specific meaning than
today and it is clear that she would not regard a passive investor in the shares
of stock market-listed shares – what she was about to become and would
remain for the rest of her life – as a capitalist either.

Mary Poovey has written persuasively of the abstracting of finance in the
middle of the nineteenth century, as the growth of share issuance and widened
ownership helped to sever the links between corporate ownership (diverse
shareholders) and management responsibility.[69] Pivotal to this transformation
was the passage, in the 1850s and 1860s of a series of legislative initiatives,
including the Partnership and Liability Acts (1855), the Joint Stock Companies
Act (1856) and the Companies Act (1862). In the debates surrounding the
build-up to the passages of these Acts – which, Donna Loftus concludes, 'gave
England one of the most permissive frameworks for business in Europe' – the
Westminster Review was an active participant, running several related articles,
some included under Eliot's editorship.[70] The debate actually split opinion
even between committed laissez-faire political economists. The opponents of
limited liability, including such prominent names as J. R. McCulloch, argued
that the removal of individual liability for the debts incurred by an investee
company beyond the value of the shares owned would substantially reduce
individual responsibility and thereby increase fraud.[71]

The *Westminster Review*, however, was in the vanguard of those leading
calls for the new legislation on both economic and social grounds. The
October 1853 article, 'Partnership With Limited Liability', argues for the
prospective benefits to all classes of society: capitalists, who, free from
the restriction imposed by unquantifiable liability, 'would embark their
money, whether for the hope of profit or in the desire to do good'; the
middle classes, previously unable to invest either in land (because of the
prohibitive cost) or what they knew best, commerce (because of excessive
risk); and the working classes, who would be able to engage in

associations, in accordance with Mill's vision of worker participation.[72] Beyond this cross-class argument, claims for the wider benefits both to society and the elevation of individual character are well attuned with Eliot's ethics of community, in which she saw art adopting a central role. For her reviewer, however, it is a freeing of the laws of *business* which would have a similarly transforming effect: 'feelings of good will, sympathy, and friendship would inevitable spring from laws which placed men in relations to mutual dependence and reciprocal benefit'.[73]

In one argument offered against the new legislation, at least, its opponents could claim some justification. The enlargement of the investing public and a dramatic increase in the issuance of listed shares in which to invest would combine, it was feared, greatly to increase stock market speculation, bubbles and the inevitable and ruinous subsequent busts and financial crises. The regional banking crisis of 1825 and the 'railway-mania' of the mid-1840s had shown that more permissive legislation was not a prerequisite for such occurrences. But the fear and censure of market speculation came to occupy a much more dominant position in the collective imagination in the 1860s and 1870s. The list of novels of this period in which financial fraud and speculation are central to both plot and moral is well documented, with Eliot herself incorporating the 'wicked recklessness' of a speculating banker and the demise of the bank as an essential plotting device in *Daniel Deronda*.[74] Newspaper coverage of finance and markets expanded in proportion to the growth of the investing public and was also on hand to expose and forensically investigate the frequent frauds and abuses enacted.

It seems clear that Eliot was never tempted into speculative trading and certainly never employed the increasingly prevalent means of making leveraged, margined bets on short-term price movements that were often the undoing of Victorian speculators, both actual and fictional.[75] She may have belonged to the growing ranks of 'invisible' capitalists but, in her own mind, she stayed firmly behind the line which separates long-term investing from the less easily differentiated activities of speculating and gambling.[76] Not all, however would agree. Barbara Hardy believes the financial ethics of the novels are, compared with the author's own life, idealised:

> Life and art are intertwined, but are not the same. Ideals are easier to promote in art than life. George Eliot's investments made her complicit with Grapnell & Co, her gambling capitalists. Her shares were not ethical, she invested in Empire.[77]

The distance she presents between art and life is overstated. Eliot, while not uncritical and suspicious of the market economy and its limitations, recognised its development as both consistent with and representative of progressive, scientific society. Investing, like other commercial practices compatible with liberal rights and the broad precepts of capitalism, could be accommodated in her ethical framework.

The introduction of a disastrous financial speculation in *Daniel Deronda* brings into focus what is a more interesting observation on investing in Eliot's life and art. By setting most of her novels in the generation of her youth, or earlier, Nancy Henry argues that 'she evaded the moral issues attending her own reliance on a system by which money generated money ("getting rich without work") and in which the value of stocks and shares differed from the "genuine value" of her own labour'.[78] This seems right and it certainly allowed Eliot to consider individual and social notions of value at transitional points in the development of a commercial money economy. It also excludes her great working-men heroes, Adam Bede and Felix Holt, from any uncertain debate about the benefits to their class of the democratisation of share ownership and market participation.[79]

However, such omissions and limitations should not obscure the fact that, in her life and work, Eliot continually reflected on and, to some extent, constantly struggled with the question of how she should deal with the fact of her ever-growing financial wealth. Daniel Deronda is unusual among her characters in explicitly owning an investment port-folio. His questioning of that ownership and its employment forms a crucial episode in his full moral awakening. Until he discovers his wider inheritance, he is content neither with the 'three or five per cent' returns on his unearned financial capital, nor with the prospect of one of the few professions ostensibly open to him: authorship, 'a vocation which is thought to turn foolish thinking into funds'.[80]

At the end of the novel, it is unknown whether Daniel has sold his stocks to fund his new life in the East or whether the 'three or five percent' continues to accrue in the Zionist cause, in much the same way as Eliot's own dividend income funded her extensive family commitments both before and after her death. The dissatisfaction that this, in many ways the most wholly virtuous of her characters, expresses echoes the author's own periodic concerns that she is not sufficiently active: 'In my private lot I am unspeakably happy, loving and beloved. But am I doing little for others?' and later 'You see my only social work is to rejoice in the labours of others, while I live in luxurious remoteness from all turmoil.'[81] Eliot shied away from what she called 'public action' in her pursuit of the good. Indeed, she has been criticised by certain feminist critics for the limited support she gave to friends including Barbara Bodichon and Bessie Rayner Parkes in their campaigning for women's rights.[82] The action in which she largely confined herself 'to help in some small nibbling way to reduce the sum of ignorance, degradation, and misery on the face of this beautiful earth' was the same vocation that she has Deronda reject as one 'which is understood to turn foolish thinking into funds'.[83] The next chapter turns specifically to the profession of authorship and the sometimes conflicting claims of the novel as art and exchangeable commodity.

CHAPTER 3

'A money-getting profession': negotiating the commerce of literature

[The author] is laugh'd at if poor; if, to avoid that curse, he endeavours to turn his Wit to Profit, he is branded a Mercenary.[1] – James Ralph, 1758

Mr. Smith the publisher called and had an interview with G. He asked if I were open to a 'magnificent offer.' This made me think about money – but it is better for me not to be rich.[2]   – George Eliot, 1862

The literary or artistic field is at all times the site of a struggle between the heteronomous principle, favourable to those who dominate the field economically and politically (e.g. 'bourgeois art') and the autonomous principle (e.g. 'art for art's sake'), with those of its advocates who are least endowed with specific capital tending to identify with a degree of independence from the economy.[3]   – Pierre Bourdieu, 1993

For Bourdieu, the field of literary production is valorised by cultural and symbolic – as opposed to economic – forms of capital. However, like all fields, at its heart is exchange and competition, creating an overlap with the key mechanism of the market for any commodity. And, as he suggests above – and Ralph's words from a distance of over two hundred years would seem to confirm – the struggle to reconcile material gain and power with an independent creative process that sits outside, indeed transcends, the market and other hierarchical constructs, has occupied the novelist since the genre's inception.

Bourdieu's insightful analysis has helped to identify shifting allegiances and balances of power within his wider, cultural 'site of struggle' and, most relevant to this study, illuminate how 'the established definition of the writer' can be transformed during periods in which long-standing relationships and power balances between groups involved in the chain of literature – from creator, via producer and distributor, to reader – are significantly altered.[4] In this way, 'the second half of the nineteenth century [was] the period in which the literary field attained its maximum autonomy'.[5] Yet while that period's growing body of professional authors was no longer beholden to the patrons who had previously financed much literary output, the free market was to create its own threats and restrictions.

Bourdieu's assertion is supported by the wide body of work examining developments in the structure of the publishing industry during this era, including the changing economic position of the novelist. In this context, some illuminating work has focused on Eliot, relating her personal dealings with the House of Blackwood and the production of her novels to her life, thought and art.[6] This chapter will extend the temporal scope of those analyses to consider the tensions and resolutions across the various stages of what Robert Darnton has called the 'communications circuit' of literary output.[7] The discussion will draw on Eliot's letters and essays, including her important final written reflections on authorship. It will also describe a particularly important and formative negotiation between the newly successful novelist and her publisher.

Eliot was unique in her progression around this circuit; for a woman in the writing profession, her range of paid employment was exceptional. The variety of her sources of income from translator to periodical journalist, from editor and publishing business advisor to best-selling novelist gave her an unusually broad perspective on the economic and artistic aspects of literature in the pivotal third quarter of the century. Looping off this main 'circuit', at each stage of her career, are (continuing in Bourdieuean terms) Eliot's own attempts to mediate heteronomy and autonomy and thereby evaluate her 'specific capital' as a novelist. These loops widened as the success of her work increased her material wealth, extended her readership and elevated her position in the hierarchy of the literary establishment. In tracing these patterns, this chapter extends the consideration of how Eliot explored the limitations of money value by reference to the competing claims for the writer of professionalism and vocation. It concludes that her inability fully to reconcile these tensions led her to consider in ever-richer and more complex ways the ethical implications of financial motivation and action within the novels.

In April 1854, Eliot wrote to Sara Hennell expressing her low expectations for the reception of her forthcoming translation of Ludwig Feuerbach's *The Essence of Christianity*:

> The press will do nothing but abuse or ridicule it – which for those who know what 'the press' means, as I do, is not of the slightest consequence to one's own view, but must always affect a publisher's. I daresay Mr. Chapman will think his case pitiable, but if he knew the amount of phosphorous it requires to translate such a book (which he does not) he would think it is still more pitiable to have only two shillings a page for it.[8]

The letter was written four years before the publication of her first novel, but her professional experience already enables her to assess a literary project from the points of view of the publisher, the reviewing press and the writer-translator. It is a multiple perspective that gives authority to her critique of both a press deficient in artistic judgement and a publishing establishment indifferent to the labour expended by the poorly paid translator.[9] The following year she was to write a short article for the *Leader*, 'Translations and Translators', in which she attempts to place her subject within a hierarchy of writing: 'Though a good translator is infinitely below the man who produces *good* original works, he is infinitely above the man who produces *feeble* original works.' Particular praise is given to those whose 'exceptional faculty and exceptional knowledge' can translate complex works of thought or science 'so as to lay open the entire uninjured kernel of meaning' – an accurate description of her own achievement in translating the work of Strauss and Feuerbach.[10] Implicit in both the letter and the *Leader* article is the disconnection between her perception of the literary value intrinsic to a particular work or genre and the monetary value ascribed by the book trade.[11]

The precarious condition of Chapman's business in the early 1850s gave a particular edge to Eliot's formative views on the relation between literary output and financial reward. When, in 1853, he apparently backed away from an agreement to publish an original work by Eliot titled 'The Idea of a Future Life', she writes angrily 'I would much rather that you should publish the work and *not* pay me than pay me and not publish it.'[12] By then, Eliot's motion around the 'communications circuit' was already under way and was about to rapidly accelerate. She was well placed to closely observe the simultaneous reshaping of long-established commercial practices and relationships within the industry and, from an early stage, she also participated in that flux. While the 'pitiable' translation earnings of which she complains relate specifically to an allocation of value between writer and publisher, Eliot was closely allied with that publisher, John Chapman, in an important mid-century site of struggle in the economics of publishing. At stake was not only how the surplus profits from the sale of books should be allocated, but also who should be able to control the level and variance of that surplus.

The Bookselling Question of 1852 arose as a result of attempts by the powerfully self-interested London Booksellers' Committee unilaterally to impose their regulations, which scaled and limited the discounts at which books could be retailed.[13] Writing in his *Westminster Review* article, 'The Commerce of Literature' (1852), which chronicled the progress of the debate, Chapman frames the argument against restrictive pricing in a broad and elevated setting: 'The facts connected with the production and distribution of books, though little heeded by the public are, nevertheless, of great social and political, as well as literary, importance.'[14] Chapman, as one of a small group of publisher-booksellers defying the committee by underselling books, was probably as much motivated by economic self-interest, if not quite necessity, given the recurrently precarious position of his business ventures.[15]

Nevertheless, his defence of 'enterprising booksellers' against the collusive and monopolistic forces of the large, established publishing houses, wholesalers and booksellers struck a chord very much in tune with the newly relaunched *Westminster Review*, under the effective editorship of Eliot. Her own letters provide further insight into Chapman's orchestration of a campaign which, in a matter of months, succeeded in effectively overturning all the committee's restrictions and establishing a free trade in books.[16] While the economic outcome placed the industry firmly in the prevailing and fast-flowing tide of liberal, free-trade ideology, the social benefit its supporters propounded – cheap literature available to a wider readership – was, in a sense, a victory for Utilitarianism against the Romantically informed conservatism of those who argued that price maintenance served to protect 'high' literature.

This last point is of particular interest because of the crucial support given to the undersellers' campaign by a number of very prominent authors, including not only economic liberals such as Mill, Gladstone and Spencer, but also Dickens and Carlyle. James J. Barnes summarises how this rare instance of unanimity came about: 'They held that the issues were clearly drawn, the interests of authors were obviously affected by the regulations, and the spirit of the age favoured liberty in all branches of commerce.'[17] That the authors' battle at this stage was with the booksellers rather than directly with the publisher (as we will see, George Eliot was at the forefront of innovative deals which were to supplant entire copyright advance purchase) should not cloud the significance of 1852. Some thirty years ahead of the formation of their own professional organisation, the Society of Authors, their concerted support for the removal of price restrictions marked a significant claim of influence over and greater ownership of the product of their own intellectual capital. The ownership debate was to intensify as the market, sales and profits from books all grew in the second half of the century and ultimately focused on the question of what constituted the public sphere in literature.[18] It was a question that was to greatly exercise George Eliot throughout her career. In her final published work, she undermines the arguments of 'Universal Utilitarianism', which holds that original authorship should be as 'free and all-embracing as the liberal air' and that any claims for the individual ownership rights of 'property in ideas' are invalid.[19]

In fact, Eliot's late writings are increasingly pre-occupied with meditations on the constitution of the author's particular form of 'capital'. In 'Leaves from a Note-Book', her contention that '[t]he author's capital is his brain-power – power of invention, power of writing', hints at an analogy between the writer and the physical inventor that Clare Pettitt has identified as a central field of nineteenth-century discourse.[20] Eliot actually makes the analogy explicit by examining the intellectual capital of authorship in terms related to, but ultimately incompatible with, marginal utility theory as applied to two imagined manufacturing businesses.[21] The first is a producer of basic, commodity calico whose profit is reinvested to create more calico, thus 'reproducing and increasing' the owner's capital: 'The wise manufacturer gets richer and richer, and the consumers he supplies have their real wants satisfied and no more.' The second manufacturer, however, has developed a new, fashionable material which sells well as a 'transiently desirable commodity' that goes beyond the consumer's 'real wants' but, containing arsenic in its colouring, has a harmful effect on both workers and purchasers. Neither demand-led model is applicable to what Eliot conceives as the proper function of authorship, which precludes both formulaic repetition and any market-driven innovation that compromises the duty of public instruction that the published writer necessarily assumes.[22]

The standardised, mass-produced item calls to mind the formulaic fiction she had so scathingly criticised twenty years earlier in her *Westminster Review* article, 'Silly Novels by Lady Novelists' (1856). Her critique of the sub-genre actually proceeds by reference to a hierarchy of capital forms: the excess financial returns these writers achieve ('they think five hundred a-year a miserable pittance') enables them to produce what Eliot describes as a 'commodity' item; but in their 'poverty of brains' they lack any corresponding intellectual capital capable of generating literary value. The article concludes with an economic explanation of why the phenomenon she describes will self-perpetuate: 'No educational restrictions can shut women out from the materials of fiction, and there is no species of art which is so free from rigid requirements.'[23] In other words, there are no barriers to entry.

By the time she came to write *Daniel Deronda* in 1875, Eliot was concerned that she too was becoming implicated in the depreciation of literature by the rapid growth in production of cheap books for a widening, but increasingly indiscriminating readership. Gallagher and Bodenheimer have both written perceptively of the doubts Eliot expressed in her journal entry of 13 January 1875 'as to the worth of what I am doing'. Her concern for her new novel is that she 'may not be able to complete it so as to make a contribution to literature and not a mere addition to the heap of books'.[24] Her fears, as an ageing and famous author, enriched by the sales of her books, are restatements of anxieties she articulated throughout her writing life. She recognised the fragility and transience of authorial capital well before the formal advent of marginal economics and struggled to contain her higher artistic purpose within a requirement to maximise the material return on that capital. While awaiting publication of her first work of fiction, *Scenes of Clerical Life*, she wrote: 'Writing is part of my religion … At the same time I believe that almost all the best books have been written with the hope of getting money for them.'[25] Lewes is less ambivalent on the question of literature in the market-place, writing to Blackwood:

> To push a book and sell it as fast as possible is the very purport of publishing. If the public won't buy they won't – and one must content oneself with reflections on their taste. If they will, they should have every chance.[26]

This conviction was to influence substantially the form in which *Middlemarch* was published some years later. Earlier in her career, when the balance of power lay less certainly with the author, Eliot and Lewes sought to negotiate deals that not only secured high financial rewards, but also promoted what was to become the 'George Eliot' brand both domestically and internationally. N. N. Feltes has been critical of such interpretations of Eliot's commercial negotiations, which, he argues, serve 'to dehistoricize the relations of production of her novels and to entertain Blackwood's private speculations about her "mercenary trait"'.[27] His overtly Marxist and feminised reading of this aspect of Eliot's life and business dealings misrepresent her position (both individually and in tandem with Lewes) within the undoubtedly male, capitalist hegemony of nineteenth-century publishing that Feltes seeks to expose. Eliot's friend Margaret Oliphant paints a more accurate and informative picture. In her history of Blackwood & Co she is forthright in her assessment of Eliot's commercial understanding and involvement: 'we find that she was an admirable woman of business, alert and observant of every fluctuation of the book-market, and determined that in every way her works should have the fullest justice done them'.[28]

Certainly, Eliot's close association with Chapman and his precarious finances in the early 1850s gave her both an important inside knowledge of the economics of publishing and a vivid illustration of the unfortunate consequences of an imbalance between literary idealism and commercial reality. Chapman came increasingly to rely on Eliot's pragmatic business sense in the re-launch of the *Westminster Review* and she became impatient of his disorganised and ill-prepared advances to potential financial support-ers.[29] Her understanding of wealthy businessmen, probably sharpened by her exposure to Bray's business circles, is evident – 'I think Mr. Combe is a capital man, who knows what he means and will not pay for what he does not mean' – and was later to inform character formation in the novels.[30]

Over the course of Eliot's career the 'commerce of literature' changed significantly. Disappointing sales of *Felix Holt* in 1866 prompted Blackwood's partner, Joseph Langford, to observe that the new market dynamic 'places everyone in a state of uncertainty and renders it impossible to know through what channels a successful book reaches the public … Looking back at the subscription paper of *The Mill on the Floss* there is evidently a great change in the book trade since 1860.'[31] Eliot and Lewes were well attuned to the new challenges and opportunities that a wider, increasingly consumerist readership presented. Lewes's proposal for the inno-vative publication form of *Middlemarch* recognised this trend, as did his suggestion that (following the precedence of Dickens and Thackeray, along-side whom he now confidently places his wife) advertisements for forth-coming parts of the novel be included in each current part-volume. The focus on the wants of the consumer provides a further justification, for 'this would not only bring in some hard cash, it would help to make the volume a lot bigger for the five shillings which in British eyes is a consideration not to be neglected'.[32] Langford, perhaps revealing something of the conservatism of the established publishing trade, is sceptical, but the progressive Lewes prevails.

In fact, an attention to advertising, marketing and presentation is a feature of the Eliot–Lewes correspondence with Blackwood from the out-set. Writing from Munich in 1858, Lewes links a complaint over a lack of advertising with another subject of occasional annoyance, Charles Mudie, who 'has never advertized "The Scenes" among his works, although many works far less significant … are named in every list'.[33] Eliot herself, with a close eye to the detail of her 'product packaging', bemoans what she regards as an ineffectual marketing campaign for *The Mill on the Floss*: 'I wish the lettering of the advertisement could be managed so as to prevent this sort of ignorance, or rather of ignoring.'[34] By contrast, the product design of the six-shilling edition of *Adam Bede* elicits praise: 'I think the advertisement and specimen pages are perfect. The utmost simplicity is the only thing that is distingue in these days.'[35] Much later in her career, her pragmatism in the face of changing consumer tastes is even more direct, when she explains her approval of a new illustrated edition of the works in 1866:

In the abstract I object to illustrated literature, but abstract theories of publishing can no more be carried out than abstract theories of politics. The form in which books shall appear is a question of expediency to be determined chiefly by public taste and convenience.[36]

The later part of this chapter will consider how Eliot's growing concern with how her books were presented and sold was linked to an increased equity ownership of her output. This involved the assumption of more risk in both the formal and the thematic elements of her later novels and in the economic terms under which they were published. Her fears surrounding the commoditising of literature persuaded her that, in order to maintain the value of her intellectual capital, or brand, she would require a greater return on that capital. Moreover, and mirroring wider trends in British commerce and investment flows (including Eliot's personal stock investments), that brand had become increasingly international. The basis of her financial deals with Blackwood was largely established as early as *The Mill on the Floss*, and while *Romola* (1862) marked the peak of her British book advances, her overseas rights continued to rise with each new book. In 1858, with only *Scenes of Clerical Life* in publication, she asks Blackwood 'Can anything be done in America for *Adam Bede*? I suppose not – as my name is not known there.'[37] Once her name was known, however, Lewes was instrumental in securing exponential increases in the size of her US advances from Harper.[38]

To illustrate a number of the points raised so far and also to construct a bridge to a consideration of the non-commercial aspects of Eliot's authorship, a brief examination of what was a pivotal point in her relationship with her publisher will hopefully be instructive. It describes a negotiation that transformed her financial position.

Discussions surrounding the publication of *The Mill on the Floss* took place during the second half of 1859, when the full extent of the success of *Adam Bede* was becoming clear. The euphoria of both publisher and author was clouded only by the unforeseen side-effect of the latter's anonymity: a claim of authorship by the impostor Liggins. It is clear that Lewes and Eliot believed, with some justification, that Blackwood was insufficiently rigorous and definitive in his denials of Liggins's bogus claim. The publisher was clearly alert to the commercial advantages of the identity of his new, best-selling author being shrouded in mystery and the subject of publicly argued dispute.[39] Indeed, the Liggins affair revealed a tension over the ownership, management and valuation of Eliot's intellectual property that was to intensify in the next negotiation and, to varying degrees, recur with each new work.

The success of *Adam Bede* had greatly shifted the basis of the financial negotiation for *The Mill on the Floss* and Eliot was clear and open in her basic requirement. John Blackwood wrote to his brother in June 1859: 'She honestly confesses to a most deep seated anxiety to get a large price for the new Tale and I think we will be well able to afford to give it. It should be a little fortune to her.'[40] In the event that Blackwood could not meet these expectations, she would have felt confident that competing firms would do so. She had already been courted to write for *Once a Week* by publishers 'perfectly prepared to meet *any* views you might entertain as to remuneration'; while Dickens, writing in effusive praise for *Adam Bede*, invited her to join him as 'a fellow labourer', promising that 'no channel that even you could command, should be so profitable as to yourself'.[41]

Blackwood, despite the ruthless open-market practices of the industry, from which not even the noble Scotsman was wholly immune, started the race in poll position.[42] His opening offer, in October 1859, was made only after careful consideration of 'what ... is right and prudent'. However, his proposal of £3,000 for serial publication in *Blackwood's Magazine* and the retention of copyright for four years thereafter was met with some annoyance.[43] To understand why, we need to wind back through the preceding months, to the time when it became clear that the author of *Adam Bede* represented an exciting, and financially lucrative, new talent.

Money was not the whole story, but it played a leading role. A week before the dispatch of the offer, Eliot had written to Blackwood from Weymouth anticipating his preferred form of publication but warning that any financial benefit accruing to the publisher from periodical serialisation should, in effect, compensate the author for what she foresaw as the inevitably negative effect on sales of the complete novel.[44] It is notable that the argument for outright publication is not made on artistic or aesthetic grounds (although the implication of Lewes's later comment that it was unlikely she would publish in *Once a Week* is that the quality of periodical was important to her), but on the basis of what constitutes a fair financial split between author and publisher.[45] Moreover, Blackwood's enthusiasm for the benefits of anonymity supplied by periodical publication – 'it would be great fun to watch the speculations as to the author's life' – was by no means shared by his author. More than half of Eliot's letter rejecting the offer is taken up with complaints about Liggins, his supporter Bracebridge and the latter's efforts to identify the original sources of Eliot's fictional characters. To maintain the mask of George Eliot – a relatively straightforward and manageable professional disguise – was one thing; further levels of concealment were not only unnecessary, but would also, she feared, serve to thicken the fog of uncertainty that might obscure, and thereby tarnish and undermine, her income-generating capital.

As the correspondence continued during October, she began to sign her letters to the Blackwoods and Langford, as 'Marian Evans Lewes', a change noted ruefully by William Blackwood, no doubt wary of the commercial implications should his author decide to remove all her various masks: 'I am rather sorry to see the change of signature. On the whole I think you may be as well without the new tale for Maga.'[46] The whole deal was now under threat. But shortly afterwards, a specific financial exchange triggered a new and threatening urgency to what had so far been a guarded, though still essentially friendly game of negotiation. The incident is a telling illustration of how 'human economics', while potentially serving to elevate and enrich the requirements of a solely commercial or contractual agreement can, because of the qualitative and subjective nature of its enactment, simultaneously engender misinterpretation and distrust.[47]

Again some background is important. Some months earlier, in May 1859, Blackwood, in response to the exceptional sales of the relatively cheaply acquired *Adam Bede* and, no doubt, preparing his ground for the negotiation of the next novel, told Eliot of his intention to pay her an additional, non-contracted fee of £400. Initially the offer was graciously acknowledged but there is little objective evidence of her real opinion of the nature and extent of Blackwood's bonus in the following months. Letters between the two Blackwood brothers and their London and Edinburgh partners indicate the presence of genuine motivations and principles in their action, although Feltes warns against taking the publisher's apparent generosity at face value. The distribution of a small part of the surplus profit of *Adam Bede* to the book's creator, he argues, merely epitomised the paternalist hegemony of the large publishers.[48] What does seem clear is that Blackwood had decided to increase the *ex gratia* payment to £800 in October, even when he genuinely feared he would be unable to secure terms for the new novel.[49] What he regarded as 'the very dry way' in which his increased payment was acknowledged, closely followed by Lewes's somewhat crude and boastful suggestion that *The Mill on the Floss* was becoming the subject of a competitive bidding war, provoked a full and frank expression of views and grievances from both parties.

This proved a turning point. Within weeks, terms for the new book were amicably agreed. While it is impossible to assess the exact roles Eliot and Lewes played in the drawn-out negotiation, the process concludes with a small but telling incident which indicates Eliot's ultimate level of control in financial as well as artistic matters. Lewes's plan to publish a serialised one-shilling edition alongside the main publication is ostensibly left open after the agreement of the principal terms, but its implementation was, in reality, never likely to pass the final sanction of the author herself: 'I think we have fairly dissipated the Nightmare of the Serial by dint of much talking' she tells Blackwood.[50]

With friendly relations restored and a new benchmark established for the novels which was to give the author a significant scaled profit share of excess sales and greater control of cheaper editions, Eliot was able to infuse the professional, commercial relationship with her own strain of human economics. Significantly, her journal entry confirms that the offer of £4,500 from Bradbury and Evans and the expectation of a firm offer from Dickens were not exaggerated negotiating counters and that she could indeed have extracted terms for *The Mill on the Floss* beyond Blackwood's capability.[51] However, the professed value of a long-standing relationship with her publisher implicitly differentiates the communications circuit of literature from those commercial activities whose participants are connected solely by economic or monetary forces: 'I prefer in every sense, permanent relations to shifting ones,' she wrote to Blackwood, 'and have the strongest distaste for the odour of mere money speculation about my writing.'[52]

On the whole, her sentiment appears sincere. This book has argued that Eliot was at least familiar with the principles of political economy in its mid- and later century variations. Her application of human economics in her professional life, however, serves to undermine the concept of 'economic man' on which much of that theory rested. In effect, she acts at odds with the overriding principle of economic self-interest.

Several years later, as we have already seen, her decision to give 'Brother Jacob' to Smith as compensation for his losses on *Romola*, removed entirely her short story from the market mechanism in favour of what she saw as a higher personal claim. This action might even be interpreted as a renunciation of the act by which she temporarily abandoned her 'permanent relations' with Blackwood: the sale of *Romola* effectively to the highest bidder. Her decision to follow the market rules of supply and demand was economically rational, indeed theoretically necessary, but the emotional realities – guilt and disappointment over Smith's losses – were more deeply felt and proved decisive in her future choice of publisher. Indeed, there are instances in her subsequent letters to Blackwood when she adopts an almost maternal concern for his and his firm's financial health. In 1867, discussing a new cheap edition of her works, she insists that 'I care comparatively little about profiting further by it myself, but I am seriously anxious that the speculation should not prove ultimately an undesirable one for you.'[53] When Blackwood admits that 'an oversight in our calculations' on the economics of the twelve-shilling editions of *The Mill on the Floss* meant that, despite high sales, he had barely covered his costs, Eliot insists that the contract for subsequent runs should be amended to give the return envisaged in the spirit, if not the final contractual terms, of the agreement.[54]

The overlay of non-monetary standards into her commercial publishing dealings both mirrored and helped inform her determination of value in the works themselves, particularly as the monetary value ascribed to them by the market escalated. The need to find a value for her work beyond the economic led her to reject financially lucrative commissions which did not fulfil a literary standard or give her sufficient artistic independence.[55] At the very time that Blackwood and his partners were bemoaning their client's lack of gratitude and mercenary motivations, she was declining an offer of £1,200 for the rights to publish a story in a New York magazine, the *Century*. Later on, at the peak of her success as a novelist, she published *The Spanish Gypsy* (1868) for a fraction of her normal advance. In a letter to Cara Bray, she explicitly distances herself from those whose measure of literary output is financial:

> Don't you imagine how the people who consider writing simply as a money-getting profession will despise me for choosing a work by which I could get hundreds where for a novel I get thousands.[56]

Her distrust of, or, at least, ambivalence towards money-valuation is again evident during the negotiation for what was to be her highest book advance. Lewes writes of George Smith's initial £10,000 offer for *Romola*, 'Polly, as usual was disinclined to accept it, on the ground that her work would not be worth the sum!'[57] Even when the final sum is settled at £7,000 – allowing for copyright reversion and a less daunting serialisation schedule – Eliot justifies her decision not even to enter Blackwood into a negotiation by conflating his assessment of the value of her work with her own, and concluding that Smith's terms were 'hopelessly beyond your usual estimate of the value of my books to you'.[58]

One way of approaching Eliot's two-tier estimation of the value of her work is to consider how she perceived, differentiated and attempted to reconcile the professional and the vocational in her writing. Susan Colón uses alternative terminology but with the same aim of probing a sometimes complex co-existence; that is, to examine 'the dialectic between materialist and idealist rationalities in order to prevent flattening the existential tension between them that the Victorians experienced'. Through specific consideration of the role of mentoring and the service ethic in readings of *Romola* and *Daniel Deronda*, Colón explores 'the tension between self-interest and public service'; a tension embodied in Eliot's attempts to reconcile maximum financial reward and higher moral purpose in literature.[59]

After the success of her early novels, Eliot describes in a letter to her old friend François D'Albert Durade a vocational awakening that is grounded in personal fulfilment: 'I have at last found my true vocation, after which my nature had always been feeling and striving uneasily.'[60] At the opposite end of her career, in 'Leaves from a Note-Book', she uses the language and imagery of the materialist, commercial world both to root the nature of artistic capital in the physical domain of human needs and wants and, simultaneously, to distinguish and distance the 'vocation' of the author whose duty is to uphold intellectual and moral standards 'which would override the rule of the market'.[61] The financial, 'professional' aspects of published literature may be negotiable and relative according to market demand, but its 'vocational' nature carries an absolute social and moral responsibility, for 'man or woman who publishes writings inevitably assumes the office of teacher or influencer of the public mind'.[62] The potential conflict is evident: the popular author secures her professional position by giving her readership more of what she knows will sell; but, by succumbing to what is transient or fashionable, she risks neglecting, or even undermining, her 'vocational' responsibility.

The moral argument for widening readership had strong liberal credentials, as illustrated in Chapman's argument in 'The Commerce of Literature'. Eliot's letters too make repeated complaints against 'the enforced dearness of good books' and call for editions of her books to be 'as cheap as my public requires'.[63] But a widening readership based on cheaper editions comes at a price. Clare Pettitt argues that Eliot was reluctant to come to terms with the trade-off:

> Over her career, Eliot was to construct a model of morally strenuous read-
> ership that satisfied her need for a 'public' sphere not defined economically,
> but rather as a sphere of moral virtue and high culture. Such a model allowed
> her to fantasize something approaching an *exchange* between the writer and
> the actively responsive reader.[64]

By the mid-1870s this model was becoming increasingly stressed, as sales of cheap editions of *Middlemarch* exceeded the best estimates of Blackwood and even the optimistic Lewes.[65] As already noted, her journal reflections reveal an attendant concern raised by popular success: the fear that her future work will merely add to the growing oversupply in the literary marketplace.[66] Ironically, her fears were realised only posthumously when, in the last two decades of the century, her publisher continued to flood the market with new popular editions, which

> were assiduously issued at an ever-increasing rate after her death in 1880, and
> as a result began accounting for an ever-increasing percentage of Blackwood's

income ... The unfortunate result was a dangerous overdependence upon this success, and a major collapse in profits when the market for Eliot's work dried up at the end of the century ... a result of overproduction of Eliot texts to the point of saturation by a firm that was increasingly at sea in a changing literary marketplace.[67]

Through the production of books 'as cheap as my public requires' she became, albeit temporarily, a posthumous victim of the market rule of surplus supply.

This chapter and, indeed, this biographically informed section will conclude by briefly considering how Eliot attempted to mediate her materialist and idealist positions by reference to her concepts of the boundaries of risk and action. Risk is often closely associated with a testing of the 'rule of the market'. In the changing risk profile of her commercial agreements, I identify almost paradoxical attempts to use and better control the market as a means towards that 'fixing of the author's vocation' which seeks ultimately to override the market. Thus, during the negotiation for *The Mill on the Floss* in 1859 she tells Blackwood, 'I don't want the world to give me anything for my books except money enough to save me from the temptation to write *only* for money.'[68] In her subsequent publishing contracts, she attempted to plot parallel routes to financial and artistic independence and progressively assumed principal ownership. And with ownership comes greater attendant risk.

From the outset of her career she is clear in her determination to retain ultimate copyright ownership, but, for the first novels, rejects Blackwood's offer of a profit-share arrangement:

> I wish to retain the copyright, according to the stipulation made for me by Lewes when he sent Amos Barton and whatever you can afford to give me for the first edition, I shall prefer having as a definite payment rather than as half profits.[69]

Her prudence, as a new novelist, is understandable, although the riskier option would have paid back extremely well with *Adam Bede*. As described earlier, her next negotiation was predicated on her desire both to maximise book sales and to have direct financial participation in the event of *The Mill on the Floss* achieving popular success. Blackwood justifies his initial, disappointing offer for this novel by reminding Eliot of the many unsold copies of *Scenes of Clerical Life* he has been left with and warns his young author of the uncertainty of the market. His understandable message is that the assessment and management of commercial risk is best left in his hands.[70] Eliot's response is definitive: 'As, from the nature of your offer, I

infer that you think my next book will be a speculation attended with risk, I
prefer incurring that risk myself.'[71]

Notably in this instance, Eliot seems prepared to accept the characterisation of her risk-action as a 'speculation'. As discussed in the previous
chapter, the term in its stock market context represented a dubious area
beyond the field of genuine investment into which she refused to cross.
Years later, the word recurs in negotiation with Blackwood over
Middlemarch when she and Lewes specifically dissociate themselves from
what they describe as a publishing speculation. Instead, Blackwood is
presented with the option of electing for either a high initial advance or a
royalty agreement: 'the choice is open to you to speculate or not as you see
fit'. In opting for the latter he increases both the risk and (as it transpired,
substantial) reward for his author who has, in effect, very much shared in the
speculation.[72] Detailed royalty negotiations recurred in 1876 with the
publication of the complete works and the extension of the copyright
lease. By then Lewes's calculations had shifted to the particular detail and
definition of the author's 'contingent advantage'.

Eliot's attitude towards risk in her writing goes beyond issues of remuneration for and ownership of the novels. It informs the very nature of her
literary creativity. Her letters and journals provide a few clues as to how
external, material circumstances shaped what and how she wrote.
Explaining, in 1861, her decision to interrupt the progress of the ambitious
Romola project in favour of *Silas Marner*, 'a story of old-fashioned village
life', she tells Blackwood, 'I think I get slower and more timid in my writing,
but perhaps worry about horses and servants and boys, with want of bodily
strength, may have had something to do with that.'[73] She was now a woman
of capital and the co-incidence of a transformed financial position and the
adoption of Lewes's sons at this time has been well noted in connection with
the emergence of the novel and its major themes.[74] Despite the author's
profession of timidity and implied narrowness of canvas, Mary Poovey's
reading of the novel places it in an important line of works attempting to
mediate concepts of material and transcendent value (most obviously
Eppie's hair which first resembles, then replaces, then becomes an embodied transformation of gold in all its scale of meaning) through the language
and concepts of the economic:

> *Silas Marner* provides a particularly clear example of the way that mid-
> century novelists subjected economic matters – in this case, the monetary
> value of gold – to the alchemy of a moral lesson by emphasizing the
> connotative capacity of language – that is, the elevation of figuration and
> suggestion over denotation and reference.[75]

Later in the decade, by which time further large advances on *Romola* and *Felix Holt* had fully secured her financial position, the form and structure of publication become areas for potential risk and innovation. Noting the previously observed changes occurring in the book trade in the mid-1860s, which in part explained the disappointing initial sales of *Felix Holt*, she proposes a strategy which again sets the author and Lewes apart from their less reactive publisher and his senior staff: 'I am quite for trying a new experiment when we publish anything again – if we can get Mr. Simpson's caution to consent.'[76] The next published novel, *Middlemarch*, did indeed constitute a new and very successful experiment, its eight half-volume publication schedule accommodating its greater length and – at least initially – the elaboration and fusion of the two main storylines. The shifting tension between the commerce of literature and its higher value is again highlighted by Jerome Beaty's analysis of the evolution of *Middlemarch*, which shows the original subjection of the novel's form of publication to its artistic integrity gradually reversing under the pressure of commercially driven deadlines.[77]

In *Daniel Deronda*, the self-reflexive narratorial admission that any attempt fully to understand character is necessarily partial and that the beginnings and ends of stories are illusory or 'make believe' serves to alert the reader to the very representative boundaries and mimetic limitations which the realist novel – not least her own – had succeeded in widening. The formal experiment became even more radical with her final work, *Impressions of Theophrastus Such*, in which the dense and sometimes obtuse reflections of a narrator of indeterminate authority constitute the whole of a text that is detached from narrated context and action. Although Eliot was as diligent as ever in negotiating the contract for *Theophrastus* with Blackwood, she knew the book would be neither as popular nor so great a commercial success as the novels that preceded it.

Eliot's inability to reconcile fully competing and sometime conflicting motivations in the production and sale of her novels gives rise to an even larger consideration: how successfully can the action of writing address the question of how best to live? The moral purpose of her writing and what she believed to be the social duty of the writer have been hinted at in this chapter and will be elaborated in the forthcoming readings of the novels, a literary form that enabled her to explore money-ethics in uniquely rich and complex ways. A starting point for this analysis is a contention that Eliot believed the circumstances of her own life in her own time – indeed of any single life – bound and confined the range of motivations, decisions and actions she wanted to explore.[78] It is in the novels themselves that the scale of her individual and social projects must be expanded, for the action of writing itself created its own confinement; what she uneasily called her 'luxurious remoteness from all turmoil'.[79]

She concludes 'Leaves from a Note-Book' with a celebration of impulsive, if ultimately futile action, of action as sympathy:

> The question, 'Of what use is it for me to work towards an end confessedly good?' comes from that sapless kind of reasoning which is falsely taken for a supreme mental activity, but is really due to languor, or incapability of that mental grasp which makes objects strongly present, and to a lack of sympathetic emotion. In the *Spanish Gypsy* Fedalma says, –
>
> > 'The grandest death! To die in vain – for Love
> > Greater than sways the forces of the world,'
>
> referring to the image of the disciples throwing themselves, consciously in vain, on the Roman spears. I really believe and mean this, – not as a rule of general action, but as a possible grand instance of determining energy in human sympathy, which even in particular cases, where it has only a magnificent futility, is more adorable, or as we say divine, than unpitying force, or than a prudent calculation of results.[80]

In writing *Daniel Deronda*, Eliot knew that any 'prudent calculation of results', limited only to domestic popularity and critical approval, would have persuaded her greatly to reduce the length and detail of the Jewish element of her novel. She recognised, but opted to ignore, what she described as the 'stupidity' of prevailing British attitudes and chose to 'treat Jews with such sympathy and understanding as my nature and knowledge could attain to'.[81] Daniel Hack sees her decision as 'resisting – even repulsing – the demands of the marketplace'.[82] It would, of course, be wrong to describe it as an act of 'magnificent futility', for, despite generally unfavourable reviews, the book was commercially successful and, indeed, fulfilled Eliot's wider social ambitions. As a novel written in the market, whose final form was determined by an ethically and socially informed aesthetic whose motivation stood essentially outside of that market, Eliot's last great novel at least partially achieves the reconciliation of professionalism and vocation with which she continually struggled. The remainder of this work will consider how she addressed issues of individual ethics and wider social good, as they relate to the economic, within the novels themselves.

CHAPTER 4

Calculating consequences: Felix Holt
and the limits of Utilitarianism

[T]here is no means of measuring pleasure & pain directly, but as those feelings govern sales and purchases, the prices of the market are those facts from which one may argue back to the intensity of the pleasures concerned.[1] — William Stanley Jevons, 1872

This is what I call debasing the moral currency: lowering the value of every inspiring fact and tradition, so that it will command less and less of the spiritual products, the generous motives, which sustain the charm and elevation of our social existence – that something besides bread by which man saves his soul alive.[2] — George Eliot, 1879

The opening section has argued that experience and observation taught George Eliot that economic strains infuse the motivations and intentions of most human action. An acute psychological understanding allowed her to analyse the complex composition of those reasons for action, and a strongly felt and intellectually forceful perception of the means and ends of literature presented the form of that analysis. Her novels were her 'experiments in life'; the characters therein the intricately compounded subjects of her ethical probing and testing.[3] This chapter will explicitly link her critique of two related, yet distinct systems that attempted to formulate economic behaviour and wider ethical choice and action: classical economics and Utilitarianism.

As the quotation above from Jevons indicates, the advent of neoclassical economics in the early 1870s more clearly formalised that discipline's link with the psychological core of Benthamism and thereby challenged some of the important modifications Mill had incorporated into Utilitarianism: a development of which Eliot was aware and which, I will argue, thematically impacted her later novels. After first contextualising George Eliot the novelist within related mid-century theoretical economic and moral philosophical debates, this argument will be tested largely by reference to a reading of *Felix Holt*, which hinges on specific developments in the late 1860s. However, because many of the critical concerns to be addressed were already apparent in her earlier work and were continually refined throughout her career, the chapter will begin with a short analysis of a piece from an earlier novel alongside related 'impressions' from her last complete work.

Mr Riley is a relatively minor character in *The Mill on the Floss*. In the first chapter of Book 3, after a long absence from the narrative, we learn that he 'had died suddenly last April, and left his friend [Mr Tulliver] saddled with a debt of two hundred and fifty pounds'.[4] However, the early chapter whose title preserves his name – 'Mr Riley Gives His Advice Concerning a School for Tom' – concludes with a dense narratorial analysis of the emotional and cognitive processes out of which his advice proceeds. The preceding descriptions of Riley's manner, opinions and conversation paint an apparently clear and simple picture of a man motivated solely by self-interest whose concept of value, as might befit an auctioneer and appraiser, has a single, monetary dimension: like one of Eliot's later self-serving value monists, 'he knew the price-current of most things'.[5]

The expectation, aroused by 'subtle indications', that a mercenary motivation will be revealed is briefly made explicit with the admission that 'Mr Riley was a man of business, and not cold towards his own interest' (22). However, the subsequent unravelling of a fragmented, loosely connected chain of causal linkages within the character's 'mind' serves to undermine the ruling principles both of classical political economy and of its symbiotically related ethical system, Utilitarianism. Riley's recommendation of the Rev. Walter Stelling stems neither from 'far-sighted designs' and 'distinct motives' (rationally calculated utility maximisation), nor from 'any positive expectation of a solid, definite advantage resulting to himself' or 'deliberate contrivance in order to compass a selfish end' (economic self-interest). It is rather the result of a somewhat haphazard mix of 'small promptings' which, while undoubtedly incorporating the intention of diverting money 'from less worthy pockets into his own', captures a wide and diverse range of psychological promptings and even an admittedly weak trace of benevolence towards Stelling, 'wishing him well so far as he had any wishes at all concerning him' (22–3).

A Benthamite interpretation of Riley's decision-making process might hold that he was in fact attempting to apply some kind of felicific calculus to maximise pleasure and minimise displeasure or pain, not only for himself, but also for the community of people who enter his evaluative equations, although the obvious flaw here is the educational outcome deriving to Tom Tulliver.[6] It is not that Riley is being a bad Utilitarian. Rather, the impressionistic jostling of the claims of memory, reputation, self-image, economic gain and mild sexual attraction presented by Eliot offers a far more compelling and identifiable behavioural pattern, one that cannot be contained within a single all-embracing system.

The measurement and comparison of diverse desires on a single scale, Eliot is protesting, demands 'too intense a mental action' for most people – even an apparently simple *homo economicus* such as Riley. Her insistence that attempts systematically to model motivation are reductive and misleading recurs throughout the novels and is forcefully made in her final work, *Impressions of Theophrastus Such*, in which the reader is again warned against confusing sagacity with

> the common mistake of supposing that men's behaviour, whether habitual or occasional, is chiefly determined by a distinctly conceived motive, a definite object to be gained or a definite evil to be avoided . . . [S]ociety is chiefly made up of human beings whose daily acts are all performed either in unreflecting obedience to custom and routine or from immediate promptings of thought or feeling to execute an immediate purpose. They pay their poor-rates, give their vote in affairs political or parochial, wear a certain amount of starch, hinder boys from tormenting the helpless, and spend money on tedious observances called pleasures, without mentally adjusting these practices to their own well-understood interest or to the general, ultimate welfare of the human race.[7]

Her perceptiveness is acute and looks forward beyond even the twentieth century to recent work in the fields of behavioural economics and situational ethics.[8] The employment of Utilitarian terminology – 'carefully appraised end to serve', 'definite consequences', the calculable weighing of 'pleasures' against 'evil to be avoided' – here serves to emphasise the system's inapplicability to the everyday reality of imperfectly informed agents making imperfect decisions, informed by an incalculable combination of multiple cognitive and emotional promptings. This is a level of critique beyond that of the early essays to which I referred in my opening chapter and, indeed, the rather blunt Benthamite-bashing of the passage in 'Janet's Repentance' in which 'certain ingenious philosophers of our own day must surely take offence at a joy so entirely out of correspondence with arithmetical proportion' and where we are reminded that 'there is a transcendent value in human pain, which refuses to be settled by equations'.[9]

As her final complete work, *Impressions of Theophrastus Such*, together with the reflective sketches in 'Leaves from a Note-Book', contains important indications of her later thoughts on many ethical issues that had exercised her throughout her life. However, it is in the full novels that Eliot achieves her most complete examinations of the complex interrelationship between ethics

and economics. Broadening a connection made earlier between Eliot and
Adam Smith, Smith's most enduring contributions to moral philosophy, the
concept of the 'Impartial Spectator' and the centrality of human sympathy,
are embodied in the form of the novel as practised by Eliot.[10] Eleanor
Courtemanche has recently made Smith's metaphor and its adaptation by
nineteenth-century novelists the subject of a book-length study. Eliot, some
of whose work Courtemanche analyses in this context, had, years before
writing her first fiction, recognised the potential of the novel to combine
the ethical and the aesthetic in a uniquely powerful way. Such a synthesis, she
believed, was achieved in the work of George Sand. In an 1849 letter to Sara
Hennell, she compares Sand to Rousseau as a moral and intellectual inspiration, but is insistent that she would 'never dream of going to her writings as a
moral code or text book'. For Eliot, the novel form is not incidental to, but a
positive embodiment of the ethical force of Sand's writing:

> I cannot read six pages of hers without feeling that it is given to her to
> delineate human passion and its results – and . . . some of the moral instincts
> and their tendencies – with such truthfulness such nicety of discrimination
> such tragic power and withal such gentle humour that one might live a
> century with nothing but one's own dull faculties and not know so much as
> those six pages will suggest.[11]

Her description of Sand's achievement connects Eliot to the school of
literary ethics a century after her own death. Martha Nussbaum, for example,
prioritises an objective 'to establish that certain literary texts . . . are indis-
pensable to a philosophical inquiry in the ethical sphere'.[12] Like Eliot,
Nussbaum rejects the implication that her readings serve to reduce literature
'into a chapter in a textbook on ethics'.[13] Rather, she promotes a critical
project which, in opposition to the long-standing dichotomy at the heart of
both nineteenth- and twentieth-century moral philosophy, sees novels 'as
helping to state a distinctive alternative to Kantian and Utilitarian conceptions'.[14] More recently, Andrew H. Miller has restated the case for literature's
ability to bypass the consequentialist and deontological arguments at the
heart of most ethical theory. Miller cites Iris Murdoch's argument for the
philosophical claims of literature in his description of 'the untidiness of
everyday ethical insistence, not captured in the language of "action" and
"choice" but apparent as story, metaphor, vocabulary'.[15]

Eliot's description of Riley and his unspoken deliberations captures this
'untidiness of everyday ethical insistence' precisely. In doing so, it creates a
sympathetic link between reader and character.[16] Riley, like a number of the
characters in *Felix Holt* about to be discussed, does not embody economic

virtue. It is unlikely that any reader will be moved either to simulate his actions or to be converted by the implicit suggestion of an alternative, 'better' way to act. Rather, by first leading us to the jaws of the trap of 'greater sagacity' (largely through external description of Riley's appearance, language and behaviour) and then steering us away from a simplistic assessment of his motivations, Eliot forces us to recognise a commonality, not with a merely fictional character, but with any individual confronting choice in the world outside the text. Miller identifies a particular 'ethical power' of Eliot's work as resting not in the moment of choice or action but in the perspectival understanding the reader uncovers in 'moments of conversion where visions are exchanged and the exercise of the will is uncertain'.[17]

Before considering how, in *Felix Holt*, she tested the economics of self-interest and consequentialist ethics, it is important to establish how the systems of classical economics and Utilitarianism coalesced in Eliot's critical sight in the mid-1860s. Once again, the figure of J. S. Mill will play a central role in delineating the intellectual context, although a note of caution must first be sounded. As one eminent economic historian of the period has warned, the stature of Mill and, to a lesser extent, his father and their close connection to Bentham have served to exaggerate the strength of the direct connection between mainstream political economy through much of the century and the far less prevalent doctrine of Utilitarian ethics.[18] Their long involvement in the *Westminster Review* undoubtedly places the Mills at the centre of the formal articulation of the overlapping philosophical underpinnings of the two systems.[19] But the ideological and institutional links went deeper. From its inception (by Bentham) in 1824, the *Westminster Review* strongly espoused an essentially Smithean vision of international free trade, laissez-faire economics and the abolition of corrupt privileges: a vision of political economy as a force for social progress.[20] Calls for the abolition of the Corn Laws gave a focus to its conviction that government interference in the economy should be minimal.

Although by the time Chapman took over the *Review* in 1851 some of the consistency of the earlier economic 'message' had been lost, a strong continuity with the previous period of the magazine's history can be traced. The younger Mill himself remained an occasional contributor, as did earlier economic commentators including W. R. Greg and Harriet Martineau.[21] Eliot herself defined the primary ongoing purpose of the *Review* in correspondence with Chapman, placing Mill at the forefront of those writers who 'are amongst the world's vanguard, though not all in the foremost line; it is good for the world, therefore, that they should have every facility for speaking out'.[22] Through her time as editor and beyond, political economy was consistently defended: favourable reviews accompanied each new edition of Mill's 1848 classic, which became the defining economic work for a generation. Eliot's personal views, as we have seen, were more ambivalent and she had little time for the exaggerated claims for political economy as an explanatory, predictive or wholly beneficial social science. She is likely to have agreed with Bray's more limited assessment in 1841, the dawn of her full intellectual maturity, that 'Political Economy is without a moral sense; it has no conscience, and its calculations are based upon the supposition that each man as necessarily seeks his own individual interest as that a stone falls on the ground.'[23]

An awareness of a similarly constrained moral sense also served to distance Eliot's own views from those championed by the *Westminster Review* on political economy's ethical counterpart, Utilitarianism.[24] Her first major periodical publication, 'The Progress of the Intellect' (1851), warns against a narrow view of human benefit that limits itself to 'the truth which comes home to men's business and bosoms in these our days', while ignoring the richer, yet less tangible and calculable appreciation of historical thought and tradition.[25] She uses the word 'utility' very infrequently in the novels and then only with its long-standing, primary meaning of usefulness. Her usage assumes neither Bentham's application to 'pleasure' nor the later appropriations of 'good' or simply 'preference' which became increasingly prevalent.[26] However, the indications in her earlier non-fiction writings that she was aware of the principles of Utilitarianism are confirmed by the language and phraseology of the novels: her greatest egoistic hedonist, Tito Melema asks, for example, 'what . . . was the end of life, but to extract the utmost sum of pleasure?'[27]

As a young woman, her understanding of the directions in which Utilitarianism was being taken in the mid-century was moved forward by Bray and accelerated by her move to London and the *Westminster Review*.[28] In this context, Collini *et al.* warn against both a simplistic 'identification of a unitary, homogenous Utilitarianism and any easy assumption of its later disappearance'.[29] More recently, Kathleen Blake has reiterated the dangers of reductive characterisation. Her reassessment of the influence and legacy of Benthamite Utilitarianism concludes that Bentham and his doctrine remain 'poorly understood and poorly regarded, and this is true even among new economic critics'.[30] Certainly, as a philosophical system it provoked heated contemporary debate both within liberal circles and beyond. Herbert Spencer's *Social Statics*, published in 1850, had attempted a reformulation of the doctrine into a wider, synthesised system, which had provoked criticism from Mill.[31] Two years later, the first edition of the re-launched *Westminster Review* under Chapman's control (and Eliot's editorship) included an important article by Mill himself, strongly attacking the criticism of Utilitarianism launched by the Cambridge Professor of Moral Philosophy, William Whewell.[32] Mill's article, while overtly a strong defence of his old mentor against the competing claims of intuitionism, marks an important step in his *adaptation* of Benthamite Utilitarianism. Most notably, this included an attempt to broaden what he saw as too narrow a definition of utility through the admission of a qualitative, rather than purely quantitative distinction among pleasures.

Mill's arguments were more fully developed in his long essay, 'Utilitarianism', which was finally published in 1861, some ten years after the Whewell article had formulated his central argument. As in the earlier piece, a personal defence of Bentham and what Mill regards as a crude misrepresentation of his ideas is accompanied by a reiteration of the core principles of Utilitarianism. Eliot was never converted to wholly believe in the scope and methodology of Mill's reiterated principles, which continued to place happiness (defined by pleasure) as the sole and ultimate end and determined the goodness of acts according to their consequences in promoting that end. She remained, in effect, teleological but non-consequentialist. Neither, however, did her criticism rest on any reductive interpretation that Utilitarianism promoted an exclusively selfish individualism. In 'Utilitarianism', Mill reasserts Bentham's promotion of a standard of wider good, or happiness: 'for that standard is not the agent's own greatest happiness, but the greatest amount of happiness altogether' (213); and again, 'the happiness which forms the utilitarian standard of what is right in conduct, is not the agent's own happiness, but that of all concerned' (218).

Where Mill largely diverged from Bentham was in his shifting of the focus of the principles of utility from his mentor's primarily social and legislative purposes, to their direct application in matters of individual morality. Altruism, as a component of the motivation driving any particular action, carries greater ethical weight for Mill and the refocusing opens the way for possibly his most significant departure from Bentham: the introduction of a qualitative distinction between pleasures, making commensurability on a single scale theoretically problematic. In making this distinction, Mill criticises Benthamite Utilitarianism and, more specifically, many of its followers on two grounds. First, that they 'have placed the superiority of mental over bodily pleasures chiefly in the greater permanency, safety, uncostliness, etc., of the former – that is, in their circumstantial advantages rather than in their intrinsic nature' (211); and, second, that in their strict application of the utilitarian standard, they 'do not lay sufficient stress upon the other beauties of character which go towards making a human being lovable or admirable' (221).

There seems little doubt that Eliot was sympathetic to Mill's main arguments here. Mill's criticism of Whewell's attack on Bentham appeared in the *Westminster Review* under Eliot's editorship and, in an essay of her own some five years later, she takes the opportunity to mock Whewell's simplistic reading of Bentham's interpretation of animal rights.[33] Perhaps even more significant is her position in relation to a much later debate, in which Mill's modification of Bentham's hedonic calculus is criticised as logically inconsistent by Jevons.[34] In 1877 and 1878, Jevons produced a series of articles in the *Contemporary Review* under the heading, 'John Stuart Mill's Philosophy Tested', which included a refutation of Mill's attempts to reconcile his concept of 'higher pleasures' within the single scale of the Utilitarian happiness principle.[35] Edith Simcox records in her diary for 1879 that George Eliot discussed the controversy sparked by Jevons's articles during a visit to Oxford.[36] The position of Lewes and Eliot is not explicitly stated, but may be surmised from the tone of the former's letter congratulating George Croom Robertson on his 'calmly crushing' response to the Jevons articles.[37] My conclusion is twofold: that Eliot agreed with Lewes that attempts by Jevons to undermine Mill's morally informed, qualitative distinction of pleasures was regressive and must be opposed; but that, equally, the logical difficulties of integrating Mill's modifications highlighted Utilitarianism's limitations as a complete ethical system.

The contention, therefore, is that during the 1860s and 1870s Eliot recognised the emergence of a tendency in economic thought towards greater system and mathematical quantification that, both independently and in its appropriation of Utilitarian ethics, ultimately threatened the line of morally informed political economy which connects Smith and the post-Benthamite Mill. This is not to exaggerate the extent of any theoretical economic shift. Much of the substance of classical economics, particularly in regard to cost of production and consumption, was incorporated into neoclassicism, while the application of advanced mathematics was already apparent in some branches of the earlier school.[38] However, the focus of Jevons and the marginalists, both on the nature of market pricing and exchange and on how that related to individual preference or utility, undoubtedly marked a significant new way of explaining economic behaviour. In doing so, it brought theoretical economics into methodological alignment with Benthamite Utilitarianism. As the latter provides a common currency (pleasure or pain) to all moral judgements in relation to their consequences, so all economic value can theoretically be gauged by a single measure: the price exchange at which marginal utility is satisfied. Both systems make assumptions concerning perfection of information and agent rationality that enable mathematical modelling and claims for universal applicability. Eliot, in the novels, undermines both.[39]

Axiomatic to neoclassical economic theory is the utility-maximising agent. Self-interest – which Smith tempered with the moral sentiment of sympathy and Mill overlaid with morally informed, socially elevating higher pleasures – thus becomes a general principle and, at least superficially, roots neoclassical economics in the same soil as Utilitarianism.[40] To some extent, this linkage over-simplifies Bentham's theory, which, as described earlier, always had a wider, non-individualistic dimension. It also under-estimates the extent to which theoretical classical economics throughout most of the century had already jettisoned the moral philosophical elements of Adam Smith in its concentration on individual wealth creation; a singleness of purpose amplified by the application of those theories in the emergent industrial capitalist society.

Felix Holt, although a product of the mid-1860s, is often included in that series of realist fictions, written mostly in the 1840s and generically described as the 'Condition of England' industrial novels.[41] The setting of Eliot's novel, around the time of the 1832 Reform Act, places it at an interesting period in the development of political economy; a period in which its ideological acceptance was starting to influence economic and social policy, while its academic credibility was being cemented by the establishment of a number of university chairs.[42] By 1865, when the novel was written, the dominance of classicism, enshrined in Mill's *Principles*, was, as described in Chapter 1, coming to an end. Widespread general agreement on a number of macro-economic issues, including free trade and the maintenance of the gold standard, could no longer obscure growing methodological fractures and the emergence of a radical new interpretation of micro-economic theory.[43] Meanwhile – and somewhat ironically given the new alliance that was forged – Mill's adaptation and resuscitation of Utilitarianism had established it as a serious and credible ethical system with a level of acceptance way beyond that prevailing thirty years earlier. J. B. Schneewind quotes letters from Mill in 1861 and F. H. Bradley in 1876 to illustrate how the former's efforts had succeeded over that period in transforming an insignificant minority school into 'our most fashionable philosophy'.[44] Stefan Collini too has drawn attention to the 'broadly Utilitarian considerations' of Fawcett's *The Economic Position of the British Labourer* (1865), which Eliot was reading during the composition of *Felix Holt*.[45]

For the economic-ethical purposes of this section, therefore, the periods of composition and setting combine in most interesting ways.[46]

Much has been written about the nature, limits and social implications of the political 'radicalism' presented in the novel, with an obvious focus on the duality of reference to the First and Second Reform Acts. Far less attention has been given to Eliot's richly perspectival analysis of individual and social ways of dealing with money. Central to the representation and development of the novel's characters is the particularity of their financial situations, motivations and aspirations; in short, what place money plays in their individual value systems. To some extent then, the novel is all about money and, as it relates to the individual in a society that is itself being transformed by the forces of the market and industrial capital, *Felix Holt*'s inclusion in the earlier industrial genre is well justified. Well-established critical consensus links the novel closely to the concerns of Eliot's essay 'The Natural History of German Life', particularly in the common opposition established between an 'organic' community subject to gradual, consensual development and a 'mechanistic' society, characterised by rapid and dis-locating change and a general descent to the common value scale of money.

The novel describes the transformation of Treby from an agrarian to an industrial society and accurately tracks the economic history of post-war England, establishing permeating links with social and political develop-ment. Indeed, the much-quoted dictum at the heart of the narrative pro-gression – 'there is no private life which has not been determined by a wider public life' – hinges on conceptions of wealth, class and value.[47] The process Eliot traces in her review of Riehl's history is essentially repeated in the development of Treby from an 'old-fashioned, grazing, brewing, wool-packing, cheese-loading' (41), essentially agrarian community to first an extractive industrial region and finally the site of Jermyn's dubious tourism speculation. The progress towards modernity and money-centring is again marked by Eliot's ironic employment of Utilitarian terminology: the new market-driven conditions 'gradually awakening in [Treby] that higher con-sciousness which is known to bring higher pains' (41). As ancient links between social classes weaken, the local economy is subsumed by 'the great circulating system of the nation' (43) in which money becomes the single measure of value. The morally corroding impact of the ascent of money crosses all social boundaries, with even the noble Sir Maximus Debarry eventually succumbing to Jermyn's promise of 'an unprecedented return for the thousands he would lay out on a pump-room and hotel' (42). Significantly, the portrayal of Sir Maximus's son, Philip, as a man whose honour and virtue transcend personal material gain is completed by the narratorial aside that he died in Rome 'fifteen years later, a convert to Catholicism'.[48]

Felix Holt is not unusual in associating Utilitarian ethics with the pursuit of wealth under the guidelines of self-interested economics. One aspect in which it differs from and greatly extends the critique at the heart of the industrial novel genre, however, is in its exploration of the pervasion of mono-value consequentialism across social classes and professions. The traditional, morally deficient capitalist is here left largely in the shadows while, as with the earlier illustration from *The Mill on the Floss*, a range of apparently minor characters reveal how money can infiltrate and dominate individual value systems.[49] Of these, Chubb, the publican, is the most straightforwardly driven by economic self-interest. His position in the community enables him to help orchestrate the unenfranchised miners in the service of the best-paying candidates while, through the supply of cheap beer, fettering the class from which he has emerged in ignorant subjection.[50] His great political idea – 'that society existed for the sake of the individual, and that the name of that individual was Chubb' (113) – is a masterful subversion of liberal thinking. His main occupation notwithstanding, he counts himself among 'those as work with your brains' (115), in some sense an accurate description of the time and mental effort he devotes to securing 'the best livelihood with the least possible exertion' (115).

He shares this calculated avoidance of authentic labour, so starkly contrasted with Felix's philosophy of work, with two other characters, whose methodical pursuit of selfish ends drives some of the novel's most pivotal plot developments: Philip Debarry's manservant, Maurice Christian (for whom 'secrets were often a source of profit, of that agreeable kind which involved little labour' (211)), and the political agent and sometime accomplice of Jermyn, John Johnson. Both believe their powers of calculation are able to shape and control events. In this they are linked to Harold Transome, for whom wealth and power create a similar illusion: he is left 'trusting in his own skill to shape the success of his own morrows, ignorant of what many yesterdays had determined for him beforehand' (161–2).

It is a critical orthodoxy that a central theme of the novel is the conflict and shifting balance between will and destiny. Eliot's first exposure to philosophical determinism dates back to Charles Bray's *The Philosophy of Necessity*, published in 1841, the same year she entered the Rosehill circle. The doctrine prioritises the effect of pre-existing and external conditions on individual will and desire. Her first *Westminster Review* article ten years later reiterated its central belief that 'human deeds and aspirations' are determined by 'that inexorable law of consequences'.[51] A revised second edition of Bray's work appeared shortly before she started writing *Felix Holt*, in which money in various forms linked to acquisition and distribution – debt, embezzlement, Eastern speculation, inheritance – binds present consequences to past actions. Hence Jermyn's realisation that 'he had sinned for the sake of particular concrete things, and particular concrete consequences were likely to follow' (104).

The inheritance plot is advanced by a series of coincidences, the implausibility of which the narrator readily acknowledges. Eliot's exaggerated point is that this is what happens in a probabilistic universe. Cause and effect are indeed deterministic, but chance and character both shape events. In *Felix Holt*, the realisation of Jermyn's feared 'concrete consequences' is largely effected by the calculated self-interest of Christian and Johnson. As with Riley in *The Mill on the Floss*, however, even the scheming of the shadowy Johnson in his decision to betray Jermyn, while lacking any identifiably virtuous impulse, is revealed to spring from a complex motivational composition. The narrator's ironic implication that such unsystematic decision-making was a characteristic specific to a past generation serves to emphasise that little in human psychology had changed in the intervening thirty years, beyond the inclination of gentlemen to wear whiskers:

> Under the stimulus of small many-mixed motives like these, a great deal of business has been done in the world by well-clad and, in 1833, clean-shaven men, whose names are on charity-lists, and who do not know that they are base. Mr. Johnson's character was not much more exceptional than his double chin. (304)

Christian and Johnson are by no means the only characters whose actions are described as calculating, a term, along with its variants, that recurs frequently in the novel, although their single-minded pursuit of personal gain combines with chance to make them more than averagely successful in their strategies.[52] Christian, a skilled gambler, is, in many senses, a schematised Utilitarian. He has given up the 'more impulsive delights of life' to 'become a sober calculator' (211) and, because 'he knew the price-current of most things' (288), he is able to re-base everything to a single monetary scale. Thus the illness for the relief of which he takes opium is a *dis*utility because it is both painful and, if perceived by others, would diminish his 'market value' (125). His strict application of egoistic hedonism contradicts Mill's theory of why those 'who are capable of the higher pleasures' are tempted to postpone these in favour of 'the lower'. Christian does not elect for 'the nearer good', knowing it to be less valuable than some higher pleasure.[53] In fact his every action is a probability-weighted calculation of personal bodily and material interest. It is therefore telling that we are told that his meeting with Johnson – the event which Jermyn had considered then discounted – came about 'by means that were quite incalculable' (242).

Felix Holt compels us to recognise the limits of calculation and system, thereby striking at the foundations of both economics and Utilitarianism. And Eliot's critique has an interesting parallel in the period during which the novel is set. The populisers of political economy at that time sought to reassure and placate a populace confronted by change on a previously unseen scale with the enumeration and certainty of precise, calculable statistics.[54] Eliot had already portrayed the dangerous ethical implications of relating moral evaluation to calculation in her first full novel. Arthur Donnithorne, seeking self-justification for his seduction of Hetty, reasons with Mr Irwine: 'It's a desperately vexatious thing, that after all one's reflections and quiet determinations, we should be ruled by moods that one can't calculate on beforehand. I don't think a man ought to be blamed so much if he is betrayed into doing things in that way, in spite of his resolutions.'[55]

Indeed, part of Eliot's intellectual journey towards becoming a novelist was the realisation of the possibilities of a form that stands outside of systems. The novel, and its cumulative, uneven transmission of authoritative and implied knowledge is mimetic of the unsystematic accumulation of ethical understanding we experience outside the text.[56] In 1855, she had begun her review in *The Leader* of Otto Friedrich Gruppe's 'The Future of German Philosophy' by approvingly quoting the author: 'The age of systems is passed . . . System is the childhood of philosophy; the manhood of philosophy is investigation.' While her specific target here is Kantian a priori thought, the criticism could equally apply to an empiricism that attempts to contain individual human motivation and behaviour – including the economic – within a theoretical system.[57] Throughout her life, from her readings of Bray to Comte and Spencer, she was to recoil from any professedly complete system, whether in the moral or social sciences.

In *Felix Holt*, all the novel's Utilitarians try to put a price on knowledge and information. Harold Transome's attempts to apply what is essentially the Jevonian method to this end has decidedly mixed results. The limits of theory are exposed when he is confronted with characters such as Rufus Lyon, Felix and the enlightened Esther, all of whom would represent outliers in any imaginary statistical sampling of economic viewpoints. They essentially stand completely outside a market, or price-driven system of value attribution. Harold's complete misconstrual of Lyon's opinion on the ballot is based on 'his best calculation of probabilities' (158), while minutes later his attempt to justify an ends-based validation of lesser evils is angrily attacked by Felix as 'a handful of generalities and analogies' (160). His justification for engaging in electioneering abuses encapsulates the moral hazard of this kind of conse-quentialism. Eliot's chosen metaphor of commercial corruption appropriately links money, politics and the brewing industry:

> it was as if he had to show indignation at the discovery of one barrel with a false bottom, when he had invested his money in a manufactory where a larger or smaller number of such barrels had always been made. A practical man must seek a good end by the only possible means; that is to say, if he is to get into parliament he must not be too particular. (162)

Like Christian, Harold conforms to a simplified, and limited, Benthamite model: as Esther comes to understand his nature, she recognises that he 'had a way of virtually measuring the value of everything by the contribution it made to his own pleasure' (345). But unlike Christian, he ultimately escapes the laws of felicific calculus. Faced with the possibility of becoming complicit with Jermyn and destroying the evidence to Esther's claim on the Transome estate, his self-interest is, unexpectedly for both him and the reader, tempered and ultimately overcome by 'his sense of honour and dignity':

> And thus, as the temptation to avoid all risk of losing the estate grew and grew till scruples looked minute by the side of it, the difficulty of bringing himself to make a compact with Jermyn seemed more and more insur-mountable. (287)

Harold's inward debate and decision closely match Jermyn's expectations, but his calculations are immediately upset by those of Christian, whose 'complete . . . survey of probabilities' leads him to take his information to Harold. The meeting and negotiation between the two (chapter 36), which first presents Harold with the idea of offsetting Esther's claim by marrying her, is a compellingly insightful portrayal of the mental machinations of two clever and calculating individuals. As our understanding of their psycho-logical processes is deftly managed by the interchange of dialogue, free indirect speech and narratorial reflection, the scene becomes a sharply perceptive exposition of high-stakes game theory. Yet Harold's understand-ing of human motivation is again deficient when, in his observation of Esther's concern for Felix, he attempts to derive the particular from a general rule: 'With all due regard to Harold Transome, he was one of those men who are liable to make the greater mistakes about a particular woman's feelings, because they pique themselves on a power of interpreta-tion derived from much experience' (351).

For Harold Transome, power and position are determined solely in relation to material wealth and, just as money establishes a standard measure of wealth, so, he believes, pleasure or utility can reconcile and rank apparently incommensurable values to determine any action. His language is infused with financial association and imagery and even his most intimate human relationships are defined as commercial transactions. His mother feels their relationship is becoming increasingly imbalanced as he surrounds her with material luxuries, while both his first marriage (to a slave girl) and his planned union with Esther are motivated by his own comfort and convenience rather than higher emotions.[58] Similarly, the extent to which the once passionate affection Jermyn felt for Mrs Transome has become degraded by self-interest is emphasised by the imagery employed in the angry confrontation during which she refuses to inform Harold of his true parentage. Jermyn's 'tenderness had turned into calculation'; her love 'into a good bargain'; she likens the process to 'a lover pick[ing] one's pocket' (337).[59]

Harold, like the similarly good-natured Arthur Donnithorne in Eliot's earlier work, essentially believes that human affection can be bought.[60] Just how antithetical this form of calculation is to Felix Holt is very cleverly expressed by Esther in her parodying of the type of logico-mathematical formulation we might expect Harold to be continually constructing in his mind:

> 'O there is no sum in proportion to be done there,' said Esther, again gaily. 'As you are to a peerage, so is *not* Felix Holt to any offer of advantage that you could imagine for him.' (352)

Felix literally renders any formula that attempts to equate self with 'advantage' (at least Harold's perception of advantage) not only unsolvable but also meaningless. Bentham's calculus – or rather a reductively simplistic and purely self-interested version of Bentham – simply breaks down.

Unlike the calculating characters discussed above, Felix is incapable of predicting and managing future consequences, particularly as they might affect his own self-interest. Consider the scene in which he assumes control of the rioters, putting his life and freedom directly at risk:

> It was not a moment in which a spirit like his could calculate the effect of misunderstanding as to himself: nature never makes men who are at once energetically sympathetic and minutely calculating. (268)

Like Adam Bede, his calculating is confined to the scientifically predictable physical world (they are both skilled craftsmen), and it is noteworthy that their inability to apply strategic, dispassionate thinking to human affairs leaves them both effectively helpless in the respective major crises that develop.[61] The saving of Hetty from the gallows and Felix's release from prison are both effected by rich, powerful men.

Whatever the limitations of Felix as a political and social radical, he undoubtedly stands radically apart from the mainstream economy in his location, or rather dislocation, of money in relation to the individual and society. Only in his support of the arguments against the abuses of monopolies and in his intention to educate working men in the basics of domestic economy is he allied to liberal economics (ch. 30). He rejects the market economy because of what he perceives to be a fundamental inequity, whereby people are 'paid out of proportion' (57). His active decision to remove himself 'from the push and the scramble for money and position' (221) carries almost religious undertones of renunciation, but his distance from the eternal-ends-focused Christianity Eliot criticised in her essay on Dr Cumming could hardly be more extreme.[62] His poverty rather 'enables [him] to do what I most want to do on the earth' (225) and, in an uncanny foreshadowing of perhaps the most famous dictum of twentieth-century economics, his focus on effecting good in the short-term is emphatic: 'But I care for the people who live now and will not be living when the long-run comes.'[63]

Significantly, Felix's motivations for action are not wholly incompatible with Utilitarianism, particularly as defined by Mill. In 'Utilitarianism', Mill specifically addresses sacrifice and renunciation and concludes that such actions are consistent with his philosophical definition of the 'good' if they are intended to promote the greater happiness, which is indeed Felix's ultimate aim.[64] His actions, however, illustrate the problems of applying even a Millean consequentialism to the incommensurable values of, say, money, leisure, education and political representation. By elevating 'higher' or 'mental' pleasures, Felix is motivated by the wider happiness of the working people. His personal utility is subservient, yet those whose happiness he is trying to promote derive pleasure from bodily, 'lower' pleasures. Moreover, it is not clear that the course of action he takes to try to achieve his ends – working and preaching among them – is most likely to produce the best consequences. Rufus Lyon's suggestion that he might achieve more good acting from a position of wealth and power is forcefully rejected by his determination to follow a path that suits his individual concept of value, thereby illustrating a circularity and contradiction inherent in solely ends-based ethical systems.

The distancing of Felix from classical liberal economics is further emphasised by the ironic use of his mother as the unwitting mouthpiece for the very theories her son is determined to undermine. Her incomprehension at his decision not to continue his father's business of peddling quack remedies is effectively a restatement of Say's Law that supply will inevitably create demand: 'And what folks can never have boxes enough of to swallow, I should think you have a right to sell' (348). She presents his actions as undermining a natural order of the market, as 'contrary to the nature of buying and selling' (299). For Felix, however, money represents not a natural order, but a containment and undermining of self. He refuses personally to return the notebook to the Debarry household because he fears being offered a demeaning money reward, while his impassioned public speeches highlight the corrosive influence of money in the practice and development of political representation (251).[65] Indeed, in his very rejection of the constraints of money, Felix articulates an insightful psychological understanding of its power:

> If I once went into that sort of struggle for success, I should want to win – I should defend the wrong that I had once identified myself with. I should become everything that I see now beforehand to be detestable. (222)

For all Felix's idealism, however, Esther's understanding of how best to deal with money is a more satisfying portrayal and, through the description of her developing insight, more ethically enlightening. It is significant that Esther's unknown mother, Annette, reaches a new level of vitality and independence only when, faced with her husband's incapacitating illness, she assumes a level of financial responsibility.[66] Esther is financially self-sufficient and, from a very different starting point from both her mother and Dorothea Brooke, undergoes a moral awakening that critically centres on an understanding and better positioning of materiality within her personal and social ethics. Her early meeting with Felix (ch. 10) opposes his 'thoughts about great subjects' with hers 'about small ones; dress behaviour, amusements, ornaments'. Her enlightenment is secured by a realisation that diverse material and human values cannot be measured on a single scale. Ultimately it is she, of all the novel's characters, who is given the opportunity to make a truly radical economic choice, rejecting both Harold and the Transome inheritance in favour of higher values. Much of the later commentary on the Transome household is actually managed through the indirect reflections and speech of Esther rather than direct narratorial observation: she identifies 'an air of moral mediocrity' and formulates an academic analogy to illustrate what Eliot herself later described as the 'debasing [of] the moral currency':

> All life seemed cheapened; as it might seem to a young student who, having believed that to gain a certain degree he must write a thesis in which he

would bring his powers to bear with memorable effect, suddenly ascertained that no thesis was expected, but the sum (in English money) of twenty-seven pounds ten shillings and sixpence. (341–2)

Felix Holt portrays how rigid Utilitarian ethics can combine with mechanistic economic systems to cause this very debasement. Felix, in the extremity of his opposition to that combination, serves to highlight its systemic limitations. A normative economics is therefore implicit but, in practice, remains distant and, like the novel's eponymous hero, somewhat abstract.[67] *Felix Holt* champions renunciation but ultimately promotes political inaction; in ethical terms, it better describes how not to live than how best to live.

CHAPTER 5

Testing the Kantian pillars: debt obligations and financial imperatives in Middlemarch

She thought the weak point of Utilitarianism, in Sidgwick and others, lay not in taking human welfare as the standard of right but in their trying to find in it the moral *motive*.[1]   – Edith Simcox, 1878

[M]y writing is simply a set of experiments in life – an endeavour to see what our thought and emotion may be capable of – what stores of motive, actual or hinted as possible, give promise of a better after which we may strive.[2]   – George Eliot, 1876

Early in 1876, the first two editions of the newly launched *Mind* featured essays, which Eliot read, on the history and present state of philosophy at the universities of Oxford and Cambridge.[3] Their inclusion is a good reminder of the common origins of and close association between psychology and philosophy during the period, while the author of the Cambridge article, Henry Sidgwick, represents the very embodiment of that connection between nineteenth-century moral philosophy and economics that underlies much of this book.[4] It is notable that both Sidgwick and his Oxford counterpart, Mark Pattison were well acquainted with the Leweses and were regular companions during the couple's visits to their respective universities: Eliot's ethical and wider intellectual opinions were as respected and sought after at both institutions as Lewes's in the scientific fields. The *Mind* articles, while, by definition somewhat parochial in their detailed assessments and criticisms, nevertheless hint strongly at the issue that dominated nineteenth-century academic moral philosophical debate: the competing claims of Utilitarianism and intuitionism.

Pattison, bemoaning the 'atrophy of philosophy here', looks enviously towards Sidgwick's Cambridge and the Moral Sciences Tripos, whose 'exactness of method and certainty of view is unfavourable to the ambitious constructions of post-Kantian metaphysics'.[5] His review of recent publications by his own academic colleagues includes a critical appraisal of probably Oxford's leading moral philosopher of the period, T. H. Green, whose

book-length introduction to *Hume's Philosophical Works* is, Pattison angrily
concludes, 'nothing less than a treatise on the insufficiency of empirical
metaphysics, of the philosophy of experience'.[6]

For most of the third quarter of the century, the claims of empiricism –
'the philosophy of experience' – had been championed by Mill in his public
battles against the intuitionist beliefs of Adam Sedgwick, William Whewell
and Sir William Hamilton.[7] Pattison now calls on a new champion to meet
the threat epitomised by Green: 'Under the disguise of an introduction,
Mr. Green has in fact issued a declaration of war, from an idealist point of
view, against the reigning empirical logic. To this challenge, Mr. Lewes's
Problems of Life and Mind may serve as the ready-made rejoinder.'[8] Needless
to say, George Eliot's position in the ensuing battle of words between Lewes
and Green was unflinchingly by her husband's side. Considerations of
loyalty and duty aside, however, Lewes's insistence on the inseparability
of psychology and ethical judgement (moral psychology and moral philosophy as two sides of the same coin), was the scientific formalisation of a
relationship she had recognised, and expressed in her writing, for many
years.[9] In an 1860 letter responding to a criticism of *The Mill on the Floss*, she
attacks a narrow and experientially inaccurate concept of ethics that fails
fully to embrace 'a widening psychology'.[10]

The previous chapter considered how, in *Felix Holt*, Eliot tested the
limitations of Utilitarian ethics. This chapter will explore further the
location of her thought in relation to the two competing schools by
examining how she exposed the claims of intuitionist, rational (as opposed
to empirical) ethics to complex financial scenarios through the medium of
fiction. It will again conclude that her syncretic mind defies categorisation
within a single ethical system. Her main intellectual associations and her
position at the *Westminster Review* would seem firmly to align her to the
Utilitarian tradition, particularly in the form modified by Mill and further
developed by Sidgwick.[11] But as earlier chapters have argued, even the more
evaluative hedonism they formulated was, for Eliot, an insufficient ethical
principle, not least because motive was subsumed by outcome and welfare
in the moral evaluation of any action.

Her opposition to Green's neo-Kantianism was, at one level, as unequivocal as her earlier criticism of Whewell and other anti-empiricist thinkers.
Edith Simcox records a conversation in February 1878 between Eliot, Mark
Pattison and Simcox concerning 'the rising school in Oxford which follows
Green and Caird to think English philosophy nowhere, Kant and Hegel on
the right track, but they themselves in some unexplained way, many leagues
in advance even of them'.[12] Her scepticism had long-standing roots. Her

1855 essay 'The Future of German Philosophy' is directly critical of Kant and is emphatic that experience and a posteriori method represent the only valid epistemological path. In this, she largely follows Lewes's assessment of Kant in the 1845 *Biographical History of Philosophy*, which argues against the existence of a priori ideas.[13]

An earlier reference to Eliot's description of her novels as 'experiments in life' clearly aligns her ethical purpose to the empirical method. Further, her melding of the moral and natural sciences seems in direct opposition to what Kant expressed in the *Groundwork of the Metaphysics of Morals* as 'the utmost necessity to work out for once a pure moral philosophy, completely cleansed of everything that may be only empirical'.[14] Precepts based on experience rather than reason, he argued, 'can indeed be called a practical rule but never a moral law'.[15] In both her essays and fiction, Eliot frequently links, either directly or through metaphor, sensory experience and morality. In her critical review of Charles Kingsley's *Westward Ho!* (1855), for example, she contrasts the author with an artist in his 'true sphere', who assumes the role of teacher 'in the sense in which every great artist is a teacher – namely, by giving us his higher sensibility as a medium, a delicate acoustic or optical instrument, bringing home to our coarser senses what would otherwise be unperceived by us'.[16]

It is notable, however, that the focus of both Eliot's and Lewes's criticism is towards Kant's epistemology rather than the content of his ethics. Indeed, Lewes concludes his remarks on 'The Consequences of Kant's Psychology' in *The Biographical History* with the regret 'that our space will not permit us to enter further into Kant's system of morality, and his splendid vindication of the great idea of duty'.[17] Both agreed that the prevailing British criticism of Kant was generally misguided and exposed an insufficient knowledge of his work. For example, in her 1865 article for the *Pall Mall Gazette*, 'A Word for the Germans', Eliot insists: 'the most eminent of German metaphysicians, KANT, is cloudy in no other sense than that a mathematician is cloudy to one ignorant of mathematics ... The recipe for understanding KANT is first to get brains capable of following his argument, and next to master his terminology.'[18]

Given the influence of eighteenth- and nineteenth-century German thought on Eliot's intellectual development, something of an ambivalence towards Kant should not come as a surprise. Rosemary Ashton has tracked the pervasive German influence, with particular focus on the work of Strauss and Feuerbach, both of whom Eliot translated.[19] While extensive Feuerbachian traces in her thought have been well acknowledged, Kant's influence is largely disregarded.[20] It may well be that Eliot herself bears some responsibility for this omission by overstating her differences with Kant, or at least failing to acknowledge their ethical alignments. If so, it is probably significant that Kant was championed in England by the Cambridge moralists, one of whose major objectives was to preserve the authority of the established church; a purpose at odds with Eliot's own move away from established religion and its institutions.[21]

However, her attention towards what she called 'the moral motive', a concept at the heart of Kant's deontology and notably absent from ends-based Utilitarianism, was central and critical to her own ethical theory. For the Utilitarian, motive, while indicative of character, has no bearing on the goodness of an action, which is determined solely by its outcome. Such philosophy runs counter to Kantianism and the 'kingdom of ends' (IV, 433). For Eliot too, literature's moral value is located not only in the artistic presentation of realistic, empirical human action but also in the revelation of motive, both real and imagined. Her appreciation of the complexity of motive distances her from instrumentalism, subjective egoism and any other rule system of ethics. It thereby establishes a crucial, though clearly incomplete, philosophical alignment with Kant. Themes of motive, duty and renunciation, which she was later to incorporate at the ethical heart of her fiction, are urgently expressed in an important 1855 review essay of Geraldine Jewsbury's *Constance Herbert*:

> It is not the fact that what duty calls on us to renounce, will invariably prove 'not worth the keeping'; and if it *were* the fact, renunciation would cease to be moral heroism, and would be simply a calculation of prudence … The notion that duty looks stern, but all the while has her hand full of sugar-plums, with which she will reward us by-and-by, is the favourite cant of optimists, who try to make out that this tangled wilderness of life has a plan as easy to trace as a Dutch garden; but it really undermines all true moral development by perpetually substituting something extrinsic as a motive to action, instead of the immediate impulse of love or justice, which alone makes an action truly moral.[22]

Unlike Utilitarianism, deontological ethics has no corresponding theoretical economic relation. However, by examining Eliot's thought and artistic method in relation to Kantian principles, this chapter aims to reveal strong and illuminating insights into wider economic ethics. A close reference to the *Groundwork* reflects both that work's status as the most succinct statement of Kant's ethics and its employment of financially informed theoretical situations to illustrate and test the validity and application of the categorical imperative.[23] The most successful of these illustrations describes a man who borrows money secured on a knowingly false promise to repay; a situation that is closely paralleled in *Middlemarch*, as described below.

By following the examination of economic ethics in *Felix Holt* with a somewhat parallel treatment of *Middlemarch*, this section of the book is in accordance with Eliot's suggestion that her novels, representing 'successive mental phases', benefit from being read in the order in which they were produced. The gap between the publications of these novels was the longest in her career and the nature and range of her reading in preparation for and during the composition of *Middlemarch* is informative. Most notably, William Lecky's *History of European Morals* (1869) considers the historical development and temporal relativity of morals within a wider context of comparative method, themes that link many of the other works referenced in her preparatory notebooks.[24] Lecky's hostile criticism of Utilitarian ethics and promotion of an a priori moral sense in his long introductory survey is a further reminder of Eliot's close familiarity with the battle lines of contemporary ethical debate.[25]

As a text through which to explore the complexity of economic motivation and action and the limits of any associated ethical system, *Middlemarch* offers an extraordinarily rich seam. All the major and many of the minor characters in the novel either exercise interpersonal financial power or are compelled to make ethically significant money-related choices.[26] Yet none of them (apart from the marvellous Joshua Rigg, who literally converts property into gold) is driven solely, or even primarily, by the acquisition of money.[27] As such, the novel marks a significant advance in the depth and complexity of Eliot's economic ethics from her earlier fiction. In *Middlemarch*, Eliot is able to explore the attractions and limitations of deontological, rational ethics – built largely on the Kantian pillars of normative universality – as an alternative to Utilitarianism and naturalistic empiricism.

As in Chapter 4, the reading that follows will focus closely on Eliot's imagined characters thinking and making decisions about money in both neutral and more morally charged situations. This chapter therefore reiterates the claim that Eliot's brand of psychologically insightful realist novels represents a uniquely enlightening ethical medium. As Robert Audi has written, 'the literature of ethics is dominated by problems awaiting judgment; it pays too little attention to conditions under which moral decisions or action is called for in the first place. Not everything we do is morally significant.'[28] While *Middlemarch* is not free from moments of 'crisis ethics' (Mary Garth at Featherstone's deathbed and Dorothea grappling with her husband's final request are obvious examples, which will form part of the discussion that follows), in general, attitudes and motivations are seen to evolve gradually with each layer of mental description.[29] By contrast, the imagined agents central to the theoretical illustrative dilemmas of academic moral philosophy are uncoloured by context or psychological complexity and yet are often confronted with extreme and morally loaded choices. Iris Murdoch draws the distinction in her argument that literature can capture a 'sense of the difficulty and complexity of the moral life and the opacity of persons … Through literature we can re-discover a sense of the density of our lives.'[30] The 'opacity of persons' is as absent from Kant and Mill as it is from academic ethicists in our own age.[31]

The academic philosophical technique is not without value. As Kwame Anthony Appiah writes in his analysis of the use of 'trolley problems' in the work of many moral philosophers of the last half-century: 'It is an interesting and unobvious assumption, which hasn't had the attention it deserves, that our responses to imaginary scenarios mirror our responses to real ones.'[32] Novels also use 'imaginary scenarios' to lead the reader to ask 'what would I do?', but potentially in ways that both enrich and expose the limitations of any ethical theory that attempts a normative solution to the question. This potential is most fully realised in *Middlemarch*.

An introductory example from *Middlemarch* will hopefully illustrate the genre's ability to unravel the finer points of theoretical distinction. Just prior to his decision to terminate his contract with Bulstrode, Caleb Garth proposes that Fred Vincy be installed as the estate manager of Stone Court.[33] Garth's suggestion is driven purely by a concern for Fred's welfare and advancement and has no self-interested motivation. By this stage of the novel, the reader has formed an understanding of Garth's particular virtues and circumstances and registers his request as that of a good man acting with a good will towards a good end for the benefit of others. Bulstrode, however, in agreeing to Garth's suggestion is motivated by selfish calculation: not only does he want to secure Garth's support in what he perceives as a gathering storm around the blackmailing Raffles, but he also perceives this as a way of deflecting his wife's criticism against his negligence of her family, in particular his refusal to offer financial assistance to the Lydgates.

In Utilitarian terms, Garth's request and Bulstrode's acquiescence have equivalent value: both combine to secure the intended beneficial consequence for Fred, while also supporting Bulstrode's selfish ends. By contrast, Kant states as a fundamental proposition in the *Groundwork*:

> an action from duty has its moral worth *not in the purpose* to be attained by it but in the maxim in accordance with which it is decided upon, and therefore

does not depend upon the realisation of the object of the action but merely upon the *principle of volition* in accordance with which the action is done without regard for any object of the faculty of desire. (IV, 400)

A good act is conditional not in the realisation of its ends, but in its very motive for action and, for Kant, the motive and the willing of the ends are rationally inseparable.

In Kantian terms, Bulstrode's violation of moral law is implicit in his failure of reason. When he first contemplates the possibility of Raffles' death, the reader is allowed to follow the cognitive train of a moral psychology that seeks justification in the separation of motive and content: 'intention was everything in the question of right and wrong. And Bulstrode set himself to keep his intention separate from his desire' (692–3). Bulstrode is here guilty of a practical, rational contradiction by willing the end (Raffles death) and not the means (his own intervention), even though the latter is conceptually contained within the former.[34] He employs a similar line of reasoning when contemplating the source of his wealth and desperately attempts to secure the boundaries of moral responsibility by reference to philosophical principle, in this case the concept of unintended consequences: 'is it not one thing to set up a new gin palace and another to accept an investment in an old one? The profits made out in lost souls – where can the line be drawn at which they begin in human transaction?' (603). The authorial intervention, after a long series of free indirect speech, powerfully captures the morally flawed reconciliation he attempts to make between two fundamentally incompatible paths: 'Bulstrode found himself carrying on two distinct lives; his religious activity could not be incompatible with his business as soon as he had argued himself into not feeling it incompatible' (603).

This attempt to (ab)use reason to correct intuitive feelings of right and wrong strikes at the heart of Kantian ethical theory. Contrary to an ethics grounded in empiricism, Kant argues that non-contingent duties (the categorical imperative) lie 'prior to all experience, in the idea of a reason determining the will by means of a priori grounds' (IV, 408). Eliot writes in *Middlemarch* that 'We are all of us born into moral stupidity, taking the world as an udder to feed our supreme selves' (205), but her most sympathetic characters in the novel all show an intuitive and deeply felt sense of duty and right which is seen to transcend practical experience. Once again the point is best articulated by Caleb Garth, here explaining to his wife how he came to the decision to employ Fred Vincy: "'It's my duty Susan . . . I've got a clear feeling inside me, and that I shall follow"' (551–2). His words are later echoed when, despite admitting to an instinctive sympathy for

Bulstrode's anguish, his decision to leave his employment is secured by a greater law: 'Caleb felt a deep pity for him, but he could have used no pretexts to account for his resolve, even if they would have been of any use.' He tells Bulstrode, 'I have that feeling inside me, that I can't go on working with you ... Everything else is buried, so far as my will goes' (684).

Throughout the novel this assertion of the pre-eminence of intuitive moral feeling is signalled by an explicit rejection of material reward.[35] Caleb's disregard for money is a repeated motif of his moral integrity and elsewhere we see Lydgate and Ladislaw actively choosing to stand apart from commercial concerns.[36]

Lydgate is morally differentiated from his fellow practitioners by his abhorrence of the commerce of medicine, which the others embrace to the clear detriment of their medical vocation. As explained below, Lydgate's flawed reason in his handling of his financial affairs comes to threaten the autonomy and integrity of his will, but his fundamental sense of duty towards his fellow man is preserved throughout his fall from grace. The instinct physically to support the disgraced Bulstrode overcomes the practical and self-interested realisation that such a gesture is likely to reinforce the widespread opinion that he has been corrupted by Bulstrode's financial patronage.[37] His action is an essentially Kantian demonstration of motive and will independent of self-interested outcome. In fact, according to Kant, Lydgate's 'unspeakable bitter[ness]' in assisting Bulstrode actually elevates the moral content of his action because it was done not from inclination but from a duty that transcends sympathy: 'It is just then that the worth of character comes out, which is moral and incomparably the highest, namely that he is beneficent not from inclination but from duty' (IV, 399).

A similar dilemma is dramatically framed in the scene of Peter Featherstone's deathbed. While Mary Garth is aware of the likely positive consequences to Fred of following Featherstone's instruction to burn one of his wills, her choice of action comes 'imperatively and excluded all question in the critical moment' (311). Mrs Garth's later assessment of the incident asserts the independence and pre-eminence of categorical duties over specific practical consequences and is again explicitly Kantian: 'a loss which falls on another because we have done right is not to lie upon our conscience' (397).

In Section II of the *Groundwork*, Kant famously reformulates the categorical imperative around specifically human ends: 'so act that you use humanity, whether in your own person or in the person of any other, always at the same time as an end, never merely as a means' (IV, 429). The extent to which characters in *Middlemarch* adopt ethical standards in accordance with this 'principle of humanity' – or 'kingdom of ends' – is marked by monetary motives and actions. Those with money, most notably Bulstrode and Featherstone, but also Casaubon, use it directly as a means of attempting to control the actions of others.[38] Monetary behaviour in the novel therefore becomes a primary indicator of the level of adherence to Kant's principle of humanity. In the case of Fred Vincy, what he thinks of, says about and does with money is central to a process whereby he comes to elevate other people from means of serving his personal pleasures to ends in themselves. Indeed, the incident that epitomises his flawed, or rather absent sense of duty early in the novel closely resembles one of the examples Kant uses to illustrate how the 'willed universal law' principle of the categorical imperative can help identify non-contingent duties. Although, unlike the agent in Kant's example, Fred does not take a loan from Caleb Garth in conscious and certain knowledge that he will be unable to repay, the maxim by which he might seem to justify his choice of creditor could be formulated as: 'When I believe myself to be in need of money, I shall borrow money and promise to repay it without any certain means of repayment from the least demanding, most trusting person I know who can least afford the loss.' The motives and actions of Kant's hypothetical debtor and Fred Vincy are equally logically incapable of being willed as universal laws.[39]

Fred's moral enlightenment following his partial default on the loan is gradual and uneven but is marked by a growing understanding of his financial obligation to others. He comes to equate his financial irresponsibility, which transgresses moral law, with a breach of criminal law and recognises the wider implications of not honouring its commitments: 'I have already a debt to you which will never be discharged, even when I have been able to pay it in the shape of money' (549).[40]

It should be noted that Kant's formulation grounds the principle of humanity in actions both towards other people and to 'your own person'. Indeed Mary Garth, while acting under the compulsion of an intuitive sense of right in refusing to follow Featherstone's deathbed instruction, also admits to a self-interested motive: 'I will not let the end of your life soil the beginning of mine.' Her words are later echoed by Ladislaw in his rejection of Bulstrode's offer of money and inheritance: 'my unblemished honour is important to me' (611). Ladislaw's positioning of money is significant in establishing his wider scale of values. Rather than accept money from a dishonourable man, he would pay everything he has to eradicate his maternal association with the sources of Bulstrode's wealth.[41] Notably, both Ladislaw and Caleb Garth subvert recognised conceptions of wealth and fortune: 'to have within him such a feeling as [Ladislaw] had towards Dorothea, was like the inheritance of a fortune' (460); while Caleb comments on a job well done: 'I'd sooner have it than a fortune' (393).

However, the character who, in following her chosen marital and phi-lanthropic paths of duty, shows least observance to Kant's duty towards self, is Dorothea.[42] Her essential struggle through much of the novel is to find a way of living that unites doing most good with doing what is most right. In some sense, therefore, she strives to combine consequentialist and Kantian ethics and Eliot explores that attempted resolution partly by reference to monetary and economic dilemmas. Specifically, her quest brings her to higher levels of enlightenment on two parallel and economically related tracks, which are discussed later in this chapter: an understanding of the limits of consequentialism; and the achievement of full moral autonomy by the assumption of monetary choice and responsibility.

Accompanying these developments, there is also a Kantian dimension to Dorothea's progressive acceptance, or de-alienation of material objects through the course of the novel. Celia notes early on that her sister 'likes giving up' (18), and Dorothea's rejection of most of her mother's jewellery is related to her disdain for the 'miserable men' who 'find such things, and work at them, and sell them' (14). Elaine Freedgood has noted Dorothea's 'highly personal and largely confused (and confusing) approach to the interpretation of objects' and concludes that her attempts to stand outside materiality and the market leave her with 'the overwhelming task of having to decide the value of things on a thing-by-thing basis'.[43] Andrew H. Miller has also observed how 'Dorothea represents herself in her dress by renunciation or negation', a form of repression that is contrasted with Rosamond's dress and spending habits, by which she becomes 'fully asso-ciated with commodified goods'.[44] Miller skilfully traces how Eliot suggests Dorothea's shifting position in relation to material culture by reference to nuanced details of and modifications to her dress, culminating in the scene with Ladislaw in which she embraces the responsibilities of domestic economic management in a house '"in a street"' (809), on 'seven-hundred-a-year' and promises to '"learn what everything costs"' (801).[45]

Despite her repeated efforts both before her marriage and after her husband's death, Dorothea fails to find a model of action that embraces political economic principles in support of a Utilitarian outcome of greater good. Her encouragement of Chettam's attempts to improve the living conditions of the farm labourers puts her at odds with political economic theory, which holds that such investment must command an increase in rent. Her enthusiasm is therefore first misunderstood and then dismissed by her uncle, who holds economic understanding to be an exclusively male preserve.[46] Even late in the novel we find Dorothea 'sat down in the library before her particular little heap of books on political economy and kindred matters, out of which she was trying to get light as to the best way of spending money' (796) for the benefit of all. In her ideals of redistribution, effectively striving for the greatest financial good for the greatest number, she demonstrates the limits of theoretical consequentialism.[47]

Her attraction to and concern for Ladislaw inspires her first attempts to locate economic ethics in a more immediate, familial context, as she ponders 'with a sympathy that grew to agitation' (362–3) questions of duty and inheritance in relation to law and natural justice. The description of her agitated thoughts is infused with Kantian language: the responsibility to recompense Ladislaw arises from 'the fulfilment of claims founded on our own deeds'; a 'just view' must be taken in order to restore a 'right footing' and the 'unfair concentration' of wealth must be redistributed to provide him with a 'rightful income'. Ironically, Casaubon's realisation of the categorical nature of Dorothea's concepts of right and duty, 'her power of devoting herself to the idea of the right and best' (467), inspires his attempt to commit her to a promise intended to bind her future in accordance with his will.[48]

The key to Dorothea's enlightenment is the Kantian realisation that the claims of an unspoken promise to a dead husband are contingent and inferior to the duty to treat oneself as an end: to strive for a personal flourishing in the widest sense. This realisation is paralleled by a modification in her money-giving plans and actions: away from the impartial spread of her 'greatest good' philanthropic dreams to the personal, focused gifts and assistance she directs to Farebrother (through the Lowick living), Lydgate's hospital project and finally Lydgate himself. As her ambitious and idealistic philanthropic plans are by necessity reined in, the true nature of the duty of beneficence, framed in Kantian rather than impartial Utilitarian terms, emerges. In her union with Ladislaw, the essential emotional component of her moral psychology is enriched by a proper 'beneficent activity' (822).[49]

The minutely described process by which Dorothea comes to recognise the misguided hopes and expectations on which she had based her decision to marry Casaubon is marked by the use of the language and imagery of confinement; the spatial dimension of her life seems to shrink with her opportunities to do good and thrive. Her attempts to rationalise her confinement by asserting the supremacy of marital duty is thwarted by the renewed and amplified pressure her husband exerts in seeking agreement to his final request: she becomes 'fettered' by the 'yoke of marriage' he has made for her (472). Her emotional and intellectual imprisonment becomes increasingly associated with her increased wealth as she concludes '[my] own money buys me nothing but an uneasy conscience' (364). Ironically, as noted below, the same images of fettering and confinement are increasingly used in relation to Lydgate as his financial situation deteriorates. In both cases, changing material circumstances have the effect of constraining the freedom of the will. Autonomy, central to Kant's conception of the rational moral agent, becomes limited and impinges upon moral motive and action.

The description of one of the money-giving acts of the more enlightened Dorothea referred to earlier, the appointment of Farebrother as the rector of Lowick, is significant in emphasising the recovery of her moral autonomy. She explains to Farebrother: 'I think it would be easier to give up power and money than to keep them. It seems very unfitting that I should have this patronage, yet I felt that I ought not to let it be used by someone else instead of me' (501). This description of a financially related motive, informed by personal responsibility and duty, in turn contrasts sharply with Bulstrode's earlier rationalisation and justification of his own money-making activities. He effectively detaches moral autonomy from financial motive by establishing divine providence as the deterministic force behind all his actions, even those he recognises as 'misdeeds'. For, 'even when committed – had they not been half sanctified by the singleness of his desire to devote himself and all he possessed to the furtherance of the divine scheme?' (515).

Bulstrode's ethical scheme is consequential but substitutes the pleasure principle, which is the motivational bedrock of Utilitarianism, with a rigid adherence to divine providence. It is strongly reminiscent of the Evangelical morality of which Eliot was so scathingly critical in her 1855 essay on Dr Cumming, whose 'perverted moral judgment' she ascribed to 'egoistic passions and dogmatic beliefs'.[50] Bulstrode's financial misdeeds, both in the accumulation of his wealth and in his attempts to preserve the providentially appointed power and social position that wealth has created, are consequently shorn of autonomous moral responsibility.[51] Thus, when he recognises the desirability of securing Lydgate as an ally during Raffles's final illness and reverses his decision not to advance a loan: 'He did not measure the quantity of diseased motive which had made him wish for Lydgate's goodwill, but the quantity was none the less actively there, like an irritating agent in the blood' (695).[52]

Although desire for financial gain does not, per se, motivate Bulstrode's actions, money assumes for him a level of critical instrumentality which leads him greatly to elevate its contingent nature. This is also the case for those characters who, from widely different ethical positions, attempt to control the actions of others by the assertion of financial obligation, such as Featherstone and Casaubon. Indeed, the contrasting moral autonomy of characters such as Caleb Garth and Ladislaw is emphasised by their adherence to non-contingent, or categorical, values that transcend the material. Thus Caleb Garth is beyond the influence of Featherstone, who 'felt himself ill at ease with a brother-in-law whom he could not annoy, who did not mind about being considered poor, had nothing to ask of him, and understood all kinds of farming and mining business better than he did' (251). In his relationship with Casaubon, Ladislaw is required to weigh duty against individual will and freedom in specific relation to money obligation and, because he genuinely does not 'care for prestige or high pay', is able to reject Casaubon's demands because: 'an obligation of this kind cannot fairly fetter me' (367).

In relation to their positioning of money in their overall ethical schemes, most characters in *Middlemarch* remain largely consistent. The greatest exception to this generalisation is Lydgate, through whom Eliot most closely explores the wider implications of debt obligations and their threat to moral autonomy. The early depiction of Lydgate standing outside the money economy – 'bent on doing many things that were not directly fitted to make his fortune or even secure him a good income' (93) – is reinforced by his unique (in Middlemarch environs) position in the medical profession. His sense of vocation and belief that medicine can best combine science and emotion establishes him as an idealist set apart from the various medical practitioners who unite in their condemnation of his 'ungentlemanly attempts to discredit the sale of drugs', by which they profit handsomely (257).[53]

Following the first of several conversations with Farebrother, which trace and measure the opposite trajectories in their relative fortunes through the course of the novel, we learn that Lydgate has a disdain for gambling. What for the vicar is a necessary means of supplementing a meagre income, represents for Lydgate a 'meanness' and a 'subservience of conduct' to material gain. Because he has never wanted for it, 'he had no power of imagining the part which the want of money plays in determining the actions of men' (175). When that very 'want of money' comes to dominate his waking existence, he is tempted by the quick potential gains of the billiard room, where Fred Vincy observes a physically transformed Lydgate, 'excited and betting' and 'acting, watching, speaking with that excited narrow consciousness which reminds one of an animal with fierce eyes and retractile claws' (661).[54] Even when he starts to lose, '[s]till he went on, for his mind was as utterly narrowed into that precipitous crevice of play as if he had been the most ignorant lounger there' (661). What Lydgate had earlier considered – with simplifying ethical detachment – a morally reprehensible activity, becomes a compulsive psychological and physiologically manifested necessity in which moral sense is apparently suspended. The exploration of the psychology of gambling, to which Eliot was to return in *Daniel Deronda*, was informed by the author's familiarity with contemporary advances in both psychological and probabilistic understanding and introduces a pathological element into considerations of money-motivation that Kantian (or indeed any extant) ethical theory could not fully incorporate.[55]

This is not to say that a large part of Lydgate's flawed financial choices and actions cannot be analysed and judged by reference to Kantian principles. His justification for allowing himself to be supported by a benefactor of whose character and integrity he was uncertain clearly fails Kant's test of willing a universal law out of the maxim on which he acted. As he attempts to justify his position to Ladislaw:

> a man may work for a special end with others whose motives and general course are equivocal, if he is quite sure of his personal independence, and that he is not working for his private interest – either place or money. (458)

He later reflects on his inability to preserve two parallel moral realms in such an interconnected relationship: 'Bulstrode's character has enveloped me, because I took his money' (753). As his personal independence is drawn in, his mind becomes 'utterly narrowed' – an image characteristic of the language Eliot uses to describe not only his gambling, but also his entire mental state during this period: he feels himself in a 'vile yoke' and 'his self was being narrowed into the miserable isolation of egoistic fears' (635).

As elsewhere in the novel, we see the inability to control financial motivation and action not only as indicative of but also as a critical contributory element in the loss of moral autonomy. The narrative technique Eliot deploys in describing the crises enveloping both Bulstrode and Lydgate serves to create a sense of slow but mounting inevitability as narrative time is split between the 'present' and explanatory scenes from the recent past. The effect is that real-time is periodically frozen and then resumed with the informed reader even more certain of the slow-motion 'crash' that is approaching. In fact, the repossession of Lydgate's house and property is averted and his fundamental virtue of acting according to duty is preserved. But the fortuitous survival of a financial crisis imposes a new and pragmatic set of practical ethics in his domestic and professional life.

His idealism gives way to scepticism as he informs Dorothea of his intention to pursue 'what will please the world and bring in money'. This, if not a crime or sin has, for the flawed Kantian, a distinct sense of moral failing: 'I have not taken a bribe yet. But there is a pale shade of bribery which is sometimes called prosperity' (758).

Mr Farebrother's observation on the malleability of character loses nothing for the frequency with which it is quoted: 'character is not cut in marble – it is not something solid and unalterable. It is something living and changing, and may become diseased as our bodies do' (725). Dorothea, speaking, as it were, for Kant, protests against Farebrother's suggestion that 'a man of honourable disposition' might succumb to dishonourable action 'under the pressure of hard circumstances' (724).[56] The natural scientific image might suggest that the scientifically practised Farebrother might here be speaking for his creator, but Eliot's position would seem to lie somewhere between that of her two characters. Farebrother surely underestimates Lydgate's ability to resist what he knows to be bribery, which Eliot would certainly have regarded as a universal moral law. And yet there is a psychological astuteness and accuracy underlying Farebrother's assertion that captures the intricacies of practical ethics, a complexity he earlier acknowledges when reflecting on his own success at the whist table: 'It's a rather strong check to one's self-complacency to find how much of one's right doing depends on not being in want of money' (633). Lydgate remains, even in Kantian terms and despite the rationally debilitating effect of the 'money craving' (635) to which he is driven, a 'good' man, consistently observant of the imperative of duty. But by becoming simultaneously bound by a financial debt that changes the nature of his obligation to Bulstrode (he is shocked, on receiving the banker's £1,000 loan 'that he should be overjoyed at being under such a strong personal obligation' (695)), his scope for 'right doing' is massively shrunk. The narrowing of his professional ideal is fittingly marked by his submission to the commerce of medicine and a specialisation in gout, 'a disease which has a good deal of wealth on its side' (821).

Neither, notwithstanding her realisation of an imperative duty to self, can Dorothea's merging of an active beneficent activity with a life of emotion be fully attributed to an adoption of Kantian principles. Ultimately, Eliot's criticism of Kant lies not in what his ethics teaches, but in what it leaves out. What Ladislaw describes as Dorothea's 'fanaticism of sympathy' (214) is something that needs a corrective to enable the attainment of a wider personal thriving or flourishing. This points more closely to classical concepts of eudaimonism, which informed Eliot's ethics as surely as they were rejected within Kant's. Ironically, this would serve to align her more closely not to Sidgwick, who continued to struggle with the 'dualism of practical reason' (self-interest versus altruism) but to Lewes's adversary, T. H. Green.[57] That Green valued highly Eliot's artistic mediations on practical ethics is evidenced by his intention to include the quotation below from *Romola* in his unfinished Prolegomena:

> We can only have the highest happiness, such as goes along with being a great man, by having wide thoughts, and much feeling for the rest of the world as well as ourselves; and this sort of happiness often brings so much pain with it, that we can only tell it from pain by its being what we would choose before everything else, because our souls see it as good.[58]

It represents a seemingly unlikely philosophical connection between the two, of which much more will be said in Chapter 8.

CHAPTER 6

Being good and doing good with money: incorporating the bourgeois virtues

Then I told [George Eliot] of a controversy as to whether Morals should be taught as a lesson in schools and that a friend of mine (Adelaide) was going to do it. She said at first that she thought it would be a most dangerous thing to do, but explained afterwards that she meant that, if it was as a set of dry maxims . . . She hoped my friend would not teach the girls to think too much of political measures for improving society – as leading away from individual efforts to be good, I understood her to mean.[1]   – Emily Davies, 1876

Seeing that Morality and Morals under their *alias* of Ethics, are the subject of voluminous discussion, and their true basis a pressing matter of dispute – seeing that the most famous book ever written on Ethics, and forming a chief study in our colleges, allies ethical with political science . . . one might expect that educated men would find reason to avoid a perversion of language which lends itself to no wider view of life than that of village gossips.[2]   – George Eliot, 1879

The previous two chapters have argued that while Eliot drew substantially from the theories of the two main competing schools of teleological and deontological ethics, she ultimately regarded neither as adequate nor complete. Utilitarianism's attempt to quantify good on the basis of outcome was incompatible with a plurality and hierarchy of values and, in common with Kantianism, denied a moral primacy to the flourishing, or eudaimonism, of the individual agent. Both she saw as ultimately bound by their respective rule-based formulations: a restriction she tested in the novels by reference to a wide and complex range of intuitive and reasoned motivations through the thoughts and actions of intricate, psychologically realised fictional characters. This chapter considers how Eliot used the novels to evaluate morality and the economic through a set of alternative, less systemised principles. Here, the ethical spotlight will be directed on the notion of 'character' itself.

Readings of *The Mill on the Floss* and *Daniel Deronda* will attempt to show how Eliot explored economically related motivation and action by reference to moral, intellectual and commercial *virtues* rather than ethical rules from duty or concepts of good outcome. By incorporating virtue concepts into the novels, she raises a number of interrelated questions: 'What is, and how does one become a virtuous character?' 'Is an ethics of virtue an adequate alternative to the two main competing systems?' and 'Within any theory of virtue, how important are those traits that relate to the economic (what Deirdre McCloskey calls the "bourgeois virtues"), including prudential self-interest?'[3] That these questions were repeated more than seventy years after Eliot's death by moral philosophers seeking to reassert the normative claims of an ethics of virtue reflects a common Aristotelian inspiration and grounding, in particular *The Nicomachean Ethics*.[4] In July 1852, Eliot tells Charles Bray that she is 'reading Aristotle to find out what is the chief good', and, as the quotation heading this chapter from *Impressions of Theophrastus Such* indicates, his guidance (not rules) continued to influence her moral philosophical thought and writing throughout her life.[5]

In Book I of *The Ethics*, Aristotle defines 'human good' as 'activity of soul in accordance with virtue [*arete*], or, if there be more than one virtue, in accordance with the best and most complete' (VII, 14). The Greek concept of *arete* does not carry the heavy moral connotations of modern usage and is often translated as 'excellence'. However, as this chapter will argue that Eliot's understanding of the concept, while clearly drawing on Christian appropriations, matches and even, in relation to commercial applications, extends Aristotle's in scope, 'virtue' remains a meaningful translation here. Aristotle distinguishes moral from intellectual virtue but, in Book 6 explains why the truly virtuous agent must combine both in the exercise of choice and action: 'This is why choice cannot exist either without reason and intellect or without a moral state; for good action and its opposite cannot exist without a combination of intellect and character' (139). Moral virtue he describes as a 'state of character', the exercise of which 'both brings into good condition the thing of which it is the excellence and makes the work of that thing be done well' (36). This internal and external promotion of the good is achieved only when the agent acts voluntarily and with deliberation *from* virtue. Robert Audi explains how this distinction links Aristotle to Kant:

> Aristotle distinguishes between acting from virtue and acting merely in accordance with it. This wording, though true to Aristotle, recalls Kant's distinction between acting from duty and merely acting in conformity with it. On the plausible assumption that acting from duty is, often, acting from moral virtue, Kantian actions from duty are often similar in important ways to Aristotelian actions from virtue.[6]

On this reading, the contention advanced in Chapter 5 that Eliot, while convinced of the primacy of character in ethics, was more attracted to and influenced by Kantian deontology than she openly admitted, seems reasonable. However, the differences between the two schools of thought are crucial to an understanding of the greater appeal of the kind of virtue ethics that Eliot advanced.

A central differentiation lies in the two philosophers' relative positioning of the agent. Aristotle's concept of acting from virtue positively promotes the good of the agent, whereas a Kantian act from duty is an others-regarding imperative that, in effect, simply exemplifies virtuous character and action. For Aristotle, character and the nurturing of the virtues is an antecedent and pre-requisite of determining right motive, rational choice and good action. As Gary Watson describes it (conflating the good and the right): 'how best or right or proper to conduct oneself is explained in terms of how it is best for a human being to be'.[7] The reading of *Daniel Deronda* that follows is crucially informed by this Aristotelian framework.

We can locate another important departure in the requirement of the dutiful Kantian agent to dissociate the motive for action from any pleasurable inclination. Conversely, for Aristotle 'the man who does not rejoice in noble actions is not even good; since no one would call a man just who did not enjoy acting justly, nor any man liberal who did not enjoy liberal actions and similarly in all other cases. If this is so, virtuous actions must be in themselves pleasant' (16). Pleasure is accordingly an intrinsic good, although still only one component of eudaimonia, thus simultaneously linking and differentiating Aristotle's ethics from Utilitarianism. The virtuous act may coincide with that of the Utilitarian calculating an aggregate, pleasure-referent outcome, but the respective scales of moral evaluation for the two agents will be completely different. Nevertheless, it seems plausible that Eliot would have welcomed (and that, arguably, she even pre-empted) more recent attempts to more precisely locate virtue ethics in relation to other ethical systems. Watson, for example, resists the traditional opposition between consequentialism and deontology to distinguish an ethical third way. Virtue ethics, he argues, simultaneously stands apart from and incorporates certain teleological and Kantian aspects. He distinguishes:

> an ethics of requirement, an ethics of consequences, and an ethics of virtue or character. This classification enables us to observe that while both ethics of consequences and ethics of virtue are teleological insofar as they are guided fundamentally by a notion of the good, Aristotle is nonetheless closer to Kant than to Bentham on the question of consequentialism.[8]

Unfortunately, Aristotle's account of those virtues attendant on economic behaviour in *The Ethics* is somewhat partial, particularly in relation to the age of widely permeating commerce into which George Eliot was writing. The Greeks had money, about which Aristotle wrote, but not capitalism. His conclusion in regard to the acquisition of material wealth in the opening Book is, however, unequivocal: 'The life of money-making is one undertaken under compulsion, and wealth is evidently not the good we are seeking' (7). Such a life, portrayed by Aristotle as akin to slavery ('under compulsion'), is incompatible with moral virtue, which requires that the agent's action is voluntary, taken with knowledge of the circumstances, and the result of previous deliberation (48–53).

He has more to say about how the virtuous man should distribute his wealth, establishing a mean of liberality, midway between the (vicious) extremes of prodigality and meanness. The economically virtuous agent who has sufficient wealth must meet this base case of liberality but, by nature of his greater distributional capacity, should aspire to magnificence. The rich man whose expenditure falls below or exceeds the standard of magnificence is guilty, respectively, of niggardliness and vulgarity (79–89). As with his early statement of the incompatibility of profit and virtue, his discussion of liberality and magnificence speaks to a patrician distaste of prudent money management and implies that the greater risk to virtue is spending too little rather than too much.

In this respect, Aristotle fails fully to extend the scope of practical wisdom (142, *phronesis*), one of the intellectual virtues – or, more precisely, 'a reasoned and true state of capacity to act with regard to human goods' – to the sphere of wealth and commerce.[9] The moral philosophical basis of such an extension in the Western tradition was to take many centuries. McCloskey traces the historical process whereby practical wisdom came to embrace financial prudence, identifying a pivotal moment of intervention by Aquinas, who sanctioned the profits of trade, including the charging of interest. This development, she argues (quoting Lester K. Little), 'brought about the emancipation of Christian merchants'.[10] In the hands of Adam Smith, described by McCloskey as 'a virtue ethicist for a commercial age', prudence, one of the four cardinal or pagan virtues, assumed a central place in Britain's fast-growing money economy.[11] As part of the argument advanced here is that Eliot was both a natural successor and a literary counterpart to Smith in presenting a commercially broadened, neo-Aristotelian unity of the virtues, McCloskey's claims for the full scope of the bourgeois virtues are worth laying out in full:

The bourgeois virtues, derivable from the seven virtues but viewable in business practice, might include enterprise, adaptability, imagination, optimism, integrity, prudence, thrift, trustworthiness, humor, affection, self-possession, consideration, responsibility, solicitude, decorum, patience, toleration, affability, peacibility, civility, neighborliness, obligingness, reputability, dependability, impartiality. The point of calling such virtues 'bourgeois' is to contrast them with nonbusiness versions of the same virtues, such as (physical) courage or (spiritual) love. Bourgeois virtues are the townspeople's virtues, away from the military camp of the aristocrat or the commons of the peasantry or the temple of the priest or the studio of the artist.[12]

Smith, of course, believed firmly in the ennobling potential of trade and commerce driven, in an open economy, by the individual profit motive, rather than any national or social character. '[W]henever commerce is introduced into any country,' he wrote, 'probity and punctuality always accompany it.'[13] His great achievement, as McCloskey explains, was to embed prudential self-interest within a range of social virtues, particularly justice and temperance; a synthesis that weakened through the course of the nineteenth century (despite Mill's best attempts) and largely disintegrated in the professionalised economics that were emerging towards the end of Eliot's life. In *The Theory of Moral Sentiments*, Smith insists that '[t]he wise and virtuous man is at all times willing that his own private interest should be sacrificed to the public interest of his own particular order or society', and he begins Section 3 of the work, 'Of Self Command', with: 'The man who acts according to the rules of perfect prudence, of strict justice, and of proper benevolence, may be said to be perfectly virtuous.' That this balance can be tested, Smith writes, 'nowhere but in the sympathetic feelings of the impartial and well informed spectator'[14] gives a strong indication of how a far-reaching exploration of the virtues in a commercial age can be achieved through imaginative literature.[15] Moreover, as Stephen Darwall has observed, 'As Smith sees it, moral judgement is always addressed to and regulated by a community of interlocutors. This makes rhetoric an important aspect of ethics for Smith.'[16]

With this in mind, this chapter will consider Eliot's rhetorical examination of economic ethics via two novels from opposite ends of her novelistic career. *The Mill on the Floss* (1860) provided Eliot with her first large advance, part of which funded her first stock investments.[17] The novel's setting, beginning in the late 1820s, enables her to explore a number of financially related transitions. The emergence from mercantilism to a more recognisable capitalist economy puts local custom and superstition under threat while at the same time multiplying individual ways of money-making. Using Aristotle's classifications, the book's almost exclusive focus on the trading and merchant classes points the reader to consider the requirements of liberality and its co-existence with other virtues.

Daniel Deronda (1876), written at the height of its author's wealth and fame, explores both liberality and, in relation to its rich and titled characters, magnificence. Uniquely among Eliot's novels, *Daniel Deronda* is set less than a decade in the past in a probabilistic, limited liability 'economy of wants'.[18] Both novels align commercial pursuits with religious traditions, but with very different outcomes; and both examine character development, in which dealing with financial loss, gain and inheritance are seminal. The money economy, whose social infiltration we observe in *The Mill on the Floss* has, by the time of *Daniel Deronda*'s setting, become hegemonic. Earlier chapters have shown that, despite her liberal inclinations and strong personal financial prudence, in both her essays and novels Eliot was not uncritical of the effects of this change; it gave rise to what she called, in her final work, a 'debasing [of] the moral currency'.[19] She also recognised the increasing complexity of economic choice and responsibility for the individual in society. Social and economic flux meant that individuals of all classes and professions (including artists such as Eliot herself, immersed in the 'commerce of literature') addressing the question 'how best to live' needed both to adapt particular concepts of balanced financial prudence and to incorporate those traits within a broad range of virtues.

In her journal for 23 January 1862 Eliot writes: 'Mr Smith the publisher called and had an interview with G. He asked if I were open to a "magnificent" offer. This made me think about money – but it is better for me not to be rich.'[20] For better or worse, the success of *The Mill on the Floss*, following on from *Adam Bede*, had secured her high market value and she was well on the road to becoming rich. While it is most unlikely that George Smith framed the 'magnificence' of his proposed offer within a context of Aristotelian ethics, Eliot's reaction to it seems to draw on the earlier-mentioned conclusion of Book 1 of *The Ethics* that 'wealth is evidently not the good we are seeking' (7). It is clear that she thought a great deal about money and it is likely that part of her reluctance to give Smith's approach her immediate consideration owes less to the prospect of a further acceleration in her already fast-growing wealth than to a realisation that changing her publisher could conflict with her other, non-financial values.

Abandoning Blackwood for largely economic reasons (which she temporarily does for the publication of *Romola*) would risk undermining the Aristotelian means of justice, temperance and benevolence towards a loyal and trusted partner, who had initially risked his own money in first publishing her work. Any justification that gave excessive ethical weight to the forces of the free market could make her complicit in the debasing of the moral currency. This concern would have been heightened by the fact that she had recently illustrated and explored the dangerous implications of constructing an ethical system on a single foundation of self-interested prudence in the novel whose great success had inspired Smith's 'magnificent offer', *The Mill on the Floss*.

According to Aristotle, the fully virtuous individual embraces a balance and completion of all the moral and intellectual virtues and always acts according to the appropriate virtue; the exclusion or underweighting of some at the expense of others risks tipping virtue into vice. These requirements of universality and consistency have, since Eliot's time, been challenged as psychologically untenable. Drawing on experimental results, situationists claim that the behaviour of individuals varies significantly according to external, non-moral factors; that character traits are simply not fixed at a certain level.[21] Eliot would not have been surprised by such empirical findings and fully recognised the difficulty even of differentiating virtue and vice in any particular situation. As she wrote in her 1855 essay, 'The Morality of Wilhelm Meister', 'the line between the virtuous and the vicious, so far from being a necessary safeguard to morality, is itself an immoral fiction'.[22] But neither would the experimental evidence have dissuaded her that, whatever its practical limitations, an ethics of virtue in which the aspiration towards a full and balanced range of inward and outward-facing, well-developed and rationally motivated character traits has considerable value.

Her portrayal of the Dodson sisters and their husbands in *The Mill on the Floss* offers a compelling illustration of how a narrowly conceived prudence can give rise to the ascendancy of the lesser side-virtues: thrift, caution and foresight. The extended Dodson family are firmly rooted in the traditions and localised economy of pre-industrial Britain. Three of the husbands have worked at occupations attached to the land that have changed little in generations – milling, wool stapling and farming – with only Mr Deane, a self-made partner in an expanding trading company, representing the transition to a modern commercial economy.

Guest & Co. embodies the archetypal, conglomerating merchant-house of the mid-century, whose trading origins were extending into a wider range of financing and banking activities. The opening description of St Ogg's places the town in an expanding network of international trade routes which the firm was well positioned to exploit. While the merchant class to which Deane belongs has emerged from a tradition of 'industrious men of business of a former generation, who made their fortunes slowly', it is also looking forward to 'these days of rapid money-getting'; the developed cash-economy from which Eliot is writing.[23] Deane's sisters-in-law and their husbands have no such progressive concept of money and wealth. Mr Pullet could 'not see how a man could have any security for his money unless he turned it into land' (85) and, while they would 'put out' money at a minimum of 5 per cent interest (and only on the strongest security), Mrs Glegg conceals any surplus funds in various locations around the house, 'for, to [her] mind, banks and strong-boxes would have nullified the pleasure of property – she might as well have taken her food in capsules' (111).[24]

Deane's financial prudence is more sophisticated. His plan to buy Dorlcote Mill and merge its operations with another Guest property based on their 'value as investments' (213) lay beyond the imagination of Mrs Glegg, but, in common with all his relations, he exercises prudence beyond the sphere of business to such an extent that it becomes the dominant motivation in his interpersonal conduct. Eliot captures this imbalance of the moral virtues by incorporating the language and images of finance into these characters' social and familial interactions. Every aspect of their lives becomes subject to what the author, in an earlier essay, described as 'calculations of prudence'.[25] For Mr Glegg, these calculations were to the fore in his choice of a wife who, as the 'embodiment of female prudence and thrift' best matches his own 'money-getting, money-keeping turn' (106). He advises his wife against calling in her loan to Tulliver, not on the basis of compassion or benevolence, but because finding a suitably secure investment paying the same rate of interest would be timely and expensive.

In relation to an ethics of virtue, the unfortunate Mr Tulliver falls equally short in approaching Aristotle's mean of liberality. The inadequacies and imbalances of his in-laws, however, are largely inverted in a character with a tendency towards what they regard as the vice of 'generous imprudence' (240). Kathleen Blake, in a recent economically focused reading of the novel, takes as her starting point 'an audit of Mr Tulliver's accounts, with an eye to his discrepant accounting between loans and gifts'.[26] His leniency towards the impoverished Moss family marks a suspension of commercial practice and legal claim in the face of familial compassion. This benevolent generosity, however, is inadequately balanced either in the moral or intel-lectual sphere as his temper and impulsiveness serve to undermine his practical wisdom. His concern with reputation and shows of supposed wealth are antithetic to the guiding principles of his wider family 'to be honest and rich'. Tulliver's affront to prudent wealth management – 'to seem rich though being poor' (239) – is exemplified by the financial risk that leads to his insolvency. As described in Appendix B, his lack of prudence draws him into a liquidity crisis at the very time a loan secured on his personal belongings becomes due and the mortgage on his land is transferred to his greatest enemy. His ignorance of the financial risk to which he has become exposed mirrors his blindness to his deficiency in the virtues and, in this at least, he is closer to his thrifty relations than any of them perceive.

The Mill on the Floss, in fact, leads the reader to an understanding of Aristotelian liberality by way of vivid psychological insights into its perversions – meanness and profligacy – that the fictional agents themselves do not recognise. In this respect, Eliot is using the medium of imaginative literature to illustrate a central theme of her important, previously cited 1855 essay, 'Evangelical Teaching: Dr. Cumming', which argues that '[t]here is not a more pernicious fallacy afloat in common parlance, than the wide distinction made between intellect and morality'.[27] The overt juxtaposition is Aristotelian and the subject – or, rather, victim – of the essay, the popular Evangelical preacher, promotes not virtue but 'intellectual and moral distortion'.[28]

The essay and the novel, therefore, implicitly argue that a properly virtuous individual should practice liberality as part of the comprehensive balance of the moral and intellectual virtues. Moreover, the exercise of practical wisdom, while incorporating a prudential self-interest appropriate to a competitive market economy, should continue to embrace the social, outward-facing guidance of *The Ethics*. Tom Tulliver never attains this status, but in some ways he approaches it and does so, contrary to his aunt's assertion that his Dodson genes were finally asserting themselves, by adapting his character according to Aristotelian principles. Aristotle insists that 'all who are not maimed as regards their potentiality for virtue may win it by a certain kind of study and care' (18), leaving the path to virtue open to all, irrespective of their individual dispositions. Later in *The Ethics*, he writes that 'we are adapted by nature to receive [the virtues], and are made perfect by habit' (28). This question of how pre-disposition, choice and practice combine in the development of the virtues (which the second half of this chapter will argue is crucial to an ethical understanding of the character of Gwendolen Harleth) is one that Eliot was able to explore through the novel in ways very similar to those which Martha Nussbaum identified in relation to the form of Greek tragedy, which 'does not display the dilemmas of its characters as prearticulated; it shows them as searching for the morally salient; and it forces us, as interpreters, to be similarly active'.[29]

The external trigger for Tom Tulliver to seek out 'the morally salient' is his father's insolvency: an awakening signalled by his simultaneous, newfound expressions of financial and ethical understanding. He quickly recognises the potential liability to his Aunt and Uncle Moss if the administration of his father's estate were to include the outstanding loan-note against them and asserts the moral probity of destroying the note. His appeal to honour and duty, insisting, correctly, that this would be his father's wish, combines with a compassionate benevolence and contrasts with the more legalistic considerations of his uncles and aunts (192).[30] An action which his aunt characterises as a 'wicked alienation of money' is, in fact, the result of Tom combining courage, justice and liberality for the first time in his life. His generous and selfless motivation links the moral and intellectual virtues in precise Aristotelian ways. Significantly, his 'intellectual' understanding relates here to the practical financial, rather than academic pursuits to which he was so unsuited: 'There were subjects, you perceive, on which Tom was much quicker than on the niceties of classical construction, or the relations of a mathematical demonstration' (196).

The further development of Tom's 'bourgeois virtues' is marked by his business partnership with Bob Jakin. Jakin combines loyalty and natural affection with prudence in practical, business matters which both promote his own self-interest and preserve the ethics of localised trading practices that rely in large part on personal relationships and trust. He belongs to the world of Adam Bede, of 'pack-horses, and . . . slow wagons and . . . pedlars who brought bargains to the door on sunny afternoons'.[31] While his knowledge of the price of the goods he trades is precise and detailed, his gift of books to Maggie stands outside the market. Not for the last time, Eliot uses books as a motif to represent higher, non-commoditised value: '"I'd ha' gev three times the money if they'll make up to you a bit for them as was sold away from you, Miss"' (247), Bob tells Maggie.[32] Tom's decision to risk money in his small-scale trading venture with Jakin puts scarce capital at risk, but the enterprise is soundly based, stepped-up gradually and leveraged by outside investment from the Gleggs. Mr Tulliver, by contrast, shows the inertia that is the consequence of complete risk aversion. In an obsession reminiscent of Silas Marner, he reverts to keeping the slowly accumulating cash savings in a tin box, from which he regularly counts it out.[33]

In the support of Glegg and Deane for Tom's determined efforts to save enough money to pay back his father's creditors in full, there are reminders that, at least in the hard practicalities of everyday life, the Dodson family's limited concept of the virtues contains some value. The 'oppressive narrowness' (238) of their moral framework contains a series of traits that actually equates closely to McCloskey's earlier-quoted list of the bourgeois, prudential virtues; here, 'a core of soundness' that includes 'obedience to parents, faithfulness to kindred, industry, rigid honesty, thrift' (239). Again, note how their ambivalent virtues are infused with financial imagery: 'The Dodsons were a very proud race, and their pride lay in the utter frustration of all desire to *tax* them with a breach of traditional duty and propriety' (239); and how the family's characteristic 'vices and virtues alike were phases of a proud, honest egoism, which had a hearty dislike to whatever made against its own *credit* and *interest*' (240, my emphases). Tom too remains unable to escape a narrowly oppressive concept of the good: in Aristotle's terms, he never approaches eudaimonism through the practice of moral and intellectual excellences. His sister recognises this when she complains to him that '[y]ou thank God for nothing but your own virtues – you think they are great enough to win you everything else' (305). As he succeeds, through prudence, in redressing his father's financial *im*prudence, that same restrictive concept of intellectual morality, which he had earlier checked in his mother's relations, becomes ascendant in him, unbalancing his emergent temperance, benevolence and justice.

In his meditations on the question 'What is temper?', Theophrastus Such bemoans 'a peculiar exercise of indulgence towards the manifestation of bad temper which tends to encourage [the bad-tempered], so that we are in danger of having among us a number of virtuous persons who conduct themselves detestably'.[34] Such an opposition is insupportable within an ethics of virtue and Eliot's complaint, via her eponymous and final narrator, is against any moral evaluation that attempts to dissociate character from conduct. A virtuous act is what a virtuous person performs, and a virtuous person is someone who possesses and acts from the virtues. In the novel that preceded *Impressions of Theophrastus Such*, *Daniel Deronda*, Eliot offers an extensive examination of the relation of character to financially related action in the attainment of the good.

Because of its near-contemporary setting, the novel addresses more specifically than any of the earlier works the question (referencing Trollope) how best to live *now*. In 1876, this question raised a particular set of economically related issues which still resonate strongly today. Following the pattern of previous readings in this section, this particular analysis will attempt to show how Eliot constructed and tested the ethical implications of how the individual 'deals' (by being good and doing good) with money and materiality by close reference to the characters she created, here focusing on how that 'dealing' process is promoted and hindered by the development of and deficiency in the relevant virtues. Partly in anticipation of the socially and politically informed chapters that follow, it will also consider how *Daniel Deronda* explores different models of late nineteenth-century trade and commerce; and how a commercial scale of value both infiltrated and remained distinct from that of more transcendent and absolute states, including marriage, art and religious inheritance.

The necessity of good character as an antecedent to good conduct is embodied in the creation of Gwendolen Harleth, a girl convinced of her destiny to live a greater life than other young ladies but unclear 'how she should set about leading any other, and what were the particular acts which she would assert her freedom by doing'.[35] Gwendolen's early character lacks the foundations and capacity for virtuous action: when she answers enquiries as to her future 'flightily', '[h]er words were born on her lips, but she would have been at a loss to give an answer of deeper origin' (57). However, Eliot's acute psychological perception, which always resists reductive descriptions of human motivation, here precludes simple and conclusive definitions of virtue and vice. An almost instantaneous mutability of feeling, which defies any straightforward motivational characterisation, is beautifully evoked by the narrator at the end of chapter 4, in reference to Gwendolen's 'contrary tendencies' and 'what may be called the iridescence of her character': 'We cannot speak a loyal word and be meanly silent, we cannot kill and not kill in the same moment; but a moment is room wide enough for the loyal and mean desire, for the outlash of a murderous thought and the sharp backward stroke of repentance' (33). Admirable character traits are not wholly absent, but, lacking practical wisdom and the habitual practice of liberal or benevolent action, Gwendolen's potential virtues are either unrealised or corrupted into egotism and vice.

Financial ignorance becomes a motif for her deficient intellectual virtue. Because the scope of her intelligence and inquisitiveness is confined to her immediate sources of self-interested pleasure and control, 'it had [not] occurred to her to inquire into the conditions of colonial property and banking, on which, as she had had many opportunities of knowing, the family fortune was dependent' (51).[36] And, lacking prudent judgement, her moral virtues in relation to money are so ungrounded that her only response to the news that her servant has offered her entire savings to support the financially ruined family is to suggest that the maid, instead of Gwendolen herself, be recommended for the position of governess to the bishop's daughter. In marked contrast to Eliot's virtuous female characters, including, in this novel, Mrs Meyrick and her daughters, she simply lacks any concept of the value of work.[37] To fill the void created by the absence of intellectual virtue, the principles of the gaming table dictate Gwendolen's interaction with the world. From the novel's opening scene, the language and uncertain motivations of gambling inform her thoughts and actions.[38]

She prefers to 'do what is unlikely' (56) and repeatedly assesses risk, particularly in relation to Grandcourt: 'she was aware that she was risking something' (111); she is made 'more conscious of the risks that lay within herself' (120); and later realises '[t]he chances of roulette had not adjusted themselves to her claims' (201).

Ironically, this gambling association links Gwendolen to Lush, a character whose complete deficiency of the moral virtues even she intuitively senses. Unlike Gwendolen, however, Lush has consciously adapted the calculating reason of the gambler to general life, with the sole aim of maximising his self-interest. 'With no active compassion or good-will, he had just as little active malevolence, being chiefly occupied in liking his particular pleasures, and not disliking anything but what hindered those pleasures' (511). Every assessment or action he makes is framed as a probability-weighted bet, although, like several other characters in the novel, his assessment of odds does not always properly account for human irrationality or the unpredictable occurrence of the improbable.[39] The epigraph from Aristotle at the head of Book VI points to the centrality of this theme within the novel: 'This, too, is probable, according to the saying of Agathon: "It is a part of probability that many improbable things will happen."'[40]

A realisation of the inadequate and flawed nature of the gambling model as applied to a wide and virtuous life therefore becomes an important indicator of Gwendolen's moral development. This gradual and uneven process begins with her first meeting with Deronda at Diplow, soon after she becomes engaged. Already questioning her motivations for and the wider implications of her forthcoming marriage, she has come to a financially centred resolution that she will 'urge [Grandcourt] to the most liberal conduct towards Mrs Glasher's children' (264). Deronda perceives an alteration in her manner and that 'the struggle of mind attending a conscious error had wakened something like a new soul, which had better, but also worse, possibilities than her former poise of crude self-confidence' (280). The nature of this 'conscious error' assumes clearer definition when she insists that Deronda explain his ethical objection to gambling. Through his explanation of how, as a zero-sum game, one person's gain necessitates another's loss, gambling takes on a wider analogical significance. Deronda's acknowledgement that, in life, another's loss is often the unintended consequence of a particular action, serves to strengthen his conviction that '[b]ecause of that, we should help it where we can' (285).

While this meeting lays down some important markers, by the time of Gwendolen's marriage the image of herself at the table, the centre of all attention, temporarily re-asserts itself. Her growing agitation 'was surmounted and thrust down with a sort of exulting defiance as she felt herself standing at the game of life with many eyes upon her, daring everything to win much – or if to lose, still with *éclat* and a sense of importance' (299). But an important process is now underway. When they next meet, Deronda is struck by her repetition of the terms of his own earlier condemnation of gambling – 'when their gain is your loss'; 'if they injure you and could have helped it' (353) – phrases which he rightly suspects are now being painfully and repeatedly applied to the choice and consequences of her own marriage. Significantly, her sense of guilt towards those she believes herself to have wronged by her actions extends, by sympathetic association, to Deronda himself and what she wrongly perceives to be his deprived inheritance. Her growing desire to restore justice, part of a wider moral awakening, finally comes to subvert within her the motivation and ends of gambling. As she awaits Lush's explanation of 'some business about property', she realises that the terms of her husband's will, including the allocation of his property, 'was all part of that new gambling in which the losing was not simply a *minus* but a terrible *plus* that had never entered into her reckoning' (511). Later still, after her husband's death, the inversion of notions of loss and gain is even more emphatic: 'I meant to get pleasure for myself, and it all turned to misery. I wanted to make my gain out of another's loss – you remember? – it was like roulette – and the money burnt into me' (593).

Over the brief time frame in which the action of *Daniel Deronda* unfolds, Gwendolen does not attain, certainly not in Aristotelian terms, a properly virtuous state of character. She learns much about how *not* to act and, in imitating Deronda, develops a sense of what it is to live for the good, without forming any distinct course of action which would accommodate the necessary virtuous practice and habit.[41] Aristotle allowed for imitation in the development of the virtues, but maintained that any truly virtuous action must be wholly voluntary. The discrimination required both in the development of a particular character trait and in the exercise of a specific choice or action must be, at least primarily, that of the agent herself. In relation to good financial action, Gwendolen certainly displays generosity in money gifts to her family but, never having developed any practical understanding and appreciation of money, she ultimately relies on Deronda to make a decision for her concerning her inheritance.[42] His advice against her proposal to renounce all but the small amount required to provide her mother with an appropriate income is based on justice and benevolence. His solution offers her the independent, voluntary opportunity to exercise prudence, temperance and liberality: 'The future beneficence of your life will be best furthered by your saving all others from the pain of that knowledge. In my opinion you ought simply to abide by the provisions of your husband's will, and let your remorse tell only on the use that you will make of your monetary independence' (657).

The combination of virtues implied in this short piece of financial advice, including a self-regarding prudence, marks an important stage in Deronda's own quest for eudaimonia, which Aristotle precisely defines as good *activity*. By nature and temperament he is well disposed to virtue and his character is seen to develop under the prescribed Aristotelian influences of habitual practice and voluntary deliberation. However, it is not until the end of the novel that he has managed to align the moral and intellectual spheres in such a way as to effectively guide him how best to live. Mordecai is the catalyst for that alignment. Prior to meeting him, an important previously cited passage sees Deronda drifting in a

> sort of contemplative mood perhaps more common in the young men of our day – that of questioning whether it were worth while to take part in the battle of the world: I mean, of course the young men in whom the unproductive labour of questioning is sustained by three or five per cent on capital which somebody else has battled for. It puzzled Sir Hugo that one who made a splendid contrast with all that was sickly and puling should be hampered with ideas which, since they left an accomplished Whig like himself unobstructed, could be no better than spectral illusions. (157)

Until he discovers his Jewish inheritance, Deronda is unable to determine how best to deploy his financial inheritance. He cannot find a route from the three professional vocations Sir Hugo urges him to consider – the law, writing and politics – to what he aspires to become, 'an organic part of social life, instead of roaming in it like a yearning disembodied spirit, stirred with a vague social passion, but without fixed local habitation to render fellowship real' (308). In Aristotelian terms, Deronda is not seeking liberality, but magnificence of action, a goal that is impeded by 'a many-sided sympathy, which threatened to hinder any persistent course of action' (307). Virtuous character and action, as defined in *The Ethics*, are characterised as benefiting and serving the needs of both the virtuous agent and other people. Deronda's 'many-sided sympathy', however, risks creating what Michael Slote calls 'agent-sacrificing self-other asymmetry'.[43] Slote argues that the conditionality (non-categorical) of the self-regarding virtues, such as prudence, in a Kantian ethical system tends to promote such asymmetry; a tendency that a sufficiently broad ethics of virtue, in which prudential self-interest is more fully harmonised within the moral and intellectual virtues, can correct. Sir Hugo's warning to Deronda, who has effectively sacrificed his own scholarship hopes in support of the incapacitated and financially needful Hans Meyrick, is well aimed: 'it is good to be unselfish and generous; but don't carry that too far. It will not do to give yourself to be melted down for the benefit of the tallow-trade; you must know where to find yourself' (156). Deronda's quest is for a cause 'that would justify partiality' (308). The discovery of his birthright answers that cause and thereby sets the terms – physical, economic and emotional – on which he is to engage in 'the battle of the world':

> It was as if he found an added soul in finding his ancestry – his judgement no longer wandering in the mazes of impartial sympathy, but choosing, with that noble partiality which is man's best strength, the closer fellowship that makes sympathy practical – exchanging that bird's-eye reasonableness which soars to avoid preference and loses all sense of quality, for the generous reasonableness of drawing shoulder to shoulder with men of like inheritance. (638)

If Deronda aspires to a concept of magnificence, the far wealthier Grandcourt represents a perversion of even the lesser liberality with which the external world generally credits him. Grandcourt has no care for money per se (which is why the maximising Lush gets him wrong so often), and exercises no intellectual virtue in its administration and distribution. Any moral virtue attendant on these acts is largely accidental. Descriptions of Grandcourt often incorporate direct reference to the virtues of *The Ethics*, which serve to emphasise the extent to which he subverts them. Mr Gascoigne justifies his decision to discount the gossip surrounding Grandcourt's affairs by invoking 'the view of practical wisdom' (118) and asks Gwendolen to consider her 'future husband's delicate liberality' (260). This, in turn, echoes Mrs Glasher's reflection that, despite his otherwise disgraceful treatment of her, 'he had always been liberal in expenses for her' (288). Even after Grandcourt's death, Gascoigne continues to 'feel confident that Gwendolen will be liberally – I should expect, splendidly – provided for' (609), before finally, and reluctantly, admitting his negligence in his 'reliance on Mr Grandcourt's liberality in money matters' (648).

Beyond his personal financial situation, with which (and usually through the agency of Lush) he is occasionally forced to deal, Grandcourt avoids all engagement with wider economic or social concerns. Ezra Cohen, with particular reference to the possession of a pawn shop, but speaking for commerce generally, tells Deronda: 'It puts you in connection with the world at large' (330). Grandcourt, however, has little interest even in the banking crisis without which Gwendolen would have escaped his clutches and classifies 'all commercial men . . . under the general epithet of "brutes"' (499).

Eliot's treatment of the same class of men in the novel is, however, more nuanced. Chapter 16 of *Impressions of Theophrastus Such*, 'Moral Swindlers', begins with an account of the narrator's conversation with a friend, Melissa, 'in a time of commercial trouble'. Melissa is bemoaning the fate of Sir Gavial Mantrap, a man of impeccable character, charitable and an excellent family man, disgraced and reduced to living on his wife's great fortune, solely 'because of his conduct in relation to the Eocene Mines, and to other companies ingeniously devised by him for the punishment of ignorance in people of small means'. No such sympathy, however, is extended to a Mr Barabbas, whose honesty in matters of business is in no way brought into question, but 'whose life', allegedly, 'is most objectionable, with actresses and that sort of thing. I think a man's morals should make a difference to us'.[44] *Theophrastus Such* establishes parallel moral spheres, which incorporate the economic, and asks the reader to consider how public and private actions interrelate. In *Daniel Deronda*, Eliot explores that same relationship by reference to secular British and Jewish business practices.

Prior to his friendship with Mordecai and his growing fondness for the Cohen family, Deronda's impressions of and prejudices against Jews are representative of his time and class. A much younger Eliot herself admitted that her 'gentile nature kicks most resolutely against any assumption of superiority in the Jews' and that '[e]verything *specifically* Jewish is of a low grade'.[45] Deronda's general repugnance (176) finds a more specific objection in his stereotypical impression of the 'grisly tradesman ... combining advantages of business with religion' (309). His heart sinks when he supposes Ezra, a pawnbroker and representative of the 'vulgar Jews' of his imagination, to be Mirah's brother. Eliot's exploration, largely through the eyes of the novel's eponymous hero, of the apparent dichotomy between the commercial and metaphysical elements of Judaism thus becomes a central ethical theme. While Mordecai and Cohen (the two Ezra Cohens) ostensibly represent opposite ends of this dualism, the novel works against reductive oppositions and, through a broader concept of the virtues, towards a synthesis and reconciliation: what Daniel Hack describes as the 'fusion of the domains of prophecy and profit'.[46]

It is only when he comes to see Cohen in a domestic setting that Deronda starts to shed his prejudice and even 'thought that this pawnbroker proud of his vocation was not utterly prosaic' (335). In return, Cohen suspends his commercial scale of value when he admits that Deronda's return to the shop was worth more to him and his excited family than any extra money that would have been otherwise earned on the pawned ring that was the pretence for his initial visit. However, even in this warm domestic sphere – in which family activities and religious observance are seamlessly linked – the language and images of commerce continue to pervade. Cohen's first, triumphant thought when Deronda prepares the family for the discovery which he tells them will substantially change Mordecai's life is 'Relations with money, sir?' (490) and the realisation that he will be leaving them to join Mirah is bemoaned as the loss of 'a property bearing interest' (491). The point Eliot is making is not that (to use her own chapter title in *Impressions*) the Cohens are thereby debasing the moral currency, but that in the commercial, domestic and wider communal spheres (and here the communal is significantly informed by ancient religious rites and traditions), the full range of virtues, including the bourgeois, can be consistently and universally applied.

The same harmonious engagement of virtues is implicit in the banking house of Joseph Kalonymos (a financier and 'wanderer') in Mainz, whose solidity and traditions contrast with the novel's representative British bankers, Grapnell & Co. Just as Lush and the unenlightened Gwendolen illustrate the corruption of individual morality by a wider adoption of the ethics of gambling, so too the blurring of the boundaries dividing investment from speculation from gambling in the commercial sphere here causes the complete collapse of an institution. The individuals responsible thought, like delusional gamblers, 'of reigning in the realm of luck' (132). Indeed, commerce and gambling conflate in the very opening scene of the book, in which the narrator observes a 'respectable London tradesman' who dispassionately risks money at the gaming table to fill the time between 'the intervals of winning money in business and spending it showily' (4).

A danger that Eliot seems to be highlighting is that, as institutions develop that are formalising and quantifying risk and probability across broad areas of experience – casinos, stock markets, life insurance offices – so their underlying guiding principles, which may lack strong moral or virtuous foundations, are likely to become more widely accepted and undermine more traditional ethical norms. Klesmer recognises this very tendency in British political life, provoking his outburst against the pragmatic and opinionated politician, Mr Bult (who is being introduced as a suitor for Miss Arrowpoint) as a representative of 'the lack of idealism in English politics, which left all mutuality between distant races to be determined simply by the need of a market' (205).[47]

At a more individual level of motivation and choice, the novel presents the incursion of ethically shallow or flawed market principles into an institution close to the heart of national culture, marriage. One of the wonderful ironies in the novel is that two characters standing at opposite extremes in relation to the virtues, Grandcourt and Miss Arrowpoint, are united in their determination, against the wishes of those around them, not to marry for money. Gascoigne is, though completely inadvertently, quite right when he reassures Mrs Davilow that Grandcourt's motivation for marrying her daughter is completely untainted by money, telling her that 'few women can have been chosen more entirely for their own sake' (301). However, while Grandcourt's motives are indeed unrelated to the acquisition of money, both his marriage and his alliance with Mrs Glasher carry wider acquisitive associations. Both women become, to some extent, commoditised and merely instrumental to what Jeff Nunokawa describes as a 'yearning for [a] more tenacious mastery' than material property can satisfy.[48] In the early stages of his passion for Mrs Glasher, we are told he 'would willingly have paid for the freedom to be won by a divorce' (287), while he later effectively pays for her compliance (through his continued, 'liberal' payment of her living expenses) not to interfere with his marriage to Gwendolen.

Gwendolen herself is groomed for the match by her uncle, who suspends the ethics of virtue by ignoring the guidance of practical wisdom to identify Grandcourt as an unworthy husband. He follows what he considers a utilitarian, ends-based strategy valorised by social rank and money.[49] His indulgence towards his niece, including the provision of a horse he can ill-afford, is part of a campaign of 'speculative investment' aimed at securing the return of a husband 'who can give her a fitting position' (65). When he fears her wilfulness may be putting his investment strategy at risk, he calls on her to accept Grandcourt's proposal as a matter of duty and responsibility under the guiding light of Providence. The exercise of voluntary, deliberative virtues (including the Christian ones) finds no recommendation. The rector is here no more acting *from* virtue than Lapidoth is when he tries to sell his daughter in marriage to a count in Vienna (185); a union also given paternal justification as a solution to the financial difficulties of the bride's family.

Having linked the motivations for marriage of Grandcourt and Miss Arrowpoint, it is necessary to emphasise, by contrast, the latter's highly virtuous disposition and assert that her marriage to Klesmer, as much as, if not more so than Deronda's to Mirah, offers a powerful and alternative affirmation of transcendent, non-material values. Mr and Mrs Arrowpoint, in the face of an event far outside any of their calculated probabilities, believe that their power to disinherit their daughter gives them a decisive advantage in determining events. The terms of their opposition again serve to emphasise an intractable perceived connection between money and marriage. Their suggestion that Klesmer is counting on them to relent on that decision provokes his wonderful retort, in which he asserts the unassailable value of love (the Judeo-Christian virtue) and art (one of Aristotle's chief intellectual virtues):

> 'Madam,' said Klesmer, 'certain reasons forbid me to retort. But understand that I consider it out of the power either of you or your fortune to confer on me anything that I value. My rank as an artist is of my own winning, and I would not exchange it for any other. I am able to maintain your daughter, and I ask for no change in my life but her companionship.' (212)[50]

What Klesmer leaves unsaid is that the religion to which he belongs also represents a value which material wealth can neither add to nor subtract from. It is a collective, inherited wealth that goes back longer than Mrs Arrowpoint's half a million, the result of 'some moist or dry business in the city' (35); longer even than the great estates of the Mallingers, now subject to the legal twists of entailment and Sir Hugo's strategic negotiations with an amoral nephew. Ultimately, that which is of greatest value, what Eliot calls 'the treasure of human affections' (103) is passed through history by stories of individual lives, a historical process whose codification is both described through the written and memorised ancient Judaic texts and represented imaginatively through the novel itself.[51] Where *The Mill on the Floss* shows us the dangers of an unbalanced reliance on the prudential virtues, *Daniel Deronda* suggests the cultural possibilities of incorporating the economic within a wider sphere of virtues to inform individual action. The place of the individual, virtuous or otherwise, in relation to social and political concepts of the good is what the final chapters of *George Eliot and Money* will consider.

CHAPTER 7

The individual and the state: economic sociology in Romola

The succession of societies cannot be represented by a geometrical line; on the contrary, it resembles a tree whose branches grow in divergent directions.[1]   – Emile Durkheim, 1895

[M]y predominant feeling is – not that I have achieved anything, but – that great, great acts have struggled to find a voice through me, and have only been able to speak brokenly. That consciousness makes me cherish the more any proof that my work has been seen to have some true significance by minds prepared not simply by instruction, but by that religious and moral sympathy with the historical life of man which is the larger half of culture.[2]   – George Eliot on *Romola*, 1863

In an 1876 review of Herbert Spencer's *The Principles of Sociology*, Alexander Bain traces an intellectual evolution and synthesis of ideas which find a particular culmination in his subject's most recent work:

Mr. Spencer's competence for rearing an advanced scheme of Sociology rests upon his having worked his way through the various preparatory stages, in a series of treatises, each admirable in itself, and all pointing to this consummation. The science that Sociology immediately reposes upon is Psychology; and in his systematic handling of this branch, Mr Spencer, while doing justice to the wide field of mental facts, has made his expositions point, by anticipation, to Sociology.[3]

The serialisation of *Daniel Deronda* began in the month following Bain's article, which appeared in the inaugural edition of *Mind*. While not suggesting that Eliot's work followed a strictly linear development – an astute sociological understanding characterised even her earlier works – the trajectory of *George Eliot and Money* traces a similar path to that described by Bain. This chapter moves on to a consideration of social networks and institutions and how Eliot portrayed them as simultaneously shaping and being shaped by individual and collective economic behaviour. Eliot was not a sociologist any more than she was either a theoretical economist or a moral philosopher, although it is worth noting that the first two disciplines only really emerged as specialised academic schools in the decades following Eliot's death and, to a large extent, evolved out of the third. Moreover, this chapter will argue that her contribution to the rise of sociological thought, or, as Wolf Lepenies characterises it, the formation of a middle ground 'between literature and science', was of considerable significance.[4] Eliot's position in relation to the intellectual developments occurring in sociology and historical method will first be considered, partly by reference to her seminal review essay, 'The Natural History of German Life'. The chapter will then progress to a reading of *Romola* that will focus on the novel's economic sociological meaning.

Eliot was undoubtedly well acquainted with the main intellectual under-pinnings of early British sociology. In fact, the first article she wrote for the *Westminster Review*, in January 1851, demonstrates a not wholly uncritical awareness of Comte's influential social theories. She associates his views with those 'thinkers who are in the van of human progress' and hold that 'theological and metaphysical speculation have reached their limit, and that the only hope of extending man's sources of knowledge is to be found in the positive science, and in the universal application of its principles'.[5] Eliot's identification of the importance of 'the positive science' was prescient. And it is significant, given his later pre-eminence in the field, that Eliot's review actually pre-dates Herbert Spencer's first reading of Comte. This occurred in 1852, when Lewes's series of articles in *The Leader* on the Frenchman's work was closely followed by Harriet Martineau's first English translation of the *Cours de Philosophie Positive*.[6]

Thus, while Spencer was starting to develop societal theories related to evolutionary science in his own early 1850s articles for *The Leader* and the *Westminster Review*, Eliot was one of a very small group in Britain already familiar with the positivism of Comte, which was to prove an important foundation in the emergence of academic sociology.[7] Prominent among that group, of course, was her future 'husband', although, amusingly, her acknowledgement of his contribution in the field is somewhat grudging. While strategising how the *Westminster Review* might best incorporate articles on Comte in 1852, Eliot observes that Lewes's early pieces in *The Leader* 'do not promise well' and concludes that Mill remains 'the chief English interpreter of Comte'.[8] As in so many fields, Mill's influence was enduring. Almost a quarter of a century later, Bain begins his *Mind* review of Spencer by locating Mill's importance in the development of the embry-onic social science: 'in the *Logic*, Mill, having imbued himself with Comte's speculations, presented a summary of theoretical Sociology, which served as a sort of text-book or compendium to a generation of learners'.[9]

While Eliot was a great admirer of the *Logic*, the importance of Comte in her intellectual life owes less to Mill's interpretation than to her direct familiarity with the texts themselves.[10] John Cross recollects her high admiration for all Comte's writing: 'I do not think I ever heard her speak of any writer with a more grateful sense of obligation for enlightenment.'[11] In the summer of 1861, just before starting to write *Romola*, she interrupts her extensive Florentine research to return to the *Cours*, telling Sara Hennell that 'I have just been reading the survey of the Middle Ages contained in the fifth volume of the Philosophie Positive, and to my apprehension few chapters can be fuller of luminous ideas. I am thankful to learn from it.'[12] At the same time, Lewes's conviction of the importance of Comte's analysis of social development (at least up to and including the *Cours*) is even stronger:

> with regard to History I venture to say that no philosopher has ever laid so much emphasis on it, no one has more clearly seen and expressed the truth, that the past rules the present, lives in it, and that we are but the growth and outcome of the past.[13]

As we shall see, Eliot's opinion of Comte's concept of history and society was somewhat more reserved. These reservations will form part of this chapter's ambitious claim that her sociological thought – and, in particular as that incorporates the economic – is more aligned to, indeed foreshadows, the work of the European sociologists who built on and greatly extended the work of Comte, Spencer and others in the decades following Eliot's death. Eliot concludes her 1855 essay, 'The Future of German Philosophy', with a call for the extension of empirical, scientific method beyond the natural sciences and formal logic 'to the investigation of Psychology, with its subordinate department Aesthetics; to ethics; and to the principles of Jurisprudence'.[14] In taking up this call, and despite their widely divergent styles, methodologies and conclusions, Comte, Mill and Spencer had a common purpose. Each sought to identify and formulate, along scientific principles, laws governing social development and individual action. While their respective investigations undoubtedly influenced Eliot's sociological thought, as was the case with the moral philosophical systems described in the earlier chapters of this work, she was prepared to discard aspects of what she considered partial or incoherent social theories. In her major novels, she came to synthesise her own multi-dimensional and dynamic (though necessarily incomplete) model of social interconnectedness. In this respect, Cross's description of her admiration for Comte is significantly qualified: 'But the appreciation was thoroughly selective . . . Parts of his teaching were accepted and other parts rejected.'[15]

To some extent, her reservations over attempts to formulate precisely a causal and predictive social science share common ground with her scepticism towards the 'laws' of political economy. As we have seen, Eliot described her particularisation of character and society as experimental. However, she presents both the conditions underlying these experiments and their outcomes as so complex and variable as to defy the natural-scientific method that tests hypothesis by empiricism to establish general predictive laws of cause and effect. By 1866, when Frederic Harrison tried to persuade her to share his 'ever present dream . . . that the grand features of Comte's world might be sketched in fiction', she had concluded that the creation of a novel overtly informed by positivist principles would be an aesthetic compromise that would transform 'the picture to the diagram', and thereby reductively misrepresent life.[16]

Her more direct qualification of Spencer's ethics and sociology is as much rooted in his idiosyncratic intellectual approach as his particular scientific method. Sara Hennell is again the correspondent to whom she confides, concluding that 'His mind rejects everything that cannot be wrought into the web of his own production.'[17] It is a method antithetical to Eliot's explorations of expansive internal and external interconnectedness. Thus Nancy Paxton argues that, as Spencer's evolutionary scientific system and biological determinism became the increasingly overarching focus of his work, Eliot distanced herself from a social philosophy which 'rigorously excluded emotion'.[18] Extending Eliot's image, Spencer's self-produced web attempts to connect ethics, economics and society in a pre-designed pattern. As Robert M. Young describes the process: 'Throughout his mature life he was seeking a scientific basis for a doctrine of inevitable progress which would justify his belief in an extreme of laissez-faire economics and social theory.'[19] Young's analysis of Spencerian method represents a critical strand that goes back many years. Durkheim's assessment at the beginning of the twentieth-century is that:

> It is abundantly plain that Spencer worked on sociology as a philosopher, because he did not set out to study social facts in themselves and for their own sake, but in order to demonstrate how the hypothesis of evolution is verified in the social realm.[20]

Like Eliot, Durkheim was critical of both Spencer and Comte (whom he nevertheless recognises as the greatest of the 'founders of the new science'), disputing aspects of their sociological method and their very different attempts 'to discover the law which governs social evolution as a whole'. Of Comte he writes:

the law of the three stages, which dominates the *Cours de philosophie positive* throughout, is essentially a sociological law. Moreover, since the demonstration of this law relies on philosophical considerations which relate to the conditions of knowledge, it follows that positivist philosophy is wholly a sociology and Comtean sociology is itself a philosophy.[21]

Eliot's investigations into the individual, economics and the evolution of society go beyond both Comte's stadial historical theory and Spencer's deterministic evolutionary progression from militancy to industrialism. In some important respects, they look forward to both Durkheim and Weber.

Bruce Mazlish in *A New Science: The Breakdown of Connections and the Birth of Sociology* is explicit in locating Eliot as an important link in the discipline's development during the late nineteenth century. If, as this chapter contends, Mazlish is correct in his assessment that she represents '[a]n especially good bridge ... between what can be called sensibility ... and sociology', an important foundation in that bridge is 'The Natural History of German Life'.[22] The essay has been exhaustively analysed and mined, most often to provide evidence of Eliot's 'social-political-conservatism' and as her clearest statement of the moral imperative of realist art and literature. The greatest art, she contends, becomes 'a mode of amplifying experience and extending our contact with our fellow-men beyond the bounds of our personal lot'.[23] However, the essay also has significant value as a pointer to the trajectory of sociological thought over the following half-century and as a guide to Eliot's position in that intellectual development.

Significantly, her commendation of Riehl establishes a link between literature and social studies in which the latter, rather than standing in rational opposition to, is given greater clarity by the adoption of a literary style.[24] The corollary, of course, is that art and literature assume high value only by the true and realistic portrayal of both the external workings of society and the inner life of those individuals, of all classes, who comprise that society. Eliot argues that Riehl, whose work 'would be fascinating as literature, if it were not important for its facts and philosophy' (294), achieves this synthesis and thereby an 'awakening of social sympathies' more completely than Dickens (271).[25] Eliot's claim, in relation to the English realist novel, that '[w]hat we are desiring for ourselves has been in some degree done for the Germans by Riehl' (273) therefore invests considerable importance in the content of his social observation and analysis. Midway through the essay she actually inserts an explanatory note that 'in our statement of Riehl's opinions, we must be understood not as quoting Riehl, but as interpreting and illustrating him' (287). Yet it is apparent that

she finds Riehl's analysis of German society both compelling in its specific-
ity and of great value as a model for studying the development of other
nations through history. It thus fundamentally informs not only many of
her domestically set novels but also the one which most specifically
addresses the 'conception of European society as incarnate history' (289):
Romola.

Eliot clearly sets Riehl apart from those who have come, 'by the splendid
conquests of modern generalisation, to believe that all social questions are
merged into economical science' (272). She traces Comte's classification of
the sciences, all of which advance from the 'general' to the 'special', in her
characterisation of the complexity of the social sciences and the reductive-
ness of applying a single, economic interpretation to its study (290).
However, she is equally dismissive of those who seek a solution to the social
problems brought about by industrial capitalism in a return to a pre-market,
patronistic economic system; what she wonderfully describes as 'the
aristocratic dilettantism which attempts to restore the "good old times" by
a sort of idyllic masquerading, and to grow feudal fidelity as we grow prize
turnips, by an artificial system of culture' (272). What her 'interpretation
and illustration' of Riehl offers, by comparison, is a nuanced analysis of
economic influences and consequences in an inevitably transforming and
urbanising society. Indeed, in her observation that changes occurring
in Germany in the 1850s mirror those 'in England half a century ago'
(i.e. around the time she set her early novels), she unknowingly links Riehl's
sociological project to her own as a novelist, with both writers exploring the
tensions created at important socio-economic transition points (273).

Riehl's description of the peasant class is unsentimental and Eliot
applauds his criticism of those novelists who impose their own emotions
on their creations. By so doing, Riehl himself writes, 'they obliterated what
is precisely [the peasant's] most predominant characteristic, namely, that
with him general custom holds the place of individual feeling' (280). This
observation explains why the adoption of a full market economy for the
transfer of agricultural produce becomes a 'disintegrating' force for both
the individual and the community. Individual responsibility comes to take
the place of custom, communal action and non-cash transactions, resulting
in 'demoralization', debt and ruin (281). Economic change is presented as
part of a wider political and institutional transformation that replaces 'the
healthy life of the Commune' with a bureaucracy controlled by the 'patent
machinery of state-appointed functionaries' (282).[26]

The descriptions of the peasantry within the structure of German society
are largely drawn from the first volume of Riehl's *Natural History*, *Die*

Burgerliche Gesellschaft (1851). Almost forty years later, Ferdinand Tonnies's highly influential *Gemeinschaft und Gesellschaft* acknowledges an explicit debt to Riehl and his ethnographic and sociological descriptions of rural communities in transition.[27] The link from Riehl to Tonnies and thereon to Simmel, Durkheim and Weber thus tangentially connects Riehl's first British reviewer with the great tradition of European sociological thought.[28] Ironically, the relatively youthful Tonnies drew the economic inspiration for his criticism of modernism and individualism, embodied by money-exchange and the cash nexus, from Marx.[29] Eliot's review of Riehl had made much of the peasantry's ignorance of theoretical Communism, surmising that any urge to revolt was inspired solely by material self-interest (284). She distances herself from Riehl's argument that the preservation of the aristocracy is defensible on both historical and rational grounds but seems content to accept his contention that, in Germany, the revolutionary tendencies of the 'Fourth Estate' represent the will not of a displaced proletariat of labourers but an educated group of discontents from across the social spectrum, a grouping he describes as the 'intellectual proletariat'. As Eliot summarises his position: 'Germany yields more intellectual produce than it can use and pay for' (297–8).

Regardless of the varying political interpretations surrounding the shift from *Gemeinschaft* to *Gesellschaft*, Riehl's insistence that social change could only be understood by the application of detailed knowledge and specific study of a particular society was the most lasting influence on Eliot and her progression as a novelist. Moreover, she realised that particularism must be historically rooted and informed by inherited social conditions:

> The external conditions which society has inherited from the past are but the manifestation of inherited internal conditions in the human beings who compose it; the internal conditions and the external are related to each other as the organism and its medium, and development can only take place by the gradual consentaneous development of both. (287)

The gradualist social change she here expresses underlies her socio-political position in *Felix Holt*, while the organic imagery to describe the interconnectedness of the individual in society recurs throughout the novels. In *Romola*, Book 2 opens with another image from nature to suggest the inseparability of private and public lives, here in a period and society far removed from the provincial surroundings of nineteenth-century England:

> Since that Easter a great change had come over the prospects of Florence; and as in the tree that bears a myriad of blossoms, each single bud with its fruit is dependent on the primary circulation of the sap, so the fortunes of Tito and

> Romola were dependent on certain grand political and social conditions
> which made an epoch in the history of Italy.[30]

The precise delineation of these 'external conditions', both social and
political, was therefore critical to her understanding of the internal motivations of the individual. In the earlier cited letter to Sara Hennell, Eliot's
praise of Comte's survey of the Middle Ages is tempered by her admission
that she agrees with her friend 'in regarding positivism as one-sided'. Her
reservation seems to relate, at least in part, to Comte's stadial historical
theory, as she explains:

> I hope we are well out of that phase in which the most philosophic view of
> the past was held to be a smiling survey of human folly, and when the wisest
> man was supposed to be one who could sympathise with no age but the age
> to come.[31]

Her point is that merely subjecting a particular period of social history to the
template of a presentist historical theory – either cyclical or progressive –
can give only a partial understanding of the past. This was why she was so
attracted to Riehl's method: 'He sees in European history *incarnate history*,
and any attempt to disengage it from its historical elements must, he
believes, be simply destructive of social vitality' (287). Five years earlier, in
'The Progress of the Intellect', she warned of a modern tendency, which she
links to Comtean positivism, to 'under-rate critical research into ancient
modes of life and forms of thought', believing it to be 'a very serious mistake
to suppose that the study of the past and the labours of criticism have no
important practical bearing on the present'.[32]

In preparing for her major undertaking in historical fiction, she was
careful to avoid such a pitfall. Her journals document the immense reading
in Florentine history she undertook, both during her trips to Italy in the
early 1860s and back in London in preparation for the composition of
Romola. The process of writing the novel was arduous and, during its
serialisation, Lewes was even more anxious than usual to protect her from
any unfavourable reviews as 'she has all along resisted writing it on the
ground that no one would be interested in it'.[33] It was an important work for
her and, while the novel's treatment of the individual making (often
economically related) ethical choices in an intricately interconnected social
environment links it particularly to the novels that followed it, the fact that
Eliot conducted her 'experiment' under such unusual historical conditions
is significant. This significance is located chiefly in the economic realm,
which the particular circumstances of a city republic, with complex social
networks and institutions at a period of transition into an identifiable form

of early modern capitalism, allowed the author to explore in ways that resonated strongly with her own period.

By the 1860s, capitalism – that is private ownership of the means of production and its attendant, profit-focused practices, including the division of labour, market expansion and innovation – had developed in Britain to a largely unrestricted form, in which social and political controls were limited. As discussed in the earlier part of this book, this process enabled the developing field of economics to theorise generalised models of the functioning of market exchange, driven by supply and demand and measured by a single, monetary scale of value. As social controls effectively contracted to the hegemony of the market, so too the conception of what constituted the 'economic' largely narrowed in focus to address the rational allocation of resources to maximise production and meet demand. However, in a society in which the market is part of a much broader-based institutional framework controlling the exchange of goods, the conception of the economic retains a wider meaning. It remains embedded in the needs and wants of individuals in the production, distribution and exchange of all goods and services. Florence in the 1490s provides a setting in which economics had not yet established a theoretical grounding nor attained autonomy from other, more traditional social structures.

In fact, *Romola* presents characters acting under economic motivation in the specific period that many of the defining characteristics of modern capitalism were starting to emerge. In *Economy and Society* (1922), Max Weber defined three principal varieties of capitalism: political, traditional commercial and rational.[34] The first two categories, which, Weber contends, can be traced very far back, are still apparent in the Florence of the novel: the political represented by the power and intervention of the state and military factions; the traditional commercial by the mostly localised and small-scale trading activities. Richard A. Goldthwaite in *The Economy of Renaissance Florence* writes, in Weberian terms, that the Florentine commercial class 'were somewhat lacking in their "spirit of capitalism"'.[35] He describes a system in which participants in the city's dominant manufacturing industry, textiles, took too little risk and employed only small amounts of capital by 'putting-out' most of their production, while deferring to the guilds (themselves a somewhat protectionist group of institutions at odds with more developed, free market capitalism) to make collective policy decisions. The model is one of co-operation rather than individual profit maximisation. Goldthwaite concludes:

> One might even go on to say that in a sense these men, however much their business practices anticipate modern capitalism, were still strongly tied into

the medieval tradition of guild corporatism, a state of mind that may not
have been altogether irrelevant to the dense networks that so characterized
their social and political life as well.[36]

Yet, as Goldthwaite suggests, in other ways this was a society already
meeting several of the requirements of the rational capitalism that Weber
actually pinpoints as coming into being in the West in the sixteenth
century. Florence was a city state under a fairly transparent and impartial
rule of law with only limited governmental interference in trade and
finance. The state had a monopoly on the issuance of money and the
Florin was widely accepted as of equal or superior standing to the currencies
of the other leading Italian city states. While, as noted, the domestic sector
was relatively conservative, a substantial and entrepreneurial international
wool and textile industry operated and supported the growth of Europe's
largest and most powerful banking sector. By the time the action of *Romola*
commences, the Medici were pre-eminent among these extensive, family-
run banking networks.[37] Florence was also instrumental in the development
of capital accounting and double-entry bookkeeping, which are prerequi-
sites of mature, rational capitalism. It is against this fluid and minutely
described socio-economic background that Eliot's characters are set in
motion. The setting is simultaneously remote and yet immediately relevant
to her contemporary readers. A review of the novel by R. H. Hutton in *The
Spectator* in July 1863 describes its setting as 'that strange era, which has so
many points of resemblance with the present'.[38]

    The opening paragraph of the 'Proem' establishes this duality – what
Eliot calls 'the broad sameness of the human lot' – within a particular
physical and temporal location. It is not only the architecture and landscape
of the city that are still clearly recognisable; 'those other streams, the life-
currents that ebb and flow in human hearts, pulsate to the same great needs,
the same great loves and terrors' (3). Not all her contemporary critics were
convinced. *The Westminster Review* argued that the moral questions raised
in the novel 'are of very modern growth and . . . would have been more
appropriately displayed on a modern stage'. Both Tito and Romola, the
reviewer contends, are essentially mid-nineteenth-century characters in
distracting and unnecessary disguise and Eliot is simply wrong 'to plead
that the great features of human life and character are determined by
conditions too permanent to offer any radical distinctions between their
manifestations from century to century'.[39] If Lewes failed to keep this article
from Eliot's view, it is likely she would have considered it a good example of
that 'philosophic view of the past' of which she disparagingly wrote to Sara

Hennell two years earlier.[40] In a letter to Hutton, responding to a more positive *Spectator* article in which he too addresses the level of period detail in the novel, she is eloquently insistent that ethical constants can be meaningfully projected against a specific and particular historical background. A later passage will discuss Tito's economic behaviour as it relates to nineteenth-century political economy and Utilitarianism, but Eliot is right to insist that the actions and development of her character in the novel are not the simple consequences of an anachronistic economic individualism, but are significantly shaped by the social environment she describes; namely 'the relation of the Florentine political life to the development of Tito's nature'.[41]

The importance of *Romola*, considered as a work contributing to the development of economic sociology, lies in the completeness of Eliot's descriptions of the institutions, more informal networks and power structures contained within the novel. Modern sociology defines a social institution as 'a set of social norms which orient and regulate behaviour and which are based on sanctions which seek to guarantee compliance on the part of individuals'.[42] This definition extends beyond collective organisations to the very rules and norms of social behaviour that control and regulate them.[43] Institutions can therefore bridge the economy and society and, to be fully understood, need to be given precise historical context. In *Romola*, Eliot shows how economic practices both shape and are shaped by social, cultural and political institutions. Unusually for her time and foreshadowing the work of sociologists long after her death, she illustrates and examines the interconnection between economics and religion, revealing how the latter exerts a powerful influence on social norms.[44] As already noted, her anticipation of Weber's famous theories in this area – albeit with a slightly different conclusion – was hinted at as early as the Riehl essay, where she compares social development in Europe with England with a specific focus on how Protestantism shaped commercial practice.[45]

As Mazlish comments in his description of Weber's pioneering work in developing a sociology of religion, unlike Spencer and, later, Durkheim he 'was concerned almost exclusively with the great religions of the world'.[46] Eliot belongs to a similar tradition. The analysis in the previous chapter attempted to identify a particular connection between the faith of the Jews in exile and commerce as an integral and unifying communal social practice. Eliot's portrayal essentially gels with Weber's conclusions in both *The Protestant Ethic* and *Economy and Society* that, contrary to accepted opinion, sought to detach capitalism from Judaism per se. Weber argued that it was rather the Jews' minority status that largely determined their concentration in commerce: 'National or religious minorities which are in a position of subordination to a group of rulers are likely, through their voluntary or involuntary exclusion from positions of political influence, to be driven with particular force into economic activity.'[47] In *Romola*, this same social phenomenon is evident. While Florence admired success in business, the opposition of the Catholic Church to usury continued to hold a powerful grip on society. Thus, Jews are depicted as a minority, 'pariah' people beyond the economic moral pale: in the novel's opening scene, the profit-obsessed Bratti decries 'those dogs of hell that want to get all the profit of usury for themselves and leave none for Christians' (13).[48]

The relationship between Catholicism and economics in the novel is more pervasive and complex. The amassing of great fortunes, epitomised by the Medici, is tolerated only so long as an appropriate percentage is sanctified by being paid to the Church or diverted to works of art and public buildings for the communal good: 'large gifts to the shrines of saints' and 'liberal bequests towards buildings for the Frati' (7). Indeed, Savonarola's political radicalism is closely connected with his efforts to undermine and invert this established relationship between the Church and money. He is reported as 'telling the people that God will not have silver crucifixes and starving stomachs; and that the church is best adorned with the gems of holiness and the fine gold of brotherly love' (345). He extends his message of redistribution to the wider society, 'teaching the disturbing doctrine that it was not the duty of the rich to be luxurious for the sake of the poor' (346). The ever-simmering dispute between Savonarola and the Papacy symbolises a struggle for the hearts and minds of Florentine society that is at once political, economic and spiritual. Under Savonarola's influence, Florentine society adjusts the accommodation it has made between earthly profit and heavenly reward but, significantly, his power finally collapses under the strain of a failing economy.[49]

While religion occupies a central position in the novel's social and ethical investigations, a dual play of the economic infiltration of social institutions and the subsequent shaping of economic norms is at work throughout *Romola*. Florence's power and prosperity by the end of the fifteenth century was built on its international trade. An outward-looking economic liberalism underlay a sharp commercial focus that comes to define the city's citizenry, as embodied in the 'spirit' of the Proem: '[The old Florentine's] politics had an area as wide as his trade, which stretched from Syria to Britain, but they also had the passionate intensity, and the detailed practical interest, which could belong only to a narrow scene of corporate action' (6). Tito is socially adept and quickly wins friends and position, but his acceptance into the influential classes (which is never wholly achieved) requires him to acquire an understanding of Florentine economic subtleties that we feel belongs to the old-established families as a kind of collective inheritance. Once his betrothal to Romola is settled, 'Tito set about winning Messer Bernardo's respect by inquiring ... into Florentine money matters, the secret of the *Monti* or public funds, the values of real property, and the profits of banking' (195).

Ultimately, however, the external events presented in the novel are brought about by a reshaping of these traditional social economics. The great financial wealth that has enabled the Medici to exert a control over the physical institutions of the city is shown in the novel to undermine the very value system on which the citizen-state was predicated. The assumption of a money value to measure or define areas that previously had a common, and therefore non-exchangeable worth, is presented as an institutional change that comes to diminish the character of individual citizens: 'For the citizens' armour was getting rusty, and populations seemed to have become tame, licking the hands of masters who paid for a ready-made army when they wanted it, as they paid for goods of Smyrna' (210). The street-trader Bratti – who appears periodically throughout the novel, each time trying to sell something different – is a mouthpiece for this subversion of values. In one of his final appearances, he is selling two types of handbills arguing the case of the forthcoming trial of the supposed Medici conspirators. One is titled 'Law' and the other 'Justice':

> 'Justice' goes the quickest – so I raised the price, and made it two denari. But then I bethought me the 'Law' was good ware too, and had as good a right to be charged for as 'Justice;' for people set no store by cheap things, and if I sold the 'Law' at one denaro, I should be doing it a wrong. And I'm a fair trader. 'Law,' or 'Justice,' it's all one to me; they're good wares. I got 'em both for nothing, and I'll sell 'em at a fair profit. (492)

Romola, in fact, is full of exchanges, although by no means all are effected by money or even made on conventionally rational economic grounds. Transactions are often personalised, reciprocal or merely distributive. Even Bratti, following a practice of 'earmarking' discreet monies, does not always seek to maximise his net returns.[50] In his first meeting with Tito, he tells of his uneasiness at his good fortune in finding the unclaimed body of a beggar whose cap was lined with coin. Mirroring the strained, self-serving logic of those wealthy Florentines troubled by guilt over their large commercial gains, he first conjures a somewhat illogical argument to justify retaining the windfall. Then, to hedge his bets, he confesses that he 'buried the body and paid for a mass – and so I saw it was a fair bargain' (11).

As the novel ascends the scale of the commercial classes, from the shop-keepers and small traders up to the wealthy merchants, Eliot illustrates the wide and often incalculable range of socially informed and individual motivations and impulses that determine economic action. Niccolo Caparra, the inscrutable blacksmith and armourer, is prepared to sacrifice short-term commercial gains for the control and knowledge he achieves by selling only to customers he knows, admitting that 'I'm rather nice about what I sell, and whom I sell to' (244). Caparra is unusual in not offering credit to anyone ('I trust nobody' (244)), including Tito, but elsewhere Tito himself benefits greatly from credit and monetary advances, often extended for non-financial reasons. His 'capital' is both intellectual and, in conse-quence of his looks and manners, human, even erotic.[51] Baldassarre's jewels provide the main collateral for his money-raising, but Tito recognises that his most valuable 'commodities' are his learning and his appearance. He overtly links the two when he tells Nello: 'It seems to me . . . that you have taken away some of my capital with your razor – I mean a year or two of age, which might have won me more ready credit for my learning' (35).[52]

Tito recognises the social dimension of economic choice yet attempts to control his own behaviour according to a reductive and strictly individu-alistic interpretation of the greatest happiness principle. His economic actions are based on instinct and character rather than theory. As Richard Goldthwaite writes of even the most successful bankers and merchants of that period: 'whatever thoughts Florentines had about their economy, none of these men ever crossed the intellectual barrier to analysis. No one ventured to devise a scheme for the justification of business, let alone to develop a theoretical understanding of economic activity.'[53] Eliot does not attempt to impose a consciously thought-out philosophy on her character, but from the perspective of her own age she uses her historical creation, Tito, to expose the empirical shortcomings and normative inadequacy of political economy. Under this reading, *Romola* provides a sociological refutation of individualistic economic determinism that complements the moral philosophical objections the earlier part of *George Eliot and Money* described. In this respect, Eliot both presents a version of the economic sociology that Weber was to formalise and foreshadows Durkheim's criticism of the individualistic Utilitarian basis of social theory as promoted by Spencer.[54]

While Weber clearly distinguishes his definition of economic action from economic *social* action, both, he concludes, have utility as their aim. It is relevant, therefore, in that context to compare the hedonistic Utilitarianism of Tito with Savonarola's very particular strain of consequentialism in search of the greater social good. Tito's hedonism is expressed in explicitly, though reductive, Benthamite terms. 'What, looked at closely,' he ponders, 'was the end of all life, but to extract the utmost sum of pleasure?' (117). The 'Chief Good' is linked to no absolute value but is relative and wholly subjective, 'a matter of taste' (119). For much of the novel, Tito is driven by impulse and seeks to justify and rationalise his actions retrospectively. However, in the scene in which he reveals to Romola that he has sold her father's library, his hedonism assumes a more reflective and philosophical tone. He asks his wife to consider her father's 'real welfare or happiness'; to 'discriminate . . . substantial good'; and to question how best to extend the books' 'usefulness' and where 'they will find the highest use and value' (288–90). Whereas Tito uses a philosophical construct (essentially an egoistic perversion of Bentham's and Mill's Utilitarianism) to valorise selfish ends, Savonarola's ideal is the common good. This idealism, 'in which every man is to strive only for the general good', is mocked by Tournabuoni as both unworldly and duplicitous, serving, he believes, to mask the Frate's own egotistical ends. Romola too comes to recognise some ambivalence in his purpose but is ultimately convinced of a motivation towards an end – 'the moral welfare of men' – that transcends individual self-interest and rationality (577–9).

The clearest statement of Tito's subversion of all socially based motivation to the principle of maximising his own pleasure is brought about by a question of economics. His calculation that, on a risk-adjusted basis, he would derive more pleasure by selling Baldassarre's gems for his own wants than by risking those same proceeds in an uncertain expedition to find and secure his adoptive father's release, gives rise to a consideration of the nature of individualism and the collective will. He is fully aware that his principle for action

> was not the sentiment which the complicated play of human feelings had engendered in society. The men around him would expect that he should immediately apply those florins to his benefactor's rescue. But what was the sentiment of society? – a mere tangle of anomalous traditions and opinions, that no man would take as a guide, except so far as his own comfort was concerned. (118)

Tito's self-exclusion from 'the sentiment of society' represents an assertion of complete individual autonomy: what he is not contracted to, he has no social obligation towards. This atomism, which Eliot undermines through the action of the novel, is formally opposed by Durkheim's alternative assertion of trust as the basis for social interrelation and by the communal underpinning of collective conscience. For Durkheim, '[s]ocial life comes from a double source, the likeness of consciences and the division of social labour'; the first representing what he calls mechanical and the second organic solidarity.[55]

Romola, in chapter 68, embraces the collective conscience both through her acts of selfless citizenship during the famine and, after fleeing the city, by her work in bringing cohesion and communal action to the plague village. She comes, in effect, to enact the new liberal programme: 'Her lot was virtually united with the general lot.' The social setting of this episode is significant: the community survives in a self-contained, completely money-free economy, in which the division of labour does not exist. In Durkheimian terms, all that remains is mechanical solidarity.[56] Eliot takes the reader out of capitalism better to focus her concern as to how best to balance individualism with the demands of the common conscience. Again she seems to anticipate Durkheim's recognition of this central sociological question, which he expresses as a kind of paradox: 'In effect, on the one hand, each one depends as much more strictly on society as labour is more divided; and, on the other, the activity of each is as much more personal as it is more specialized.'[57] Chapter 8 will consider further how Eliot questioned the limits of market exchange and sought to define how individual economic rights and freedoms should co-exist with wider social duties.

The politics of wealth: new liberalism and the pathologies of economic individualism

What, then, is the rightful limit to the sovereignty of the individual over himself? Where does the authority of society begin? How much of human life should be assigned to individuality, and how much to society?[1]
　　　　　　　　　　　　　　　　　　　　　　　　– J. S. Mill, 1859

The most arrant denier must admit that a man often furthers larger ends than he is conscious of, and that while he is transacting his particular affairs with the narrow pertinacity of a respectable ant, he subserves an economy larger than any purpose of his own.[2]
　　　　　　　　　　　　　　　　　　　　　　　　– George Eliot, 1878

The result [*Middlemarch*] is a justification of all that it was then usual to sum up in the word altruism, which for this generation it is necessary to translate as meaning living for others, and for this justification George Eliot has been damned by those that have come after her.[3]
　　　　　　　　　　　　　　　　　　　　　　　　– L. T. Hobhouse, 1915

The dominant political figure of the second half of the nineteenth century memorably described John Cross's biography of George Eliot as 'a reticence in three volumes'. W. E. Gladstone did not open *George Eliot's Life* in search of an examination of the novelist's political theory. However, Cross's single reference to his wife's political opinions illustrates well the reserve that frustrated Gladstone along with many of the book's early readers. Cross's observation is accurate, as far as it goes. Her 'many-sidedness', he writes, 'makes it exceedingly difficult to ascertain, either from her books or from the greatest personal intimacy, what her exact relation was to any existing religious creed or to any political party'.[4] In fact, to ascertain the exact relation of many politically engaged individuals – and not least Gladstone himself – to a specific party during this period, was an increasingly difficult and complex exercise.[5] Eliot was not politically active, even in the limited spheres open to women in her age, and, in her letters and journals, rarely propounds extensive personal views on contemporary political events and characters.[6] However, this chapter will argue that Eliot's moral and

139

sociological concerns were informed by essentially political questions around the role of the state in the governance of individual citizens and that, moreover, central to these questions lie considerations of economic duty and responsibility.[7] This process is evident in both her personal and her early non-fiction writings and more fully explored in the novels.

The period her writing covers, up to her death in 1880, was one that saw great and seminal developments in concepts both of liberalism and of the Liberal Party itself, whose main ideological underpinnings were increasingly strained by the policy demands of actual government in an age of widening enfranchisement. Eliot's professional life in the 1850s, and her main body of friends and acquaintances thereafter, presented her with an unusually prominent vantage point from which to observe the fast-flowing and eddying current of liberal thought. The influence of J. S. Mill has been discussed elsewhere, but it is worth recollecting that she re-read *On Liberty*, alongside Henry Fawcett's *The Economic Position of the English Labourer*, while writing her most overtly political novel, *Felix Holt*, in 1865.[8] Mill's classic statement of individual rights and freedom from state interference – subject only to the absence of causing harm to others or to society – was written in response to the growth of democracy, which had served to replace the despotism of the absolute ruler with the equally powerful force of public opinion, what he called 'the tyranny of the majority'.[9]

The assertion of individual rights was an extension of the principle of non-governmental intervention in trade and commerce, a triumph of economic liberalism that had been secured by the repeal of the Corn Laws in 1846. *On Liberty* emphasises the absolute right of *individuality*, but the hegemony of the free-trade doctrine served to secure the ascendancy of a less-nuanced economic *individualism* that underlay theoretical political economy and thereby came to define mid-century liberalism in overwhelmingly economic terms.[10] The most prominent voice of economic liberalism, *The Economist* magazine, placed economic laws both ascendant and prior to social laws and institutions. It insisted that 'unerring natural laws determine the creation and distribution of wealth – that is, of subsistence and of all the products of industry – and determining these, must determine also all the subordinate phenomena of society'.[11] The intellectual biographer of the most influential advocate of individualism (and one-time writer for *The Economist*), Herbert Spencer, explains succinctly how an inexorable connection between economics and politics was theorised: 'men who had acquired wealth by responding to the needs of the market deserved to possess political power, for they had thus shown their moral and intellectual worth'.[12]

By the late 1870s, however, the experience of a number of Liberal administrations revealed that a non-interventionist political theory was becoming inconsistent with the realities of policy implementation. Spencer, echoing a number of the concerns voiced by Mill in *On Liberty*, had predicted just such a dislocation in his 1860 *Westminster Review* article, 'Parliamentary Reform: the Dangers and the Safeguards'. The article reiterated the central principles of individualism and voluntarism against the coercion of the State that he had expounded nine years earlier in *Social Statics*. By 1884, his worst fears had come to pass:

> Dictatorial measures, rapidly multiplied, have tended continually to narrow the liberties of individuals; and have done this in a double way. Regulations have been made in yearly-growing numbers, restraining the citizen in directions where his actions were previously unchecked, and compelling actions which previously he might perform or not as he liked; and at the same time heavier public burdens, chiefly local, have further restricted his freedom, by lessening that portion of his earnings which he can spend as he pleases, and augmenting the portion taken from him to be spent as public agents please.[13]

In the collection of articles that comprise *The Man Versus the State*, Spencer maps the development of Liberal government over the last twenty years of Eliot's life, a period which saw an increasingly positive concept of government translate into widening social legislation, supported by escalating tax revenues.[14] This marked a distinct shift from the Whig and Radical policies following the First Reform Act of 1832, whose primary focus was the repeal of restrictive laws in both the social and, more prominently, the economic spheres. It prompted Spencer to ask: 'How is it that Liberalism, getting more and more into power, has grown more and more coercive in legislation?' Surprisingly, his attempted answer identifies both Utilitarian and socialist explanations for the growth in essentially welfarist policies, a dual evolutionary course indicative of the gathering tensions within the party.[15]

Turning to Eliot, it seems clear that the atomistic economic individualism at the heart of the 'old' liberalism celebrated by Spencer remained a target of her satire and criticism to the end of her life.[16] *Impressions of Theophrastus Such*, written only two years before her death, includes a penetrating sketch of a rich industrialist. Spike, the eponymous 'Political Molecule' is variously self-described as a Progressive, a Liberal and a Radical, 'who voted on the side of Progress'.[17] In reality, the extent of his political philosophy amounts to a simple laissez-faire capitalism in service to his own economic interests. Spike's concept of well-being is strictly, and crudely, Benthamite: 'his notions of human pleasure were narrowed by his want of appetite' (64–5), and it is by accidental circumstance rather than any positive motivation that he 'becomes a representative of genuine class-needs' and is 'raised . . . to a sense of common injury and common benefit' (66). There is more than an echo of Smith's 'invisible hand' and the laws of political economy in the conclusion that 'the nature of things transmuted his active egoism into a demand for a public benefit' (66).

Eliot, throughout her work, contests the idea that economic self-interest and egoism are the necessary foundations of the common good. Part of the argument of this chapter is that, in her insistence that individual self-realisation is both an absolute end in itself and yet simultaneously con-stitutive of wider social benefit, she was morally and intellectually aligned with the new liberal theorists who, drawing on the work of Green and the English idealists, were starting to come to prominence around the time of her death.

This is not to argue that she actively thought herself particularly connected to that or any other branch of liberalism. Most readings of *Felix Holt* and the later 'Address to Working Men' conclude rather that the author's politics matched exactly the 'social-political-conservatism' she admired in Riehl.[18] Certainly, her belief that political action and an enlarged democracy were insufficient in themselves to drive social progress is borne out in her 1878 letter to D'Albert-Durade: 'You remember me as much less of a conservative than I have now become. I care as much or more for the people, but I believe less in the help they will get from democrats.'[19] However, social conservatism can wear many political colours and Donald Winch is right to remind us of 'the intellectual historian's need to distin-guish labels from those which the historical agents themselves would have recognised'.[20] In fact, influential voices from both ends of the contemporary political spectrum confirm that political parties and their contending philosophies were in a state of unusual flux at this time. One of T. H. Green's earliest disciples, Arnold Toynbee, welcomed the very contradic-tion between old liberal principles and interventionist policy against which Spencer railed, as he describes 'startling legislative measures [which] . . . have been defended by arguments in sharp contradiction to the ancient principles of those who have pressed these arguments into their service'.[21]

Toynbee and Spencer, from radically different perspectives, were in agreement on the ultimately socialist implications of an extension of such policies. Spencer, however, sees the very foundations of party politics and traditional labels being steadily undermined. He describes the mainstream liberalism of the 1880s as 'a new form of Toryism' and he presciently anticipates an inversion of the two parties in their location of individual rights relative to society and the State: 'if the present drift of things continues, it may by and by really happen that the Tories will be defenders of liberties which the Liberals, in pursuit of what they think popular welfare, trample under foot'.[22] In what follows, particular economic questions will be brought to bear on a consideration of how Eliot perceived this connection between individual liberties and 'popular welfare', how this perception changed during her writing life and how, towards the end of her life, it related to new liberal thought on land ownership, property rights and education.

While recognising the dangers of over-simplifying complex historical processes and shifting political terminology, Stefan Collini, in his still-important study of new liberal thought, argues that the debate over the role of the state in the final decades of the nineteenth century was increasingly 'conceptualized in terms of the opposition between Individualism and Collectivism'.[23] It was in this context that Spencer published *The Man Versus the State* and that Toynbee, Ritchie and later new liberals theorised an alternative vision of society. Both Spencerian individualism and new liberal collectivism, however, claimed to be the inheritors of an older liberal heritage, and there are strong threads of continuity running between the two camps that should warn against dichotomising their respective political visions. As Regenia Gagnier writes of the diverse mid-century theorists who preceded new liberalism – a list whose span includes Spencer, Mill, Smiles and Bagehot – '[i]n all cases the relative function of the individual and state were interdependent and mutually constitutive'.[24] The continuity with some branches of new liberalism was further advanced by Spencer's appropriation of organicism in support of his theories of the individual in society in a biologically informed, competitive social model. Collini describes the popularity of these theories in the 1880s:

> Here was a scientific description that Progress in the natural and social world alike resulted from the free adaptation of individual to environment; the laws of evolution prescribed a policy of Individualism.[25]

The organic social model had something of a contested ontology. Hobhouse was prominent among new liberals who took inspiration from Spencer's organicism and expanded it into a more encompassing concept of the progressive social state. Hobhouse effectively reformulated evolutionary theory in a 'co-operative-altruistic version of Darwinism'.[26]

The liberal critical heritage to which Eliot was connected was, therefore, heterogeneous and complex. Her early periodical writings, at a time when, through the *Westminster Review*, she was in close contact with

Spencer and other Liberal and Radical intellectual figures, unsurprisingly show some alignment with a doctrine of ascendant individual rights, including economic freedom from government interference.[27] Even her literary reviews are informed by a political opinion that underpins wider ethical judgement. Thus, her criticism of Tennyson's *Maud* is based less on the work's poetic quality than on its distinctly anti-Liberal 'ground-notes', which she regards as 'nothing more than hatred of peace and the Peace Society, hatred of commerce and coal mines, hatred of young gentlemen with flourishing whiskers and padded coats, adoration of a clear-cut face, and faith in War as the unique social regenerator'.[28] Her 1865 *Fortnightly Review* article, 'The Influence of Rationalism', shows her enthusiasm for the progressive aspects of the industrial, contract age still burning strong. Superstition, she writes, however much bound up in social custom, is powerless against 'railways, steam-ships, and electric telegraphs, which are demonstrating the interdependence of all human interests, and making self-interest a duct for sympathy'.[29]

This is undoubtedly a more optimistic image of how 'self-interest' can serve the common good than the earlier example I cited from *Impressions of Theophrastus Such*, where external, social benefit is presented as a merely accidental benefit of private industry. In the *Fortnightly Review* article, commerce embodies intrinsic qualities – sympathy and the promotion of interdependence – that elsewhere Eliot ascribes to art and literature. Thus, when liberalism (either political or economic) fails to produce good that transcends that of the self-interested individual agent, it becomes a subject not of praise but censure. Once again, her 1856 review of Riehl in 'The Natural History of German Life' is important in providing clear illustrations of how she drew such distinctions. Close to the point of her transition into fiction, the article provides markers of her developing political philosophy that were to be imaginatively developed in the novels. In this, as in all intellectual areas, Lewes was almost certainly a formative influence, and his interest in and attraction to the theory of socialism is of particular interest in the context of Riehl's work.[30] In her article, Eliot differentiates the movement, on one level, from the abstract political theorising of the 'democratic doctrinaires'. Their commitment 'to inquire into the actual life of the people' she describes as 'the glory of the Socialists' and the basis of what she calls the 'secret of their partial success'.[31] However, the success is only 'partial' because, whatever the attractions of the doctrine, its practical application was at best unproven and at worse unworkable. Eliot is likely to have agreed with Lewes's conclusion that 'socialist systems [were] premature'.[32]

The 'Natural History of German Life' therefore serves to support two of the principal old liberal arguments against any tendency towards collectivism: the moral and the economic.[33] Moreover, the political developments that are shown to characterise the transformation from *Gemeinschaft* to *Gesellschaft* throughout most of Germany seem to exemplify aspects of the 'modern liberalism' of which Spencer and others were so suspicious. Eliot describes how urban industrialisation has been accompanied by a growth in the size and power of the state so that the German peasant's 'chief idea of a government is of a power that raises his taxes, opposes his harmless customs, and torments him with new formalities' (282). The effect of an increased level of bureaucracy also supports Mill's argument in *On Liberty* that the self-esteem and self-development of the citizen falls as the interference of the state rises. For Eliot, this is 'the surest way of maintaining him [the citizen] in his stupidity' (282). What is interesting here is that her criticism of 'modern liberalism' appeals to both the individualist tradition (limit state intervention) and the emerging communitarian branch of new liberalism, which strove to maintain and reinvigorate the finer elements of social custom. To some extent this duality epitomises the ambivalence many liberals felt around the third quarter of the century when attempting to answer the questions posed by Mill which head this chapter: 'How much of human life should be assigned to individuality, and how much to society?' Eliot's own treatment of custom and tradition in *The Mill on the Floss* illustrates the point well. These communal functions simultaneously represent narrow and constraining forces and higher, cohesive values; they are seen as antiquated and out of place in an age of widening trade and modern commerce and yet constitutive of individual and communal worth that transcend the abstraction and atomism of a developing money economy.[34]

Eliot the novelist was aware that the specific conditions created by the combination of industrial market capitalism and political reform complicated and called for a reassessment of the relationship between citizen and state in all spheres, including the economic. However, she recognised earlier in her career that the potential conflict between individual conscience and social obligations was one that was fundamental to any human community. Her 1856 *Leader* article, 'The Antigone and its Moral', goes beyond literary criticism to universalise the 'dramatic collision' between individual impulse and 'the duties of citizenship'.[35] It is a conflict that will inevitably recur, subject to the particular social duties determined in any particular time and place: 'Wherever the strength of a man's intellect, or moral sense, or affection brings him into opposition with the rules which society has sanctioned, *there* is renewed the conflict between Antigone and Creon.'[36]

Mill's rhetorical questions around the definition of individual and social assignment, therefore, were constantly in Eliot's mind and her inability to answer them definitively places her in company with a wide range of thinkers trying to navigate the individualist–collectivist divide. Indeed, Suzanne Graver argues that the shifting socio-political stress of the novels is an essential component of their enduring power: 'The irresolutions force her readers to experience and confront the problems of community in the modern world, as is palpably evident from her Victorian readers' responses to her novels and modern critics' disagreements about whether her priorities lie with the individual or with community.'[37]

Graver's *George Eliot and Community* was published in 1984, and the 'modern critics' to whom she refers include a number of Marxist commentators who, in general and in common with many political theorists of the day, perpetuated the established dichotomy between communitarianism and liberalism.[38] In recent years, however, a growing body of scholars has sought to reconcile these theories, some by particular reference to the new liberal writings of the late nineteenth century.[39] The quotation from L. T. Hobhouse at the head of this chapter provides a tangible, if somewhat tangential link between Eliot and one of the most prominent new liberal thinkers.[40] Hobhouse was greatly influenced by Mill and, particularly, Green, under whom he studied at Oxford. In his most enduring work, Hobhouse links the two great theorists in his analysis of what he sees as the very heart of liberalism, wherein lies 'the organic conception of the relation between the individual and society – a conception toward which Mill worked . . . and which forms the starting point of T. H. Green's philosophy.'[41] Hobhouse, like Green asserts the supremacy of morality within political theory and explains how the morally informed action of the individual is necessarily compatible with the good of the society within which he is acting: 'in Green's phrase, he finds his own good in the *common good*.'[42] It is a concept at the very heart of new liberalism.

Eliot's partial yet significant intellectual alignment with Green has already been broached and a further crucial connection is advanced here.[43] For Hobhouse, writing from the dark days of 1915, Eliot's novels embodied an 'altruism' representing that same reconciliation of individual self-realisation and promotion of the common good that underpinned Green's philosophical idealism and which was to directly inform new liberal theory. Avital Simhony's analysis of Green's 'complex' concept of the common good concludes succinctly: 'Green's common good aims at rejecting private society as the ethical basis of liberalism.'[44] Green does not reject individual rights, including those to private property ownership. He argues rather that these rights can be consistent with a wider concept of public society that can be served by the actions of fully realised moral citizens. Philosophically, his ideal of the common good avoids the 'dualism of egoism and altruism' by creating 'a non-dichotomous moral framework which aims to occupy a moral terrain of human connectedness where one's good and the good of others are intertwined'.[45] The exploration of the 'moral terrain of human connectedness' could equally well describe a central aim of what Eliot sought to achieve through her novels.

In 'The Natural History of German Life', she compares the study of the social with the natural sciences, noting a progression from general, law-based methodologies to the complex and special conditions that constitute the actual practice of the social and natural world. In the social sciences, she locates the *laws* of economics within the former fields of study and observed economic behaviour in the latter. Significantly, Eliot's survey of the progressive analytical stages concludes with a dual observation: what she calls life's 'special conditions, or Natural History, on the one hand, and ... its abnormal conditions, or Pathology, on the other'. And because 'a wise social policy must be based not simply on abstract social science, but on the Natural History of social bodies', it is implicitly necessary to identify and understand the abnormal, pathological conditions of social behaviour, including the economic.[46] In the novels, Eliot presents economic pathologies as those financially related motivations and actions that attempt to bypass the society to which the particular economic agent is bound. Where these pathologies are treated and cured, the widened social benefit is a secondary consequence of the enlightenment and self-realisation of the individual agent. It is a process that mirrors Green's perception of all good individual action being compatible with and constitutive of the common good, for

> Only through society is any one enabled to give that effect to the idea of himself as an object of his actions, to the idea of a better part of himself, without which the world would remain like that of space to a man who had not the senses either of sight or touch.[47]

Financial pathology in the novels is very rarely identifiable by its transgression of civil or criminal laws.[48] The 'abnormal conditions' of economic behaviour therefore relate to moral or social norms rather than legal definitions. Indeed, the strict legality of, for example Tito's sale of Bardo's library and Bulstrode's deceptively achieved inheritance serve to emphasise the scale of their respective moral breaches.[49] In 'Brother Jacob', even the outright theft of his mother's sovereigns is rationalised and effectively decriminalised by David Faux's accurate prediction that she is certain not to report him: 'Besides, it is not robbery to take property belonging to your mother: she doesn't prosecute you.'⁵⁰ Faux has no moral objection to stealing: '[he] would certainly have liked to have some of his master's money in his pocket, if he had been sure his master would have been the only man to suffer for it; but he was a cautious youth, and quite determined to run no risks on his own account' (51). He is, however, comfortable with the more legally ambivalent practice of blackmail ('charitably abstaining from mentioning some other people's misdemeanours' (77)) which here, and elsewhere in the novels, Eliot exposes as morally and socially equivalent to property theft. All David's economic choices are, in fact, based on a crude Utilitarianism of pure self-interest: 'he calculated whether an action would harm himself, or whether it would only harm other people. In the former case he was very timid about satisfying his immediate desires, but in the latter he would risk the result with much courage' (58).

Where Eliot's critique of this economically driven social atomism becomes more interesting is in the second part of the story when David, now Edward Freely, establishes a legal confectionary business and, as a result of his skills and labour, prospers in a free, competitive market. It is a market at a particular stage of social and commercial evolution, which Eliot describes in explicitly Smithean terms. As a result of the 'division of labour', increasing disposable income and a greater value ascribed to leisure time, the housewives of Grimworth 'had their hands set free from cookery to add to the wealth of society in some other way' (66). This may represent progress, but not in a way that creates any net addition to the wealth of society: the liberated women turn to idle gossip and the reduced household wealth is simply transferred to Freely. Grimworth is a microcosm of an apparently modern and progressive commercial society in which economic individualism unalloyed by individual virtue or social purpose thrives, but with zero net gain to the overall wealth of the community. In Green's terms, the standard of the common good – which must benefit any individual or section of society neither to the exclusion nor detriment of others – is not met.⁵¹

The simple metric of whether a net economic gain has been achieved is, in fact, a meaningful, if ultimately inadequate, indicator of the value of a particular financial action or behaviour. Gambling, in ignorance or defiance of calculable probabilities, undermines human rationality, but the moral objection, as voiced by Daniel Deronda lies in the fact that the gain of one gambler necessitates the loss of another. Similarly, speculation in stocks and shares, as opposed to the kind of long-term investments Eliot herself made, requires the balancing of a profit and loss equation, usually the result of the kind of information asymmetry exploited by Sir Gavial Mantrap in *Impressions of Theophrastus Such*. However, this net gain shorthand is not always sufficient. Silas Marner provides a skilled and valuable service for the Raveloe community, for which he is paid a fair market rate. There is an economic argument that his hoarding of gold coins and minimal personal expenditure on goods and services (under-consumption) is a constraint to growth and therefore not in the best public interest.[52] But a high rate of saving and low consumption can, in certain economic conditions, be socially beneficial. And, in any case, any duty to spend must surely be subservient to the right to liberty of action, subject only to that action not causing harm to others. This was the central theme of Mill's *On Liberty*, which necessarily supported the individual's right to non-conventional or eccentric ways of behaviour.[53] Silas would appear to exercise this right while causing no harm to others, so should we regard his miserliness as pathological? Green's conception of individual self-realisation and the common good provides a useful framework for how Eliot approached the question.

When he first moves to Raveloe, Silas's reclusiveness is still distinct from his money hoarding. His focus on his work as 'an end in itself' both maintains a direct, non-exclusively financial link to the community and, internally, provides him some comfort and consolation against the injustices he has suffered, 'so to bridge over the loveless chasms of his life'.[54] Notably, his work is compared to that of a spider; clearly lacking in some essential human completeness, but nonetheless vital and organic, in contrast to the mechanistic imagery that describes his later obsession with the accumulation of gold. Over time the money becomes an end in itself with 'no purpose beyond it', so that 'every added guinea, while it was itself a satisfaction, bred a new desire' (18). Unlike the things that money can buy, the medium itself is theoretically limitless in supply and its acquisition can therefore create insatiable wants. Gold, rather than more abstract representational money, has a talismanic quality that makes the individual coins humanised and familiar in Silas's eyes; 'He began to think [the money] was conscious of him . . . and he would on no account have exchanged those coins, which had become his familiars, for other coins with unknown faces' (18).

Money ultimately loses its use and exchange value and literally becomes non-economic. Its substitution for any kind of social contact marks an extreme of individualism that, in its isolation, is dehumanising. As his hoard grew, so Silas's life was 'narrowing and hardening itself more and more into a mere pulsation of desire and satisfaction that had no relation to any other being' (19). The loss of his money exposes him to the individuals and institutions through whom he eventually re-engages with society, but, until Eppie appears, '[t]he fountains of human love … had not yet been unlocked, and his soul was still the shrunken rivulet' (84). His eventual spiritual and physical epiphany approximates closely to Green's concept of full self-realisation: 'his soul, long stupefied in a cold narrow prison, was unfolding too, and trembling gradually into full consciousness' (124). The process is finally characterised by a transformation of his social and economic habits to 'the ties and charities that bound together the families of his neighbours' (124) and immersion into their communal institutions, including the Church.

If Eliot was broadly aligned with Green and new liberalism in an understanding of the common good that distinguishes a liberal tradition of individual freedoms from a purely *individualist* conception of society, it remains to consider whether there was similarly common ground with regard to the theory and policy implications of state interference in economically related rights. New liberalism came to prominence in the years after Eliot's death and the ways in which its leading theorists and practitioners envisaged the adaptation of the old liberal tradition for the modern age varied greatly, particularly on the question of how far central government should support social welfare. Amidst this diversity, however, are recurrent themes that find their most common link in Green, most of whose work was produced during Eliot's lifetime.

Despite the more collectivist directions in which some of his followers attempted to steer late century liberalism, the main economic aspects of Green's political theory, particularly with regard to wealth creation, are actually broadly compatible with the central theories of political economy. In his *Lectures on the Principles of Political Obligation*, Green opens his discussion of the problems of 'an impoverished and reckless proletariate' (175) by declaring the optimistic foundation of capitalism. This maintains that 'the increased wealth of one man does not naturally mean the diminished wealth of another', but that rather 'supposing trade and labour to be free, wealth must be constantly distributed throughout the process in the shape of wages to labourers and of profits to those who mediate the business of exchange'.[55] There is an unexpectedly conservative thread to Green's writing here; for example, in his reluctance to ascribe the extant great inequalities of wealth, and particularly in land ownership, to capitalism but tracing them rather to historic abuses stretching back to feudalism.[56] It is a nuanced and historically informed approach that accords well with Eliot's own.

Neither does he propose any form of redistribution by limiting private ownership of land or restricting its bequest. He does, however, recognise that land, because it is a limited commodity from which many natural resources originate and on which the housing stock and communications of the whole of society depend, is a special case of economic concern, distinct from wealth in general. These factors 'necessitate a social control over the exercise of property in land'.[57] Green recognises that this social responsibility is, ideally, best exercised by the enlightened landowner, for 'the possessor of an estate, who has contributed nothing by his own labour to its acquisition, may yet by his labour contribute largely to the social good, and a well-organised state will in various ways elicit such labours from possessors of inherited wealth'.[58]

The opening chapter of *George Eliot and Money* described how Eliot uses land husbandry and concern for the well-being of tenants as an important moral marker for her landowning characters, often making use of a generational contrast in attitudes. Thus, the desire of Arthur Donnithorne and Godfrey Cass to reform the land-management abuses of their fathers is indicative of an altruistic core to their characters which, through the course of the respective novels, gains an ascendancy over the egoism that underlies their earlier actions. Suzanne Graver makes a related but wider point when she describes the greater communal emphasis of Eliot's earlier period settings, in which a 'simple family life of common need and common industry prevailed'.[59] In the resolution of both *Adam Bede* and *Silas Marner*, she traces how 'the movement from alienation to integration is marked by Gemeinschaft images of a holiday world'.[60] The interaction between landowner and tenant is flawed but still sufficiently strong to root both in the same patterns of custom, ritual celebration and seasonal rotation.

As the settings of the novels move forward in time, however, landed estates become the sites of social alienation. As Graver observes, 'The Squires fall far short of the feudal ideal they should represent; still, the central role they play in the life of the community contrasts sharply with the peripheral function of the great houses in the fiction set nearer to the present.'[61] In Henleigh Grandcourt, Eliot creates her most socially atomised egoist. Indeed, his detachment from the responsibility of managing his estates to promote the common good seems to grow as his landholdings expand. However, neither in *Daniel Deronda* nor in the other novels in which land inheritance features does Eliot suggest that the state should interfere either in the bequest or ownership of land or in any extensive redistributive schemes linked to its value.[62] Her natural gradualism here again aligns her more closely with Green than, say Mill, whose distinction between the earned and unearned increments produced by land became the basis for proposed state appropriation of the latter by socialist theorists later in the century.[63]

Beyond the specific conditions relating to the ownership of land, the nature of rights to any individually owned property was at the heart of new liberal theory and debate. The interdependence of the individual and the wider community is again a unifying theme and serves to reinforce the morally informed link between the leading theorists and Eliot. John Morrow clearly differentiates the varying perspectives of new liberalism with regard to the limitation of individual property rights by the state but concludes that: '[u]nderlying these different perspectives . . . was a common commitment to the idea that property rights were of simultaneous and corresponding significance both to individuals and to the communities to which they belonged. The common good was furthered through the exercise of rights, but so too was the good of individual rightholders'.[64] Like Eliot, the new liberals, as part of their project to disassociate their political heritage from a self-serving individualism, sought to establish a mutually reinforcing link between property rights and social embeddedness.

Hobhouse, in *Liberalism*, idealises society as 'a whole which lives and flourishes by the harmonious growth of its parts, each of which in developing on its own lines and in accordance with its own nature tends on the whole to further the development of the others'.[65] This is a statement of individuality as opposed to individualism that is strongly reminiscent of Mill and which highlights the requirement of self-development in the attainment of true individuality – Green's concept of self-realisation. Where this process connects back to property rights is that the very act of responsibly exercising those rights, they insisted, was both morally significant for the individual and served to cement his participation in the community. For Green, 'Appropriation is an expression of will; of the individual's effort to give reality to a conception of his own good; of his consciousness of a possible self-satisfaction as an object to be attained.'[66]

Under such a definition, a political theory that either promoted state collectivism or merely denied the universalisation of the right to the social benefits of individual appropriation was essentially obstructive to the self-development of its citizens. Moreover, to the extent that ownership is linked to an individual's *future* well-being, incorporating his desire to provide for others, it is expressive of a particularly human virtue and freedom that should not be limited by the state: 'If we leave a man free to realise the conception of a possible well-being, it is impossible to limit the effect upon him of his desire to provide for his future well-being, as including that of the persons in whom he is interested.'[67]

As the earlier reading of *The Mill on the Floss* attempted to show, conceptualising future well-being in exclusively material terms can result in a strain of excessive prudence which serves to elevate economic over non-economic values while relegating the legitimate claims of *present* well-being.[68] Where the bourgeois virtues are in proper balance, however, Eliot shows how property ownership is not only compatible with but also constitutive of a virtuous character. Silas Marner, when freed from his obsession with gold and fully immersed in his community, is, we feel, better able to defend his natural right to be Eppie's 'father' when he proudly tells Cass that '"I'm in no fear o' want ... There's few working-folks have got so much laid by as that. I don't know what it is to gentlefolks, but I look upon it as a deal – almost too much."'[69] His assessment of what constitutes an appropriate level of monetary wealth is reminiscent of Adam Bede's description of having 'just enough and some to spare'. Throughout the novel, Adam's heightened and persuasive concept of the value of labour is accompanied by a desire to elevate his own position. His plans to support a family of his own involve the accumulation of capital, initially out of wages, to finance his own business.[70]

The new liberals' position on property rights in which, I contend, George Eliot was in essential agreement, effectively accepted that great inequalities of wealth were an unfortunate but inescapable consequence of liberal rights. But beyond ensuring that these rights were protected – an essentially negative concept of government – did the state have additional, positive responsibilities to promote the common good? New liberalism moved beyond Mill and his most direct descendants, including Sidgwick, in defending such intervention. However, the extent to which its leading proponents believed this should be extended varied widely and eventually precipitated the split in the party out of which the Labour Party came into being.[71] Green, despite his wide-ranging social concerns and enormous influence on later theorists and liberal politicians, advocated little direct policy intervention. Political change, he argued, should be the result of the voluntary action of socially engaged individuals. He therefore insisted that 'it is the business of the state, not indeed directly to promote moral goodness ... but to maintain the conditions without which a free exercise of the faculties is impossible'.[72]

But what exactly should these 'conditions' be and where, along a wide spectrum of interpretations, did George Eliot stand? On the little evidence available, Eliot was most likely in broad agreement with Mill and Sidgwick, whose theories of taxation were the most comprehensive and influential in the third quarter of the century. They concluded that income and inheritance taxes were, subject to strict limitations, legitimate means of the state providing services that would contribute to the common good.[73] For many new liberals, including Hobhouse and Hobson, this meant the provision of welfare payments, derived from the proceeds of socially enabled wealth, to give every citizen the means to participate fully in society. This participation would, they argued, subsequently inspire a cumulative swell of moral self-development that would progressively serve to lessen dependency. However, the rejection of individualism in favour of a communitarian theory of state did not necessarily mean the rejection of old-fashioned economic liberalism. Bernard Bosanquet was a follower of Green who stood against the increasingly welfarist tide, believing that public charity was morally damaging for both individual recipients and the state. Free trade and market capitalism, he argued, were capable of providing conditions of equal opportunity for individuals to acquire ethically significant property ownership without direct assistance from the state.[74]

It is a viewpoint with which the fiercely financially independent Eliot was sympathetic. One of her earliest fictional representations of a charitable and socially minded character is Mr Jerome, the 'good old man' who befriends the eponymous heroine of 'Janet's Repentance'. His belief that the improvement in the condition of the poor is best served by voluntary, directed and localised charitable giving is supported by a long-term economic argument against smaller but ineffectual welfare payments that perpetuate dependency. He therefore explains the object of his charity as being

> to keep industrious men an' women off the parish. I'd rether give ten shillin' an' help a man to stan' on his own legs, nor pay half-a-crown to buy him a parish crutch; it's the ruination on him if he once goes to the parish. I've see'd many a time, if you help a man wi' a present in a neeborly way, it sweetens his blood – he thinks it kind on you; but the parish shillins turn it sour – he niver thinks 'em enough.[75]

The Poor Law to which Mr Jerome refers remained a touchstone in the debates surrounding the nature and extent of state-funded relief throughout much of the century. Recall Eliot's 1874 letter and its expression of an essentially 'old' liberal attitude towards poor relief, which 'remains a huge system of vitiation, introducing the principle of communistic provision instead of provision through individual, personal responsibility and activity'.[76] This quotation in isolation, however, risks giving a false impression that Eliot was both categorical in her views on how society should help the poor and somehow indifferent to their plight. There is, in fact, a tone of sadness and frustration in the letter, which was written to Jane Senior, a woman whose work and pioneering success in an increasingly government-supported area of social research and improvement Eliot greatly admired.[77] In a letter to Blackwood later the same year, she describes Mrs Senior's work as 'serious social labour'.[78]

It is also significant that Eliot's letter, while addressing the more general problems of poor relief, was written in direct response to Senior's Parliamentary Report on 'Education of Girls in Pauper Schools'.[79] Eliot agrees 'heartily' with Senior's educational conclusions, including 'the superiority of that home education which calls out the emotions in connection with all the common needs of life, and creates that interest in means and results which is the chief part of cleverness'. While Eliot's thoughts on education were never collected, as were, for example, Spencer's, they are a frequent and prominent feature of her letters and essays and are widely explored in the novels.[80] Her conviction that a complete education, at all levels of society, should combine the moral, intellectual and practical led her to question and criticise established syllabuses from primary to tertiary levels.

In December 1875, she wrote to Mark Pattison congratulating him on the contribution she believed a paper he had just published made to 'that *most important* of all reforms – reform of the theory of Education'.[81] Pattison was then Rector of Lincoln College, Oxford and, together with another friend of Eliot and Lewes, Benjamin Jowett, was at the forefront of far-reaching reforms of courses and teaching methods at the university.[82] The narrowness of the earlier century Oxford educational experience and its intellectually and morally flawed fictional products (including Arthur Donnithorne, Walter Stelling, Fred Vincy, Edward Casaubon and Thomas Lush) feature recurrently in the novels. The practical Caleb Garth is appalled by the useless expense incurred in Fred's university education. Cambridge is less prominent in Eliot's work, although Leslie Stephen provided her with detailed information in preparation for *Daniel Deronda*. Tellingly, Daniel chooses to leave the university 'to pursue a more independent line of study abroad', while Lydgate notably eschews the ancient English universities in favour of the scientifically advanced institutions of London, Edinburgh and Paris.[83]

In her calls for a more equal educational provision for girls and a wider conviction that education was the key to the social development of the lower classes, Eliot was very much in tune with progressive liberal thought over the period.[84] After 1860, the party's long periods in government enabled it to extend the economically related social reforms enacted earlier in the century, which progressively limited the working hours of children, into specifically educational legislation.[85] The most significant landmark was the Education Act of 1870, which, by enabling local school boards to create bye-laws making school attendance compulsory, embodied a commitment to nationwide provision. A decade later, the Education Act of 1880 actually compelled the boards to enact compulsory attendance bye-laws. Thus, by the year of Eliot's death, 'the formal legal position was clear and unequivocal. Every parish was expected to have an elementary school and all the children of the labouring poor between the ages of five and ten were expected to attend it on a full-time basis.'[86]

As government was increasingly drawn into educational provision at elementary level and beyond, the debate on how this should be funded intensified. Old liberals drew on Adam Smith's argument, in *The Wealth of Nations*, that teaching should not stand outside the market mechanism and that, for example, university teachers should be paid in relation to the number of students they were able to attract.[87] Spencer's 1850 *Social Statics*, which Eliot read, included a chapter entitled 'National Education' which insisted that his overarching principle of non-state interference should extend to educational provision. Mill's *On Liberty*, nine years later, agreed that the provision of a prescriptive and uniform syllabus by the state would be an unjustified interference in individual liberty, what he called a 'despotism over the mind'.[88] However, because he believed that for a child to receive no education was a 'moral crime' against both the individual and society, the ability of the state to compel parents to educate their children was an acceptable limitation on their freedom of choice.[89] Moreover, he argues, if the state enacts compulsion, it also has a duty to provide sufficient funding to enable the poor to comply with the requirement. Mill therefore justifies economic intervention by the state, funded by and on behalf of society in order to prevent a positive harm to society, thereby satisfying his central condition of personal liberty.

Eliot shared many of the main educational theories of both Mill and Spencer and the later new liberals, but on the economic aspects of the debate she is largely silent. In 'The Address to Working Men, by Felix Holt' (1868), probably her most direct statement of political philosophy, education is a central theme. The education, or 'rescue of our children' is, Felix insists, 'a part of our good, without which everything else we strive for will be worthless'.[90] However, Felix's appeal is not to government but to the working man directly and through the trades union mechanism of 'extended co-operation'. It is therefore a matter of social duty to persuade one's fellow-workers not to forsake their children's education and push them, prematurely, into waged labour. Emphatically, Felix argues, '[n]o political institution will alter the nature of Ignorance, or hinder it from producing vice and misery'.[91] From this allocation of moral and social responsibility follows an economic requirement that the 'common fund' drawn from union subscriptions is used to finance the 'common benefit' of compulsory education.

Both *Felix Holt* and its hero's subsequent 'Address' have been given in evidence by critics over many years in support of the case that Eliot was, at heart, politically conservative and became increasingly so as she aged. However, if we accept that both works represent attempts to reconcile individuality with community, it seems plausible to place them and their author in the developing current of liberal thought. While Eliot's resistance to the extension of government into widespread welfare provision may align her more closely to the old liberals of her *Westminster Review* days, Felix's certainty 'that a society, a nation is held together ... by the dependence of men on each other and the sense they have of a common interest' emphatically secures a link with Green and the new liberalism he inspired.[92] Like the new liberals, Eliot, in her life and her work, sometimes struggled to make the further reconciliation between individual economic responsibility and the social adjustments that were required to ensure a level of meaningful, universal citizenship that went beyond the quantitative level of enfranchisement. The market and competition therefore remained ambiguous, even confused concepts for both.[93]

A modern-day communitarian philosopher, Michael J. Sandel, tells us that '[t]o know whether a good should be subject to market exchange ... we need to know what mode of valuation is fitting or appropriate to that good. This is different from knowing how much the thing is worth. It involves a qualitative, not just a quantitative judgment.'[94] The great success of her books *within* the market exchange brought Eliot influence with a widening readership and wealth; yet simultaneously it brought a fear that she was merely adding to the 'heap of books'.[95] In one of her final meditations on the art and commerce of 'Authorship' in 'Leaves from a Note-Book', her commercial analogies can only go so far before they break down amidst incommensurable considerations of capital, replication and value. The new liberal attempt to '*combine* an "ethically-orientated" social rights perspective ... with a liberal market ontology', while never fully succeeding, essentially informed the course of British politics for the next hundred years.[96] So too, Eliot's incorporation of the economic into her moral philosophical, sociological and political thought was a constant and profound influence on her novelistic art.

George Eliot's final stock portfolio, 1880

	£	% Portfolio	% Yield
Consols	963	3	2.9
USA Government	4,000	13	4.9
New South Wales	1,000	3	6.9
Victoria	1,000	3	6.3
Cape of Good Hope	1,000	3	2.0
Total Government	*7,963*	*25*	*4.7*
Melbourne and Hobsons Bay Railroad 5%	700	2	4.9
Bueonos Ayres 6% Perp. Debenture	500	2	5.9
Sambre et Meuse Railroad 5.5% pref	1,000	3	5.6
Pittsburg, Ft Wayne & Chicago Railroad 7%	500	2	3.6
South Eastern Railway 5% pref	800	3	4.9
Midland Railway 5% pref	780	3	4.9
Colonial Bank	1,400	5	3.6
East & West India Dock Co. Ord.	1,000	3	5.0
Scottish Australian	1,100	4	7.2
Gas Light & Coke Ord.	240	1	8.4
Phoenix (South Metropolitan Gas)	300	1	5.1
Improved Industrial Dwellings Ord.	500	2	6.0
Grand Junction Canal	2,000	7	4.0
Surrey Commercial Dock	450	1	8.0
Midland Railway Debentures	1,650	5	3.9
Great Indian Peninsula 5% Guaranteed Stock	1,900	6	5.2
Madras Railroad 5% Guaranteed Stock	1,580	5	4.9
London and Northwestern Railway 4% Debentures	3,000	10	2.0
Regents Canal Ord.	1,125	4	4.7
London Docks (St. Katherine's) Ord.	1,700	6	3.0
Total Corporate	*22,225*	*75*	*4.4*
TOTAL	30,188	100	**4.5**

Geographical Exposure

UK	48%
Empire	32%
US	17%
Europe	3%
	100%

Sector Breakdown
(Excluding Government Bonds)

	% Eliot	% Market Average 1880
Railways	56	64
Canals & Docks	28	3
Banks	6	15
Mining	5	2
Gas	2	2
Other	2	15
	100	100

Was Edward Tulliver made bankrupt? An analysis of his financial downfall

Despite its central importance to the plot of *The Mill on the Floss*, the details of Mr Tulliver's financial collapse are somewhat opaque, if not absent from the narrative. Mary Poovey has suggested that this was a deliberate obfuscation by Eliot in order to direct the reader's attention from the financial plot towards what she calls the 'sentimental plots'.[1] The summary that follows attempts to explain the detailed circumstances leading up to and following Tulliver's insolvency. It gathers together the relatively few facts contained in the text and makes what I believe are some reasonable deductions therefrom. One conclusion I draw is that the long-standing assumption that Tulliver became legally bankrupt is technically incorrect, a fact that Eliot draws the reader's attention to on more than one occasion and which is borne out by British bankruptcy law prevailing at the time the novel was set. I begin with a breakdown of Tulliver's known assets and liabilities from which I construct an illustrative table. The events and process leading up to and following his financial collapse are then described, followed by some conclusions.

A. TULLIVER'S ASSETS

1 Dorlcote Mill and the attached house together with stock, farm equipment and household possessions. These are held outright, although the household possessions are pledged as security against a specific loan (see B3 below). No value is disclosed for any of these assets.

2 A holding of land – size and value unspecified – over which is held a privately financed mortgage (see B1 below).

3 Cash. Although no details of bank or other cash holdings are given, we know that whatever he did have has been greatly reduced by a series of commitments, described in B2 below.

4 Debtors. An unsecured £300 loan to his brother-in-law, Moss, a poor farmer who is unable to make either interest or capital repayments (68).

B. TULLIVER'S LIABILITIES

1 The mortgage on the land in A2. The two thousand pounds mortgage is held by a Mr Furley who, Tulliver believes, would be inclined to take ownership of the land and buy the house and mill at a fair price when the loss of the lawsuit requires Tulliver to raise a substantial sum (171). This hope is dashed when he discovers that Furley ('lately much straitened for money') has sold the mortgage to Tulliver's great enemy, the lawyer Wakem (174).

2 Bank debt. Tulliver 'was held to be a much more substantial man than he really was' (67). The impression is that he lived slightly beyond his means, a tendency not helped by his history of 'going to law'. His resources have been further diminished by the payment of school fees for Tom – the subject of a heated disagreement with his wife's family that results in the aggrieved Tulliver rashly repaying a £500 loan from his sister-in-law, Mrs Glegg. In addition, his provision of surety for Riley left him 'saddled with a debt of two hundred and fifty pounds' when his impoverished friend died the previous year (171–2). Including this debt, I assume he has relatively small net bank borrowings, implicitly supported by a later reference to 'the deficiency at the bank' (213).

3 Creditor A. Having hastily repaid Mrs Glegg (B2) and unable to call in his loan to Moss (A4), Tulliver borrows £500 on a fixed term from an unnamed lender. The lender was a client of Wakem's who 'was the only convenient person to be found' (114). Creditor A very significantly receives a charge over Tulliver's furniture and household possessions as security (172).

4 Costs of the lost law suit. While the extent of damages and fees are not disclosed, we know there is a 'defendant's claim for costs' (213). I assume a substantial amount becomes due to Pivart (the defendant, represented by Wakem) and Tulliver's own counsel, Gore.

5   Other creditors. It seems evident from the creditor repayment sub-plot
    that there were other undisclosed (probably trade) creditors, although
    numbers and quantum are not known. We are told later that 'several
    creditors . . . had accepted a composition from [Tulliver]' (243).

C. NET ASSETS SUMMARY

As per B1, it is clear that although he realises that the loss of the Pivart case
will require him to sell his principal assets, Tulliver is confident that the
value of these assets comfortably exceeds his liabilities and that he will be
able to continue living in his home, surrounded by his possessions and
running the mill, albeit now as a tenant and employee. He also realises that
the £500 loan secured against his possessions is about to come due, but
seems to believe that this can be re-financed by his wealthy in-laws: 'it was
nothing but right and natural that Bessy should go to the Pullets and
explain the thing to them' (172). However, the transfer of the mortgage on
his land to Wakem destroys his dream of an orderly realisation of his assets
at a fair market value. He falls from his horse and slips into semi-conscious
delirium while his 'downfall' gathers pace.

The table below is illustrative only, but summarises Tulliver's assets and
liabilities under two scenarios. The first represents his delusional expectation that the £500 loan would be refinanced and his property bought at a
generous price by Furley; the second the distressed auction process that
actually transpires. Many of the numbers are 'guesstimates' but, as well as
illustrating how Tulliver initially manages to convince himself that he has
positive net assets, the figures are consistent with two facts that emerge from
the text: (i) that the unsecured creditors received an interim payment of 'ten
or twelve shillings in the pound' (213); and (ii) that this left outstanding
debts of more than £500 (243).

	Fair Market Asset Value	Liabilities	Distressed Asset Value
Land (1)	2,000	2,000	2,000
Property (2)	900		650
Possessions (3)	500		250
Moss Loan (4)	300		0
Cash (5)	−50		−50
Legal Case (6)		700	
Creditor A (7)		500	

Other Creditors (8)		150	
Total	3,650	3,350	2,850
Total Ex-Land	1,650	1,350	850
NET ASSETS	300		−500

Notes:

[1] Tulliver took out the mortgage partly to fund his sister's dowry when she married (67), presumably around the time the war with France ended (1815). The high inflation of the war years gave way to a fall in prices over the period that followed. I assume that the value of the land matches the mortgage. If there was significant equity value in the land holding, Tulliver would have been able to sell it and repay the mortgage, leaving him with a cash surplus; his reaction on discovering the transfer to Wakem suggests this was not an option.

[2] My valuations of the house and mill are, to a large extent, back-solved, but illustrate the substantial discount that can result from the forced sale of illiquid assets.

[3] Similarly, although Tulliver may have thought his household possessions were adequate security for the £500 loan from Creditor A, auction values (with no minimum reserves) are often heavily discounted. I assume only £250 was raised in the first auction, including the items purchased by the Dodson family for the basic living requirements of the Tullivers.

[4] Prior to the financial crisis, Tulliver decided against enforcing this debt. After his accident, Tom rightly predicts that his father, facing a possible bankruptcy process that would transfer the claim against Moss to Tulliver's creditors, would want to cancel the debt (191). Before the loan note is destroyed, Mr Glegg tells us that the £300 would be a significant amount in determining whether Tulliver enters or stays out of bankruptcy (190).

[5] Guess for illustrative purposes. See B2 above and note 6 below.

[6] Incorporates possible damages, fees owed to Gore and reimbursement of Pivart's fees paid to Wakem: 'For when the defendant's claim for costs had been satisfied, there would remain the friendly bill of Mr Gore' (213).

[7] See B3 above.

[8] Guess for illustrative purpose – the fact that Tulliver is ashamed to face his trade creditors on market days and later hosts a party for all the creditors he eventually makes good suggests there were a number of merchants on the list. See B5.

D.   THE PROCESS

1   Unbeknown to the stricken Tulliver, Creditor A calls in the debt – 'the debt we're going to be sold up for' (187). In response to Tom's request that his uncles and aunts advance any future inheritance they might leave him and Maggie to pay this off so they may keep their possessions, Glegg explains that they too would then become impaired unsecured creditors (188). This must imply that other creditors apart from Creditor A were demanding repayment – presumably Pivart, Gore, the other trade creditors and possibly the bank.

2   After a period of two months and 'under a decree of Chancery' (212), notices for the auction of the farming and other stock, mill and land are posted. Mr Deane's intention to buy the assets on behalf of his firm is

thwarted when Mrs Tulliver discloses the plan to Wakem. Wakem buys everything and employs Tulliver to run the mill: 'the very thing that would cause Mr Tulliver the most deadly mortification' (220).

3   As noted above, Mr Deane predicts that the sale will allow an interim payment to creditors of 50–60 per cent of par, leaving around £500 outstanding. Using my illustrative model and assuming that Wakem simply takes possession of the land (on which he held the mortgage), we have the sale proceeds of the house, mill and possessions less bank debt amounting to £850. The first £250, raised in the auction of household possessions goes to the secured Creditor A, leaving £600 to be distributed to Creditor A (still owed £250) and all other creditors: a total owed of £1,100. Therefore a payment representing 55% of par (£600) is made, with a further £500 outstanding.

4   Four years later, largely as a result of profits from Tom's trading speculations, which greatly supplemented Mr Tulliver's meagre savings out of earnings, all outstanding creditors are repaid in full, including accrued interest (309).

E   CONCLUSIONS

1   The initial auction of the household possessions followed on quickly from Tulliver's accident and the expiry of the fixed term of the loan from Creditor A, who called in the bailiffs to claim his security. The subsequent auction of the mill and other assets took longer and involved a formal court process: 'By the beginning of the second week in January, the bills were out advertising the sale, under a decree of Chancery, of Mr. Tulliver's farming and other stock, to be followed by a sale of the mill and land' (212). Indeed this chapter opens with a narratorial reflection on the collateral damage imposed by the weapons of legal process: 'Allocaturs, filing of bills in Chancery, decrees of sale, are legal chain-shot or bomb-shells' (212). So it certainly looks like some form of court-appointed bankruptcy proceeding has commenced.

2   And indeed Tulliver's son Tom believes bankruptcy to have occurred, as disclosed in a crucial sentence: 'That might have cheered the lad and fed his hopes a little, if there had not come at the same time the much-dreaded blow that his father must be a bankrupt, after all; at least, the creditors must be asked to take less than their due, which to Tom's untechnical mind was the same thing as bankruptcy' (213). Taken in the context of the 1825 Bankruptcy Act, this strongly suggests that a composition was reached *outside* the bankruptcy process.[2] The term

'composition' is explicitly used when describing Tulliver's shame: 'Even the days on which Wakem came to ride round the land and inquire into the business were not so black to him as those market-days on which he had met several creditors who had accepted a composition from him' (243).

3   I conclude that Tom and Maggie wrongly assume their father is bankrupt, although to them it seems a truly accurate description of his financial and wider emotional collapse. When the broken Tulliver starts to comprehend the extent of his downfall and asks 'have they made me a bankrupt?', Maggie tellingly 'thought that terrible word really represented the fact' (225). His shame within his community and reliance on Wakem for his home and livelihood could hardly have been more devastating if he had become technically bankrupt. But the composition agreement that keeps him out of a bankruptcy process that would have discharged him from the obligation to repay his creditors in full enables him to achieve that very end. For Tulliver and his son, the discharge of all debts finally restores honour to the family name.

Notes

INTRODUCTION

1. D. Morier Evans, *The History of the Commercial Crisis 1857–1858, and the Stock Exchange Panic of 1859* (London: Groombridge, 1859), 33.
2. Terry Eagleton, review of Paul Auster and J. M. Coetzee, *Here and Now: Letters 2008–2011* in *The Times Literary Supplement*, 31 May 2013, 11.
3. Tamara Wagner, *Financial Speculation in Victorian Fiction: Plotting Money and the Novel Genre, 1815–1901* (Columbus: Ohio State University Press, 2010), 3.
4. David R. Green *et al.*, 'Men, Women, and Money: An Introduction', in David R. Green, Alastair Owens, Josephine Maltby and Janette Rutterford (eds.), *Men, Women, and Money: Perspectives on Gender, Wealth, and Investment, 1850–1930* (Oxford University Press, 2011), 21.
5. George Eliot, *The Journals of George Eliot*, ed. Margaret Harris and Judith Johnston (Cambridge University Press, 1998), 149. Hereafter, '*Journals*'.
6. William Baker, *The George Eliot–George Henry Lewes Library: An Annotated Catalogue of Their Books at Dr Williams's Library, London* (New York and London: Garland, 1977), xxvi.
7. Contributors to the series included Gary Becker, Alan Greenspan, Robert Shiller, Joseph Stiglitz and Amartya Sen.
8. One of the most critically acclaimed analyses of the crisis was by another *FT* journalist which drew on the author's doctoral research in social anthropology. Gillian Tett, *Fool's Gold: How Unrestrained Greed Corrupted a Dream, Shattered Global Markets and Unleashed Catastrophe* (London: Little Brown, 2009).
9. Steven D. Levitt and Stephen J. Dubner, *Freakonomics: A Rogue Economist Explores the Hidden Side of Everything* (London: Allen Lane, 2005); Tim Harford, *The Undercover Economist* (Oxford University Press, 2006).
10. Diane Coyle, *The Soulful Science: What Economists Really Do and Why it Matters* (Princeton University Press, 2007).
11. Jeffrey Sachs, *The Price of Civilization: Economics and Ethics After the Fall* (London: Bodley Head, 2011); Michael Sandel, *What Money Can't Buy: The Moral Limits of Markets* (London: Allen Lane, 2012); Robert Skidelsky and Edward Skidelsky, *How Much is Enough? The Love of Money, and the Case for the Good Life* (London: Allen Lane, 2012); Robert J. Shiller, *Finance and the Good Society* (Princeton University Press, 2012).

12. Richard Bronk, *The Romantic Economist: Imagination in Economics* (Cambridge University Press, 2009); George A. Akerlof and Robert J. Shiller, *Animal Spirits: How Human Psychology Drives The Economy, and Why It Matters For Global Capitalism* (Princeton University Press, 2009).

13. Philip Mirowski (ed.), *Natural Images in Economic Thought: 'Markets Read in Tooth and Claw'* (Cambridge University Press, 1994); D. McCloskey, *The Rhetoric of Economics* (Madison: University of Wisconsin Press, 1995).

14. Martha Woodmansee and Mark Osteen (eds.), *The New Economic Criticism: Studies at the Intersection of Literature and Economics* (London and New York: Routledge, 1999). More recent collections, representing a range of disciplines and methodological approaches to the broad interconnections of Victorian economics and literature (and some limited reference to George Eliot) include: Francis O'Gorman (ed.), *Victorian Literature and Finance* (Oxford University Press, 2007); and Nancy Henry and Cannon Schmitt (eds.), *Victorian Investments: New Perspectives on Finance and Culture* (Bloomington: Indiana University Press, 2009).

15. Donald Winch, *Wealth and Life: Essays on the Intellectual History of Political Economy in Britain, 1848–1914* (Cambridge University Press, 2009), 6.

16. Deanna Kreisel, *Economic Woman: Demand, Gender, and Narrative Closure in Eliot and Hardy* (University of Toronto Press, 2012); Eleanor Courtemanche, *The 'Invisible Hand' and British Fiction, 1818–1860: Adam Smith, Political Economy, and the Genre of Realism* (Basingstoke: Palgrave Macmillan, 2011).

17. Courtemanche, *The 'Invisible Hand'*, 3.

18. See Clare Pettitt, *Patent Inventions: Intellectual Property and the Victorian Novel* (Oxford University Press, 2004); Paul K. Saint-Amour, *The Copywrights: Intellectual Property and the Literary Imagination* (Ithaca: Cornell University Press, 2003); and Jennifer Ruth, *Novel Professions: Interested Disinterest and the Making of the Professional in the Victorian Novel* (Columbus: Ohio State University Press, 2006).

19. See John Guillory, *Cultural Capital: The Problem of Literary Canon Formation* (University of Chicago Press, 1993), esp. ch. 5, 'The Discourse of Value from Adam Smith to Barbara Herrnstein Smith'; and Mary Poovey, *Genres of the Credit Economy: Mediating Value in Eighteenth- and Nineteenth-Century Britain* (University of Chicago Press, 2008).

20. The literature on Victorian materiality and 'thing' theory is large. For particularly interesting interpretations with specific reference to Eliot, see Elaine Freedgood, *The Ideas in Things: Fugitive Meaning in the Victorian Novel* (University of Chicago Press, 2006); Daniel Hack, *The Material Interests of the Victorian Novel* (Charlottesville: University of Virginia Press, 2005); Andrew H. Miller, *Novels Behind Glass: Commodity Culture and Victorian Narrative* (Cambridge University Press, 1995); Jeff Nunokawa, *The Afterlife of Property: Domestic Security and the Victorian Novel* (Princeton University Press, 1994); and Deborah Wynne, *Women and Personal Property in the Victorian Novel* (Farnham: Ashgate, 2010).

21. Simon R. Frost, *The Business of the Novel: Economics, Aesthetics and the Case of Middlemarch* (London: Pickering and Chatto, 2012).
22. Alexander Welsh, *George Eliot and Blackmail* (Cambridge, Mass.: Harvard University Press, 1985).
23. Gordon S. Haight, *George Eliot: A Biography* (Oxford: Clarendon Press, 1968); Rosemary Ashton, *George Eliot: A Life* (London: Hamish Hamilton, 1996); Nancy Henry, *The Life of George Eliot* (Chichester: Wiley-Blackwell, 2012).
24. Gillian Beer, *George Eliot* (Brighton: Harvester Press, 1986); Deirdre David, *Intellectual Women and Victorian Patriarchy: Harriet Martineau, Elizabeth Barrett Browning, George Eliot* (Ithaca: Cornell University Press, 1987).
25. Pettitt, *Patent Inventions*; Rosemary Bodenheimer, *The Real Life of Mary Ann Evans: George Eliot, Her Letters and Fiction* (Ithaca: Cornell University Press, 1994). For earlier critics and biographers who addressed Eliot and economics from various perspectives, see, for example: Daniel Cottom, *Social Figures: George Eliot, Social History, and Literary Representation* (Minneapolis: University of Minnesota Press, 1987); Ruby V. Redinger, *George Eliot: The Emergent Self* (New York: Alfred A. Knopf, 1975); Kristin Brady, *George Eliot* (New York: St Martin's Press, 1992); and Dorothea Barrett, *Vocation and Desire: George Eliot's Heroines* (London: Routledge, 1989).
26. Nancy Henry, *George Eliot and the British Empire* (Cambridge University Press, 2002).
27. Most notably Martha Nussbaum, *Love's Knowledge: Essays on Philosophy and Literature* (Oxford University Press, 1990).
28. Alasdair MacIntyre, 'Moral Philosophy and Contemporary Social Practice: What Holds them Apart?', in *The Tasks of Philosophy: Selected Essays, Volume 1* (Cambridge University Press, 2006), 113.
29. Bernard J. Paris, *Experiments in Life: George Eliot's Quest for Values* (Detroit: Wayne State University Press, 1965), vii.
30. William Myers, *The Teaching of George Eliot* (New Jersey: Barnes & Noble, 1984), qtd 1; Valerie A. Dodd, *George Eliot: An Intellectual Life* (Basingstoke: Macmillan, 1990); Elizabeth Deeds Ermath, *George Eliot* (Boston: Twayne, 1985); and K. M. Newton, *George Eliot: Romantic Humanist* (London: Macmillan, 1981).
31. Barbara Hardy, *George Eliot: A Critic's Biography* (London: Continuum, 2006), 23.
32. Avrom Fleishman, *George Eliot's Intellectual Life* (Cambridge University Press, 2010).
33. George Gissing, *New Grub Street*, ed. John Goode (Oxford University Press, 1993), 9.
34. Pettitt, *Patent Inventions*, 214.
35. George Eliot, *Impressions of Theophrastus Such*, ed. Nancy Henry (London: William Pickering, 1994), 79–80.
36. George Eliot, 'Leaves from a Note-Book', in *Essays of George Eliot*, ed. Thomas Pinney (London: Routledge & Kegan Paul, 1963), 446. Hereafter, '*Essays*'.
37. Bruce Mazlish, *A New Science: The Breakdown of Connections and the Birth of Sociology* (University Park, Pa.: Pennsylvania State University Press, 1989),

129–143. See also John R. Searle, *Making the Modern World: The Structure of Human Civilization* (Oxford University Press, 2010) for a recent analysis of the structure of human institutions.

1 'A SUBJECT OF WHICH I KNOW SO LITTLE': GEORGE ELIOT AND POLITICAL ECONOMY

1. John Ruskin, 'The Roots of Honour', in '*Unto this Last': Four Essays on the First Principles of Political Economy* (London: George Allen, 1907), 1. The essays first appeared in the *Cornhill Magazine* in the last four months of 1860.
2. Walter Bagehot, 'The Postulates of English Political Economy – I', in *Economic Studies* (London: Longmans, Green, 1880), reprinted in *The Collected Works of Walter Bagehot*, ed. Norman St John-Stevas, 15 vols. (London: The Economist, 1965–86), XI, 238. First published in the *Fortnightly Review*, 1 February 1876, 215–42. Bagehot died in March, 1877.
3. *Westminster Review*, 22 (July–Oct. 1862), 531.
4. The 1885 edition. See Bagehot, *Collected Works*, XI, 196.
5. *Ibid.*, XI, 223.
6. Winch, *Wealth and Life*, 2.
7. David Carroll, *George Eliot and the Conflict of Interpretations: A Reading of the Novels* (Cambridge University Press, 1992), 9.
8. John Maynard Keynes, 'Alfred Marshall 1842–1924', in A. C. Pigou (ed.), *Memorials of Alfred Marshall* (London: Macmillan, 1925), 57.
9. George Eliot, *The George Eliot Letters*, ed. Gordon S. Haight, 9 vols. (New Haven: Yale University Press, 1954–1978), I, 45. Hereafter, '*Letters*'.
10. *Ibid.*, I, 104.
11. *Ibid.*, VIII, 28.
12. *Ibid.*, I, 351. The phrase is taken from a letter from Chapman to Mill, attempting to clarify the aims of the *Review* under its new ownership.
13. *Ibid.*, II, 414.
14. For colourful descriptions of the various financial crises and a history of the currency debates, see David Kynaston, *The City of London, Volume I: A World of its Own 1815–1890* (London: Chatto & Windus, 1994). The best contemporary accounts were provided by Evans, *History of the Commercial Crisis*, and *Speculative Notes and Notes on Speculation, Ideal and Real* (London: Groombridge and Sons, 1864). The 1857 crisis temporarily brought down John Cross's family business, Dennistoun Cross, for whom he was working in New York at that time. See Stanley Chapman, *The Rise of Merchant Banking* (London: Allen & Unwin, 1984), 74.
15. See note 79 below for Smith's definitive statement on labour value.
16. Poovey, *Genres*, 16.
17. Martin Daunton, *Wealth and Welfare: An Economic and Social History of Britain, 1851–1951* (Oxford University Press, 2007), 276.
18. *Essays*, 46.

19. *Ibid.*, 216.
20. *Letters*, III, 411.
21. Baker, *The George Eliot–George Henry Lewes Library*, xxvi.
22. The collection at Dr Williams's Library totals 2,405 items. In addition, about 1,200 were sold at auction in 1923 and a catalogue of 1,046 was made by a descendant of Lewes of books remaining in the family. It is not known what proportion of these collections comprise the original library.
23. George Eliot, *Felix Holt, The Radical*, ed. Fred C. Thomson (Oxford: Clarendon Press, 1980), 192.
24. The very opening sentence of the work draws the battle lines: 'The produce of the earth – all that is derived from its surface by the united application of labour, machinery and capital, is divided among three classes of the community; namely, the proprietor of the land, the owner of the stock or capital necessary for its cultivation, and the labourers by whose industry it is cultivated.' David Ricardo, *On the Principles of Political Economy and Taxation*, Volume I of *The Works and Correspondence of David Ricardo*, ed. Piero Sraffa, 11 vols. (Indianapolis: Liberty Fund, 2004), 5.
25. George Eliot, *Silas Marner*, ed. Terence Cave (Oxford University Press, 2008), 21.
26. George Eliot, *Middlemarch*, ed. David Carroll (Oxford: Clarendon Press, 1986), 16.
27. *Letters*, VI, 163.
28. *Ibid.*, IV, 196.
29. *Journals*, 124–6. Fawcett himself was greatly influenced by Mill. *The Economic Position of the British Labourer* (London: Macmillan, 1865) takes up one of the more disputed areas of Mill's *Principles*: 'You will then be able to perceive that employers and employed would both be benefited by the introduction of some system of Co-partnership between capital and labour' (9).
30. Leslie Stephen, *The English Utilitarians*, 3 vols. (London: Duckworth, 1900), III, 53.
31. *Letters*, II, 68.
32. John Stuart Mill, *Collected Works of John Stuart Mill*, gen. ed. John M. Robson, 33 vols. (University of Toronto Press, 1963–1991), III, 805–6.
33. *Ibid.*, III, 811.
34. *Letters*, II, 70.
35. *Ibid.* Mill, in the *Principles*, also describes tax on newspapers as 'objectionable'. *Collected Works*, III, 861. The economic boundaries of the state and the individual is discussed further in Chapter 8.
36. Mill, *Collected Works*, II, 199: '[The distribution of wealth] is a matter of human institution solely.'
37. *Letters*, II, 62.
38. Eliot, *Middlemarch*, 18.
39. Smiles is characteristically forthright on the subject of 'Money': 'the patriotism of this day has but little regard for such common things as individual economy and providence, although it is by the practice of such virtues only that the

genuine independence of the industrial classes is to be secured'. Samuel Smiles, *Self Help: With illustrations of Character, Conduct and Perseverance*, ed. Peter W. Sinnema (Oxford University Press, 2002), 243.

40. Maurice Dobb, *Theories of Value and Distribution since Adam Smith: Ideology and Economic Theory* (Cambridge University Press, 1973), 137. Dobb refers specifically to William Thompson, Thomas Hodgskin, J. F. Bray and John Gray.

41. *Letters*, I, 161.

42. *Essays*, 285.

43. Quoted and discussed in D. Weinstein, *Equal Freedom and Utility: Herbert Spencer's Liberal Utilitarianism* (Cambridge University Press, 2006), 182–96. See also W. C. Owen, *The Economics of Herbert Spencer*, 1891 edn (Honolulu: University Press of the Pacific, 2002) for a late nineteenth-century socialist perspective.

44. *Letters*, II, 14.

45. Mill, *Collected Works*, II, 214.

46. Most notably bk. 4, ch. 7, 'On the Probable Futurity of the Labouring Classes', Mill, *Collected Works*, III. He writes in the *Autobiography* that this chapter 'is entirely due to' Harriet Taylor. *Ibid.*, I, 255.

47. See Chapter 8 below for the couple's position on socialism and Eliot's politics more generally.

48. *Letters*, VI, 46.

49. Mill, *Collected Works*, III, 763.

50. Her own views were in direct contrast to those voiced by her earlier character Tomlinson, the rich miller who, in the opening chapter of 'Janet's Repentance', argues against any form of education for the lower classes: 'Give me a servant as can nayther read nor write, I say, and doesn't know the year o' the Lord was born in.' George Eliot, *Scenes of Clerical Life*, ed. Thomas A. Noble (Oxford University Press, 2000).

51. Eliot, *Felix Holt*, 249.

52. George Eliot, *Adam Bede*, ed. Carol A. Martin (Oxford: Clarendon Press, 2001), 200–1. The labour theory of value united orthodox political economics and the science's opponents, including Carlyle and Ruskin, and is affirmed in Eliot's portrayal of virtuous working heroes and characters (Adam Bede, Felix Holt, Caleb Garth). See Kreisel, *Economic Woman*, Chapter 2, for a reading of Adam Bede that traces the passing of the pastoral way of life and the movement from a barter to a credit economy.

53. Thomas Carlyle, 'Signs of the Times', in *The Works of Thomas Carlyle*, Centenary Edition, 30 vols. (London: Chapman and Hall, 1898), XXVII, 'Critical and Miscellaneous Essays II', 60. Note also how Silas Marner's work in Raveloe is first described by reference to the unnatural but still-organic imagery of the spider, before increasingly mechanistic metaphors take over as his obsession with gold intensifies (ch. 2).

54. *Essays*, 213. See, for example, Mill, *Collected Works*, II, 105, on the need of the English to 'moderate the ardour of their devotion to the pursuit of wealth'.

55. *Essays*, 288. For Eliot's relation to later economic sociology, see the reading of *Romola* in Chapter 7 below.
56. *Letters*, II, 46.
57. See Henry William Spiegel, *The Growth of Economic Thought*, 3rd edn (Durham: Duke University Press, 1991), 24–34.
58. *Letters*, II, 422.
59. Quoted in David Carroll (ed.), *George Eliot: The Critical Heritage* (London: Routledge & Kegan Paul, 1971), 167. Ruskin was writing in 1881, the year after Eliot died.
60. See Chapter 3 below. For Ruskin's economics, see Gill G. Cockram, *Ruskin and Social Reform: Ethics and Economics in the Victorian Age* (London: Tauris Academic Studies, 2007). Ruskin's influence on later socio-economic thought, discussed by Cockram in ch. 6, 'Hobson, Ruskin and New Liberalism', is also relevant to the discussion of Eliot's moral and intellectual allegiance with new liberalism in Chapter 8 below. For how Ruskin's overall notion of economics linked the consumer to the producer in an act of sympathetic projection, see David M. Craig, *John Ruskin and the Ethics of Consumption* (Charlottesville: University of Virginia Press, 2006).
61. Eliot, *Scenes of Clerical Life*, 270.
62. *Essays*, 272.
63. Baker, *The George Eliot–George Henry Lewes Library*, xxvi.
64. Henry Fawcett, *Manual of Political Economy* 4th edn (London: Macmillan, 1874), v–vi.
65. *Ibid.*, 132. The wage-fund concept stems from Adam Smith, who viewed wages as an advance or sacrifice by the provider of capital, thus adding a temporal dimension to capital.
66. As discussed in Chapter 4 below, in relation to the publicly aired dispute between Jevons and the defenders of Mill, Eliot and Lewes were very much allied to Cairnes in this respect. Cairnes, however, disagreed with Mill's socialist tendencies: see Winch, *Wealth and Life*, 210.
67. Quoted and discussed in *ibid.*, 195. This should not imply that Cairnes proposed restrictions in free, international trade, which he strongly supported.
68. *Ibid.*, 134. In his obituary of Cairnes, reprinted in Bagehot, *Works*, IX, Bagehot wrote that 'he defines better, as we think, than any previous writer, the exact sort of science which political economy is, the kind of reasoning which it uses, and the nature of the relation which it, as an abstract science, bears to the concrete world' (401–3).
69. See Stefan Collini, Donald Winch and John Burrow, *That Noble Science of Politics: A Study in Nineteenth-Century Intellectual History* (Cambridge University Press, 1983), chs. 7 and 8.
70. Bagehot, *Works*, XI, 222.
71. Mill, *Collected Works*, II, xci.
72. The term derives from Julie A. Nelson, *Economics for Humans* (University of Chicago Press, 2006). A central argument of the book is that 'economies are vital, living, human-made, and shaped by our ethical choices' (4).

73. It seems clear from a number of references in the novels that she was very familiar with Smith's work. See my discussion of 'Brother Jacob' in Chapter 8. Note also the opening passage of Chapter 29 of *Felix Holt*: 'Imagine what a game at chess would be if all the chessmen had passions and intellects, more or less small and cunning . . . Yet this imaginary chess is easy compared with the game a man has to play against his fellow men with other fellow-men for his instruments' (383). This extended metaphor chimes with Smith's chessboard image in *The Theory of Moral Sentiments*. Adam Smith, *The Theory of Moral Sentiments*, ed. D. D. Raphael and A. L. Macfie (Oxford: Clarendon Press, 1976), 234.
74. Eliot, *Adam Bede*, 63.
75. Mill, *Collected Works*, I, 243. His own work attempts to treat 'Political Economy not as a thing by itself, but as a fragment of a greater whole; a branch of Social Philosophy, so interlinked with all the other branches, that its conclusions, even in its own peculiar province, are only true conditionally.'
76. Alfred Marshall, *Principles of Economics*, 8th edn (1920) (New York: Prometheus, 1997), 4.
77. W. Stanley Jevons, *The Theory of Political Economy*, ed. R. D. Collison Black (Harmondsworth: Penguin, 1970), 44.
78. *Letters*, III, 396.
79. Adam Smith, *An Inquiry into the Nature and Causes of the Wealth of Nations*, ed. R. H. Campbell and A. S. Skinner, textual ed. W. B. Todd (Oxford: Clarendon Press, 1976), I, 51: 'Labour alone, therefore, never varying in its own value, is alone the ultimate and real standard by which the value of all commodities can at all times and places be estimated and compared. It is their real price; money is their nominal price only.'

2 'INTENTIONS OF STERN THRIFT': THE FORMATION OF A VERNACULAR ECONOMICS

1. *Letters*, III, 118.
2. [W. R. Greg], 'Political Economy', *Westminster Review*, 84 (Jan. 1865), 106–33 (125).
3. See Harold Perkin, *The Origins of Modern English Society, 1780–1800* (London: Routledge & Kegan Paul, 1969), 420. Stefan Collini, *Public Moralists: Political Thought and Intellectual Life in Britain 1850–1930* (Oxford: Clarendon Press, 1991), 35–50, gives data on the comparative earnings of different professions.
4. Smiles, *Self Help*, 17. Eliot read Smiles's *Life of George Stephenson* (1857) – in which many of the virtues promoted in *Self Help* are given human embodiment – in the year of its publication, finding it 'a real profit and pleasure' (*Letters*, II, 369). Adrian Jarvis, in his biography of Smiles, shows how the hagiographic treatment of the great engineer involved the suppression of his financial acumen during the speculative railway boom of the 1840s, including practices of which Smiles was otherwise extremely critical. Adrian Jarvis, *Samuel Smiles and the Construction of Victorian Values* (Stroud: Sutton Publishing, 1997), 27–28 and 86–91.

5. For Spencer, individualism and thrift as an essential component of 'character' in the 1880s; see Regenia Gagnier, *Individualism, Decadence and Globalization: On the Relationship of Part to Whole, 1859–1920* (Basingstoke: Palgrave Macmillan, 2010), 31.

6. Boyd Hilton, *The Age of Atonement: The Influence of Evangelicalism on Social Thought 1785–1865* (Oxford: Clarendon Press, 1988), viii.

7. T. Chalmers, *On the Power, Wisdom and Goodness of God as Manifested in the Adaptation of External Nature to the Moral and Intellectual Constitution of Man* (London, 1853), quoted in G. R. Searle, *Morality and the Market in Victorian Britain* (Oxford: Clarendon Press, 1998), 12. Eliot records her excitement on receiving a six volume edition of Chalmers's Sermons in 1841. *Letters*, I, 104.

8. A. M. C. Waterman, *Revolution, Economics and Religion: Christian Political Economy, 1798–1833* (Cambridge University Press, 1991), 3.

9. See pages 26 and 154 regarding Eliot's letter to Jane Senior.

10. *Letters*, III, 168.

11. Robert Evans to Francis Newdigate, 13 September 1834, quoted in Ashton, *Life*, 15.

12. *Ibid.*, ch. 2.

13. *Letters*, III, 351.

14. *Ibid.*, VII, 106.

15. Boyd Hilton, *The New Oxford History of England: A Mad, Bad, and Dangerous People? England 1783–1846* (Oxford: Clarendon Press, 2006), 366. Marcet's *Conversations on Political Economy* appeared in 1824 and Martineau's *Illustrations of Political Economy* in 1832.

16. *Letters*, III, 69.

17. *Ibid.*, II, 145.

18. *Ibid.*, II, 350. Redinger, *The Emergent Self*, 337–41, describes perceptively how, in the months after her elopement, she adopted various strategies to ensure that she was able to preserve that independence by continuing to receive the income from her inheritance while initially concealing then obscuring from her brother Isaac the facts of her change in situation.

19. The Married Women's Property Acts were passed in 1870 (allowing women to legally own their earned income and inherit property) and, more substantively, in 1882. For data on the growing prevalence of women investors around this time, see Green *et al.*, *Men, Women and Money*; and David R. Green and Alastair Owens, 'Gentlewomanly Capitalism? Spinsters, Widows, and Wealth Holding in England and Wales, c. 1800–1860', *Economic History Review*, LVI (2003), 510–36.

20. See Margot C. Finn, *The Character of Credit: Personal Debt in English Culture, 1740–1914* (Cambridge University Press, 2003). Eliot's views on debt, however, are very much in line with those of Smiles, and, interestingly, contrary to those of both St Simon and Comte who, according to Patrick Brantlinger, 'treated credit as a social-mystical category . . . Credit was the spiritual energy that fuelled materialist, industrial progress.' Patrick Brantlinger, *Fictions of State: Culture and Credit in Britain, 1694–1994* (Ithaca: Cornell University Press, 1996), 138.

21. George Eliot, *The Mill on the Floss*, ed. Gordon S. Haight (Oxford: Clarendon Press, 1980), 244.
22. *Letters*, III, 351.
23. See Krista Lysack, *Come Buy, Come Buy: Shopping and the Culture of Consumption in Victorian Women's Writing* (Athens: Ohio University Press, 2008) for a discussion of the contrast between Rosamond's status-defining extravagance and Dorothea's thrift and an attempt to locate both behavioural patterns in relation to more traditional forms of domestic management. These themes are also explored by Miller, *Novels Behind Glass*. Dorothea's relation to 'things' is perceptively analysed by Elaine Freedgood as an illustration of Eliot's narratorial reduction of the metonymic to the metaphoric as an attempt 'to reduce or anticipate the random way in which things, as they are read by readers, take on meaning' (*The Ideas in Things*, 112). For related discussion, see Chapter 5 below.
24. Barbara Weiss, *The Hell of the English: Bankruptcy and the Victorian Novel* (Lewisburg: Bucknell University Press, 1986).
25. *Ibid.*, 29.
26. *Ibid*, esp. ch. 2.
27. *Letters*, IV, 375 – a consequence of the banking and stock market crisis of 1866–7.
28. *Ibid.*, II, 163.
29. Her final act of benevolence to the family was financial and substantial, with the bequest in her will of £5,000 to Chrissy's daughter, Emily.
30. Stefanie Markovits, *The Crisis of Action in Nineteenth-Century Literature* (Columbus: Ohio State University Press, 2006), 97, describing Eliot's somewhat utilitarian weighing of the consequences of eloping with Lewes.
31. *Letters*, I, 236. See also Bodenheimer, *The Real Life of Mary Ann Evans*, who characterises Eliot's letter-writing 'as a system of credits and debts' (20); and describes her use of 'moral mathematics' (100) in confronting ethical choices involving conflicting claims of duty.
32. Eliot, *Middlemarch*, 250; *Silas Marner*, 169; *Romola*, 430.
33. *Letters*, VII, 138. The incident gives an indication of the breadth of the calls on her money: Vivian Lewes was Lewes's niece, the daughter of his brother, Edward; Mde Belloc was Eliot's old friend, Bessie Rayner Parkes.
34. See Ashton, *Life*, 34–5. Frank Christianson, *Philanthropy in British and American Fiction: Dickens, Hawthorne, Eliot and Howells* (Edinburgh University Press, 2007) argues that philanthropy could be read as both a critique and a redeeming consequence of capitalism and its widening of wealth inequality (140).
35. See J. D. Y. Peel, *Herbert Spencer: The Evolution of a Sociologist* (London: Heinemann, 1971), ch. 8, 'Militancy and Industrialism'.
36. *Letters*, I, 141.
37. *Ibid.*, II, 74.
38. *Ibid.*, II, 97.
39. 'The Progress of the Intellect', *Westminster Review*, 54 (Jan. 1851), 353–68, in *Essays*, 27.

40. See T. R. Wright, *The Religion of Humanity: The Impact of Comtean Positivism on Victorian Britain* (Cambridge University Press, 1986), 173. See also Peel, *Evolution of a Sociologist*, and Thomas Dixon, *The Invention of Altruism: Making Moral Meanings in Victorian Britain* (London: British Academy, 2008). Fleishman, *Intellectual Life*, is the latest of Eliot's intellectual biographers to question the extent of Comte's influence on her thought (59–68).

41. Wright, *The Religion of Humanity*, 174, in reference to 'Evangelical Teaching: Dr. Cumming' (Oct. 1855); and 'Worldliness and Other-Worldliness: The Poet Young' (Jan. 1857). For the influence of Feuerbach in relation to altruism, see, for example, Myers, *The Teaching of George Eliot*, 4–8.

42. She uses a financial image to argue that Cumming reduces human motivation for justice and compassion to a fear of divine consequences: 'Dr Cumming's Christian pays his debts for the glory of God; were it not for the coercion of that supreme motive, it would be evil to pay them' (*Essays*, 187).

43. Hilton, *Atonement*, esp. part 3 'After the Age of Atonement'. See also David Payne, *The Reenchantment of Nineteenth-Century Fiction: Dickens, Thackeray, George Eliot, and Serialization* (Basingstoke: Palgrave Macmillan, 2005).

44. Searle, *Morality*, 15–26.

45. John Lalor, *Money and Morals, A Book for the Times* (London: John Chapman, 1852), 132.

46. See Winch, *Wealth and Life*, 59–60.

47. 'The Morals of Trade', *Westminster Review*, 71 (Apr. 1859), 357–90 (385).

48. *Ibid.*, 356.

49. *Ibid.*, 389.

50. See Gagnier, *Individualism*: 'Essential to the story told in *The Wealth of Nations* (1776) was its many ironies that yoked Hobbesian self-interested rationality and the altruism of the civic humanists into a theory of social Progress' (28).

51. Smith, *Wealth of Nations*, 1, 267.

52. *Essays*, 93.

53. Eliot, *The Mill on the Floss*, 103. The passage is quoted and discussed by Miller, *Novels Behind Glass*, 5, in his introductory comments on the impact of glass-making technology, shop-window displays and consumer culture in the mid-nineteenth century.

54. Henry, *George Eliot and the British Empire*, 91. Ch. 3, 'Investing in Empire' is the most detailed investigation of Eliot as an investor I have yet come across.

55. *Letters*, II, 184.

56. *Letters*, III, 360.

57. British overseas investment was estimated to be £208 million in 1850, rising to £1.065 billion in 1875 and to £2.397 billion by the end of the century. Lance E. Davis and Robert E. Gallman, *Evolving Financial Markets and International Capital Flows: Britain, the Americas, and Australia, 1865–1914* (Cambridge University Press, 2001), 55.

58. Benson's name lives on in the City to this day. Cross withdrew from the partnership in 1884 and the business reverted to Robert Benson & Co which, in 1947, merged with Lonsdale Investment Trust. This entity in turn merged with

Kleinwort, Sons & Co to create Kleinwort Benson in 1961. Despite a number of changes of ownership since the mid-1990s, the Kleinwort Benson name has survived.

59. See Chapman, *Merchant Banking*, ch. 5.

60. Henry, *George Eliot and the British Empire*, 141–9.

61. My own analysis shows the following geographical exposure of her final portfolio: UK 48 per cent, Empire 32 per cent, USA 17 per cent, Europe 3 per cent, although all the securities were denominated in sterling. Railways were easily the largest weighting by industry group, followed by smaller exposures to banks, canals, gas and miscellaneous. Mining represented just 5 per cent. See Appendix A.

62. In preparation for writing *Daniel Deronda*, Eliot took notes on R. A. Procter's article 'Gambling Superstitions', *Cornhill Magazine*, 25 (June 1872), 704–17. Procter refers to the probability calculations and elaboration of the law of large numbers described in Steinmetz's *The Gaming Table* and cites de Morgan on probability. For Venn's work on probability, including his rebuttal of Henry Buckle's influential theories of determinism, see Helen Small, 'Chances Are: Henry Buckle, Thomas Hardy, and the Individual at Risk', in Helen Small and Trudi Tate (eds.), *Literature, Science, Psychoanalysis, 1830–1970: Essays in Honour of Gillian Beer* (Oxford University Press, 2003), 64–85.

63. Henry Lowenfeld produced the earliest substantive work on portfolio diversification theory in 1907.

64. Bank runs formed part of the collective financial memory of Eliot's generation. In *Felix Holt*, Mr Nolan recalls a story from an old banker friend from the crisis of 1816, three years before the author was born: 'a gentleman came in with bags of gold and said "Tell Mr. Gottlib there's plenty more where that came from"' (179).

65. Davis and Gallman, *Evolving Financial Markets*, 165.

66. *Letters*, vi, 344.

67. See Appendix A.

68. *Letters*, iii, 323.

69. Mary Poovey, *Making a Social Body: British Cultural Formation, 1830–1864* (University of Chicago Press, 1995), 23. In *Genres of the Credit Economy*, Poovey explores the social processes that served to 'naturalise' money and money derivatives in their evolution from precious metals to complex and abstract credit and equity instruments (16).

70. Donna Loftus, 'Capital and Community: Limited Liability and Attempts to Democratize the Market in Mid-Nineteenth-Century England', *Victorian Studies*, 45, 1 (2002), Special Issue, 'Victorian Investments', 93–120. See also Timothy L. Alborn, *Conceiving Companies: Joint-Stock Politics in Victorian England* (London: Routledge, 1998), and James Taylor, *Creating Capitalism: Joint-Stock Enterprise in British Politics and Culture, 1800–1870* (Woodbridge: Boydell Press, 2006).

71. J. R. McCulloch, *Considerations on Partnerships with Limited Liability* (London: Longman, Brown, Green & Longmans, 1856).

72. 'Partnership With Limited Liability', *Westminster Review*, 60 (Oct. 1853), 382–5.
73. *Ibid.*, 414.
74. See Wagner, *Financial Speculation in Victorian Fiction* for an extensive analysis. John R. Reed, 'A Friend to Mammon: Speculation in Victorian Literature', *Victorian Studies* 27 (1983–4), 179–202, provides a still useful summary. More recently, Mary Poovey has wryly observed: 'It is a truth universally acknowledged that mid-nineteenth-century novelists represented financial matters in ethical and moral terms' (*Genres*, 373).
75. See David C. Itzkowitz, 'Fair Enterprise or Extravagant Speculation: Investment, Speculation, and Gambling in Victorian England', *Victorian Studies*, 45, 1 (2002), Special Issue, 'Victorian Investments', 121–47.
76. It is interesting, however, that, in a memorable passage in 'The Lifted Veil', she seems to recognise the urge to speculate as an instinctive characteristic of the unfettered individual: 'if the whole future were laid bare to us beyond to-day, the interest of all mankind would be bent on the hours that lie between; we should pant after the uncertainties of our one morning and our one afternoon; we should rush fiercely to the Exchange for our last possibility of speculation, of success, of disappointment'. George Eliot, 'The Lifted Veil', in '*The Lifted Veil' and 'Brother Jacob*', ed. Helen Small (Oxford University Press, 1999), 29. Nonetheless, Claire Pettitt's observation that 'Capitalist activity is figured by Latimer throughout the story as violent and repugnant, unreflective and grossly material' (*Patent Inventions*, 242) is surely correct.
77. Hardy, *A Critic's Biography*, 65.
78. Henry, *George Eliot and the British Empire*, 89.
79. The argument Felix uses against the immediate widening of the franchise – that the working classes must first be educated in order properly to understand and employ their increased rights – was one used in the context of democratising the capital markets by opponents of limited liability.
80. George Eliot, *Daniel Deronda*, ed. Graham Handley (Oxford University Press, 1984), 157. In 'Brother Jacob', the morality of monetising literary creation is called into even greater question by David Faux, who applies his knowledge of 'imaginative literature' (i.e. the creation of Freely) to 'practical purposes' (79).
81. *Letters*, v, 127, and vi, 65.
82. Bodichon founded *The English Woman's Journal* in 1857, which was edited by Rayner Parks. Bodichon's influential essay 'Women and Work', which Eliot read, was published in the same year. The heart of the criticism against Eliot lies in comments she made such as the following, in an 1869 letter to Jane Senior: 'There is no subject on which I am more inclined to hold my peace and learn, than on the "Woman Question." It seems to me to overhang abysses, of which even prostitution is not the worst. Conclusions seem easy so long as we keep large blinkers on and look in the direction of our own private path' (*Letters*, v, 58). See Beer, *George Eliot*, ch. 6, '*Middlemarch* and "The Woman Question"'.
83. *Letters*, iii, 293. Leslie Stephen, for one, was in doubt of the wider social value of her novels. Writing to his sister-in-law, Anny Thackeray, in 1875 on the relative

merits of charitable giving versus writing, he proclaims: 'Good literature has an immense influence. George Eliot has influenced people more than if she had given away millions.' Quoted in Noel Annan, *Leslie Stephen: The Godless Victorian* (London: Weidenfeld and Nicholson, 1984), 74.

3 'A MONEY-GETTING PROFESSION': NEGOTIATING THE COMMERCE OF LITERATURE

1. Quoted in John Brewer, *The Pleasures of the Imagination: English Culture in the Eighteenth Century* (London: Harper Collins, 1997), 149.
2. *Journals*, 108.
3. Pierre Bourdieu, *The Field of Cultural Production: Essays on Art and Literature*, ed. and intro. by Randal Johnson (Cambridge: Polity Press, 1993), 40.
4. Bourdieu, *Cultural Production*, 42.
5. *Ibid.*, 46.
6. For example, Pettitt, *Patent Inventions*; Bodenheimer, *The Real Life of Mary Ann Evans*; Saint-Amour, *The Copywrights*; Poovey, *Genres*; and N. N. Feltes, *Modes of Production of Victorian Novels* (University of Chicago Press, 1986).
7. Robert Darnton, 'What is the History of Books?', *The Kiss of Lamourette: Reflections in Cultural History* (New York: W. W. Norton, 1990), 107.
8. *Letters*, II, 152.
9. Poovey traces the development of the pre-modern literary critic around this time: 'even though reviewers were trying to acquire the social authority to make their judgements more decisive than the crude measure of popularity or sales, they had yet to cultivate a *technical* vocabulary that would immediately distinguish between the way they evaluated novels and the way less expert readers did' (*Genres*, 378). Cottom, however, highlights the developing hierarchy of the reviewing industry itself, an institutional delineation associated with the formation of the 'middle-class intellectual', a process in which Eliot directly participated: 'As Blackwood's and the *Edinburgh*, *Quarterly* and *Westminster* reviews especially assumed a position as cultural arbiters, they catered to ... the growing assumption among the middle and upper classes that matters of public interest were matters of intellectual argument before all else' (*Social Figures*, 5).
10. 'Translations and Translators', *Leader, VI* (20 October 1855), in *Essays*, 207–11.
11. Her calculation of the price per page she earned from her translation of Feuerbach is an ironic foreshadowing of Trollope's dryly quantitative enumeration and analysis of his literary output and earnings. Anthony Trollope, *An Autobiography*, ed. Michael Sadlier and Frederick Page (Oxford University Press, 1998), 363.
12. *Letters*, II, 130–1. For background to this incident, see Rosemary Ashton, *142 Strand: A Radical Address in Victorian London* (London: Chatto & Windus, 2006), 196.
13. See James J. Barnes, *Free Trade in Books: A Study of the London Book Trade Since 1800* (Oxford: Clarendon Press, 1964) for a detailed discussion of the debate.

14. [John Chapman], 'The Commerce of Literature', *Westminster Review* 57 (Apr. 185), 511–54 (511).
15. Ashton, *142 The Strand*, 146–51.
16. *Letters*, II, 23, records her first sighting of Dickens, who chaired the meeting of the association's opponents at Chapman's house on 4 May 1852.
17. Barnes, *Free Trade in Books*, 90.
18. See Saint-Amour, *The Copywrights* for a description of attempts by free trade liberals to abolish copyright in the late 1870s, a position opposed by Herbert Spencer.
19. Eliot, *Impressions of Theophrastus Such*, 91, 88.
20. 'Leaves from a Note-Book', in *Essays*, 439. First published four years after her death by Charles Lewes, who loosely dates their composition 'some time between the appearance of "Middlemarch" and "Theophrastus Such"'. Pettitt argues that the formation of ideas of literary ownership and value, including debates on copyright, did not occur in academic isolation 'but, in fact, took place as part of a much wider reconceptualization of labour, and particularly of mental labour' (*Patent Inventions*, 2).
21. The passage is discussed by Gallagher, *Body Economic*, 118–20.
22. *Essays*, 438–40.
23. *Essays*, 303–4, 324. For an informative discussion of this article alongside the earlier 'Woman in France: Madam de Sable' (1854), see David, *Intellectual Women*, 181–7.
24. *Journals*, 145. See Gallagher, *Body Economic*, 118; and Bodenheimer, *The Real Life of Mary Ann Evans*, 175.
25. *Letters*, II, 377. See also, Trollope, *Autobiography*, on the great historical and contemporary writers: 'I may say that none of those neglected the pecuniary results of their labour' (106).
26. *Letters*, III, 212.
27. Feltes, *Modes of Production*, 46.
28. Quoted in Redinger, *The Emergent Self*, 384.
29. *Letters*, II, 247.
30. *Ibid.*, II, 47. A good example is her portrayal of Mr Deane in *The Mill on the Floss*; see pp. 109–10, below.
31. *Ibid.*, IV, 274.
32. *Ibid.*, V, 184.
33. *Ibid.*, II, 467.
34. *Ibid.*, III, 334.
35. *Ibid.*, III, 465.
36. *Ibid.*, IV, 313. For product advertising in the serialised editions of *Middlemarch* and *Daniel Deronda*, see, respectively, Gillian Beer, 'What's Not in *Middlemarch*', in Karen Chase (ed.), *Middlemarch in the 21st Century* (Oxford University Press, 2006), 15–35; and Hack, *Material Interests*, ch. 5, 'Moses and the Advertisement Sheet: *Daniel Deronda's* Earthly Mixtures'.
37. *Letters*, II, 508.

38. The progression, quoted by Haight, was as follows: *Adam Bede* £30, *The Mill on the Floss* £300, *Middlemarch* £1,200, *Daniel Deronda* £1,700 (*Letters*, II, 509).
39. *Ibid.*, II, 73, 75, 78. See Bodenheimer, *The Real Life of Mary Ann Evans*, 121–43, 169 for the commercial aspects of the distance initially preserved between 'Marian Evans/Lewes' and 'George Eliot'.
40. *Letters*, II, 94.
41. *Ibid.*, II, 115.
42. See David Finkelstein, *The House of Blackwood: Author–Publisher Relations in the Victorian Era* (University Park, Pa.: Pennsylvania State University Press, 2002), esp. 28–34.
43. *Letters*, II, 160.
44. *Ibid.*, II, 151.
45. *Ibid.*, II, 204.
46. *Ibid.*, III, 118. See Bodenheimer, *The Real Life of Mary Ann Evans*, 129, for the evolution of Eliot's signature: 'the connection between the fictional married name and the pseudonym is a tantalising one. If she could be George Eliot, why not Marian Lewes?'
47. See note 72, Chapter 1, above for 'human economics'.
48. Feltes, *Modes of Production*, 46.
49. *Letters*, III, 172–3.
50. *Ibid.*, III, 235.
51. *Journals*, 82.
52. *Letters*, III, 219.
53. *Ibid.*, IV, 373.
54. *Ibid.*, III, 369.
55. See 'Worldliness and Other-Worldliness: The Poet Young', *Westminster Review* 67 (Jan. 1857), in *Essays*, 335–85, for the potential of patronage to suppress independent artistic expression. Pinney characterises the essay as 'an episode in the long history of the nineteenth century's revolt from the eighteenth' (335).
56. *Letters*, IV, 438.
57. *Ibid.*, IV, 18.
58. *Ibid.*, IV, 34.
59. Susan E. Colón, *The Professional Ideal in the Victorian Novel: The Works of Disraeli, Trollope, Gaskell, and Eliot* (Basingstoke: Palgrave Macmillan, 2007), 13. See also Barrett, *Vocation and Desire*, for whom 'vocation and desire . . . in their widest possible senses . . . form a dichotomy in all George Eliot's work' (17); and Alan Mintz, *George Eliot and the Novel of Vocation* (Cambridge, Mass.: Harvard University Press, 1978), which considers, in particular, characters' vocational striving in *Middlemarch*.
60. *Letters*, III, 186.
61. *Essays*, 438.
62. *Ibid.*, 440. William R. McKelvy, *The English Cult of Literature: Devoted Readers, 1774–1880* (Charlottesville: University of Virginia Press, 2007),

explores how the vocation of literature assumed a kind of sacred function during the period.

63. *Letters*, IV, 316; and V, 441.
64. Pettitt, *Patent Inventions*, 242.
65. Bodenheimer pinpoints the Bracebridge–Liggins affair years earlier as a time when '[t]he gap between sympathetic individual readers who "recognized her" in her books and an ignorant gossiping public that recognized only a lowest common denominator was being firmly established as a paradigmatic image of her audiences' (*The Real Life of Mary Ann Evans*, 143).
66. *Journals*, 145.
67. Finkelstein, *The House of Blackwood*, 34. In October 1876, with Eliot at the peak of her popularity, Blackwood wrote to his brother urging that 'We must risk a good deal and go in for the whole works' (*Letters*, VI, 297).
68. *Letters*, III, 152.
69. *Ibid.*, II, 388.
70. *Ibid.*, III, 161.
71. *Ibid.*, III, 161.
72. *Ibid.*, V, 179.
73. *Ibid.*, III, 371.
74. See, for example, Pettitt, *Patent Inventions*, 258, and Bodenheimer, *The Real Life of Mary Ann Evans*, 230.
75. Poovey, *Genres*, 383. Gillian Beer's analysis of the 'acquired cultural language' of science during the period makes somewhat similar claims: 'It offers an imaginative shift in the valency of words, new spaces for experience to occupy in language, confirmation of some kinds of vocabulary, increased prowess in pruning, in which diverse senses are held in equipoise within the surveillance of consciousness.' *Darwin's Plots: Evolutionary Narrative in Darwin, George Eliot and Nineteenth-Century Fiction* (London: Routledge and Kegan Paul, 1983), 140.
76. *Letters*, V, 309.
77. Jerome Beaty, *Middlemarch, From Notebook to Novel: A Study of George Eliot's Critical Method* (Urbana: University of Illinois Press, 1960).
78. Her reservations towards autobiography and biography hardened with age. Just a year before she died, she wrote that 'the best history of a writer is contained in his writings' and that 'Biographies generally are a disease of English literature' (*Letters*, VII, 230).
79. *Ibid.*, VI, 65.
80. *Essays*, 451.
81. *Letters*, VI, 301.
82. Hack, *Material Interests*, 150.

4 CALCULATING CONSEQUENCES: *FELIX HOLT* AND THE LIMITS OF UTILITARIANISM

1. William Stanley Jevons, letter to J. E. Cairnes, 14 January 1872, quoted in Sandra Peart, *The Economics of W. S. Jevons* (London: Routledge, 1996), 149.

2. Eliot, *Impressions of Theophrastus Such*, 337.
3. *Letters*, VI, 216. See Paris, *Experiments in Life*, 37–9, for how the experimental elements of Eliot's art as a novelist relate to Lewes's argument, in *The Principles of Success in Literature*, that the scientific and artistic processes have a strong imaginative commonality, that is, '[t]he experimental process employed by the scientist to test his hypotheses is analogous to the novelist's invention of a story'. Victorian understandings of experimentation are discussed by Beer, *Darwin's Plots*, 148–9, 151. See also Carroll, *Conflict of Interpretations*: 'each experiment proceeds by the testing, juxtaposing, comparing, and contrasting of different ways of making sense of the world until coherence reaches its limit and breaks down into incoherence' (2).
4. Eliot, *The Mill on the Floss*, 172. Subsequent references will appear in the text.
5. Eliot, *Felix Holt*, 288: a description of Maurice Christian, who features in the discussion later in this chapter. See Miller, *Novels Behind Glass*, 209–12, for a discussion of auctions in *Middlemarch*. Trumbull, the auctioneer, 'uses language to inflate the worth of the objects he sells', a practice in which authors are also potentially implicated.
6. Mill repeatedly defends Utilitarianism against those who claim that it is invalidated by the impossibility of accurately predicting consequences. Mill's argument is that general (rather than individual) classes of actions can identifiably be predicted to give rise to pleasurable or painful consequences. Riley does not appear to apply principles of either Act or Rule Utilitarianism in calculating Tom's educational utility.
7. Eliot, *Impressions of Theophrastus Such*, 53–4. Just eleven days before she died, Eliot emphasises the complexity of individual motivation. Defending the decision of a Mrs Menzies (a friend of Eliot's correspondent, Elma Stuart) to convert to Catholicism, she explains, 'I for my part would not venture to thrust my mind on hers as a sort of omniscient dictatress, when in fact I am very ignorant of the inward springs which determine her action' (*Letters*, VII, 346).
8. The literature on behavioural economics continues to expand, despite ongoing hostility from certain schools of theoretical economics. See, for example, George Loewenstein, *Exotic Preferences: Behavioural Economics and Human Motivation* (Oxford University Press, 2007). For empirical ethics, see Kwame Anthony Appiah, *Experiments in Ethics* (Cambridge, Mass.: Harvard University Press, 2008).
9. Eliot, 'Janet's Repentance', *Scenes of Clerical Life*, 270–1.
10. For Smith's moral philosophy see: Emma Rothschild, *Economic Sentiments: Adam Smith, Condorcet, and the Enlightenment* (Cambridge, Mass.: Harvard University Press, 2001); Robert Sugden, 'Beyond Sympathy and Empathy: Adam Smith's Concept of Fellow-Feeling', *Economics and Philosophy*, 18, 1 (2002), 63–87; and D. D. Raphael, *The Impartial Spectator: Adam Smith's Moral Philosophy* (Oxford: Clarendon Press, 2007). Raphael concludes that the concept of the impartial spectator was 'the most important element of Smith's ethical theory' (11). Mill uses curiously similar terminology when describing the process to be followed by the rational, calculating agent: 'As

between his own happiness and that of others, utilitarianism requires him to be as strictly impartial as a disinterested and benevolent spectator'. 'Utilitarianism', *Collected Works*, x, 218.

11. *Letters*, 1, 278. Coincidentally, Lewes was also already a great admirer of Sand at this time. Valerie Dodd traces the influence of Sand on both Eliot's and Lewes's (largely similar) theories of fiction and her part in the former's decision to write novels. See Dodd, *An Intellectual Life*, 132–42 and 213–15.

12. Nussbaum, *Love's Knowledge*, 23. She later expands her proposal, 'that we should add the study of certain novels to the study of these works [seminal Kantian and Utilitarian philosophical texts], on the grounds that without them we will not have a fully adequate statement of a powerful ethical conception, one that we ought to investigate' (26). Nussbaum's thesis that ethical perception is both cognitive and affective is also articulated by Eliot: 'And how can the life of nations be understood without the inward light of poetry – that is of emotion blending with thought' (*Letters*, vi, 124).

13. Nussbaum, *Love's Knowledge*, 29.

14. *Ibid.*, 23. The 'ethical turn' in literary studies was roughly contemporaneous with the re-emergence of an essentially Aristotelian ethics of virtue in academic moral philosophy. See Chapter 6, below, which concludes the argument that Eliot's examination of economic ethics in the novels followed a parallel progression.

15. Andrew H. Miller, *The Burdens of Perfection: On Ethics and Reading in Nineteenth-Century British Literature* (Ithaca: Cornell University Press, 2008), 62. Nussbaum's linkage of literature and 'everyday' ethics echoes Miller's lack of tidy system: 'Our actual relation to the books we love is already messy, complex, erotic' (*Love's Knowledge*, 29).

16. Courtemanche argues a similar point by reference to what she describes as an interplay between 'the worm's-eye view of the characters and the bird's-eye view of the narrator' (*The 'Invisible Hand'*, 3) in realist fiction.

17. Miller, *Burdens of Perfection*, 70. Cora Diamond makes a similar point in relation to 'classic realist novels ... [which] contain scenes of deliberation and choice, and this is necessary to the moral view they express'. Cora Diamond, 'Martha Nussbaum and the Need for Novels', in Jane Adamson, Richard Freadman and David Parker (eds.), *Renegotiating Ethics in Literature, Philosophy, and Theory* (Cambridge University Press, 1998), 49.

18. D. P. O'Brien, *The Classical Economists Revisited* (Princeton University Press, 2004), 29–31. Bentham, when enumerating 'the several simple pleasures of which human nature is susceptible', places 'the pleasures of wealth' at number two, aligning it closely with the science of wealth with which political economy was exclusively concerned. Jeremy Bentham, *Introduction to the Principles of Morals and Legislation*, in John Stuart Mill, *Utilitarianism*, ed. Mary Warnock (Glasgow: William Collins, 1962), 68.

19. Both Mills were significant contributors of economic articles from the *Review*'s earliest years, and, over a long period, had direct editorial and proprietorial

interests. John Mill's financial support – and occasional reviews – continued into the Chapman years.

20. See Frank W. Fetter, 'Economic Articles in the *Westminster Review* and Their Authors, 1824–51', *Journal of Political Economy*, 70, 6 (1962), 570–96. 'To the writers in the Westminster political economy was not the dismal science, it was a message to all men except "aristocrats" and "monopolists," and to them it was the handwriting on the wall' (573).
21. *Ibid.*, 577.
22. *Letters*, ii, 49.
23. Charles Bray, *The Philosophy of Necessity or, Natural Law as Applicable to Moral, Mental, and Social Science*, 2nd edn (London: Longman, Green, Longman & Roberts, 1863), 201.
24. Mill claims to have been the first to bring the term into common usage. 'Utilitarianism', *Collected Works*, x, 209–10. Subsequent references to the essay will appear in the text.
25. 'The Progress of the Intellect', *Westminster Review*, 54 (Jan. 1851), in *Essays*, 27–8.
26. However, one – possibly ironic – reference to the Benthamite meaning is Eliot's description of the wholly egotistical Duncan Cass, 'whose delight in lying, grandly independent of utility, was not to be diminished by the likelihood that his hearer would not believe him' (*Silas Marner*, 83). For an illuminating debate on the changing meaning of 'utility' in economic and philosophical literature from Bentham to the present, see John Broome, 'Utility', *Economics and Philosophy* 7 (1991), 1–12, and 'A Reply to Sen', *Economics and Philosophy* 7 (1991), 285–7.
27. George Eliot, *Romola*, ed. Andrew Brown (Oxford: Clarendon Press, 1993), 117.
28. Bray's *Philosophy of Necessity* has strong Utilitarian leanings, with moral ends and happiness closely linked (see, for example, 29). Bentham is frequently quoted.
29. Collini *et al.*, *That Noble Science*, 281.
30. Kathleen Blake, *Pleasures of Benthamism: Victorian Literature, Utility, Political Economy* (Oxford University Press, 2009), 31.
31. See J. B. Schneewind, *Sidgwick's Ethics and Victorian Moral Philosophy* (Oxford: Clarendon Press, 1977), 175. Mill's belief that *Social Statics* was opposed to Utilitarianism was disputed by Spencer.
32. Mill, 'Whewell on Moral Philosophy' (1852), reprinted in *Collected Works*, x, 165–201.
33. *Essays*, 376: 'This is a notion of loftiness which may pair off with Dr Whewell's celebrated observation, that Bentham's moral theory is low, because it includes justice and mercy to brutes.'
34. The debate is well covered, in the context of Jevons's wider and complex ambivalence towards Mill in Winch, *Wealth and Life*, ch. 6.
35. See Peart, *The Economics of W. S. Jevons*, 137–54.
36. 'They turned back and there was more conversation, concerning Jevons on Mill.' *Letters*, ix, 217.
37. *Ibid.*, ix, 211.

38. Fetter points to an early *Westminster Review* article by Perronet Thompson, 'On the Instrument of Exchange', which is thought to be the first English economic writing to employ calculus ('Economic Articles', 571).

39. It has been a powerful and long-standing combination. As Amartya Sen concludes, twentieth-century welfare economics 'was dominated by one particular approach, to wit, utilitarianism, initiated in its modern form by Jeremy Bentham, and championed by such economists as Mill, Edgeworth, Sidgwick, Marshall, and Pigou'. Amartya Sen, 'On the Foundations of Welfare Economics: Utility, Capability, and Practical Reason', in Francesco Farina, Frank Hahn, and Stefano Vannucci (eds.), *Ethics, Rationality and Economic Behaviour* (Oxford: Clarendon Press, 1996), 50–65 (50).

40. As Sugden explains, Bentham marks a distinct shift from Hume and Smith, both of whom were sceptical about the limits of reason, while 'the Benthamite tradition appeals to universal principles of rationality and favours stylised models of human psychology' ('Beyond Sympathy and Empathy', 64).

41. See Josephine M. Guy, *The Victorian Social-Problem Novel: The Market, the Individual and Communal Life* (Basingstoke: Macmillan, 1996); Catherine Gallagher, *The Industrial Reformation of English Fiction* (University of Chicago Press, 1985); and Brantlinger, *Fictions of State*.

42. Brantlinger, *Fictions of State*, includes a chapter on 'Benthamite and Anti-Benthamite Fiction' of the 1830s and 1840s.

43. Jevons was publishing somewhat unrelated work (known to Lewes) in the 1860s, though *The Theory of Political Economy* did not appear until 1871.

44. Schneewind, *Sidgwick's Ethics*, 174. Schneewind concludes that Mill's incorporation of common-sense morality, while, as we have seen, unacceptable to Jevons, opened the door for Sidgwick's definitive work on Rule Utilitarianism.

45. Collini, *Public Moralists*, 176. Collini quotes Fawcett's use of explicitly Benthamite terminology: 'the greatest happiness to the community in general'; 'this augmented wealth has tended not to promote but to diminish the comfort and happiness of the people'.

46. Mill, whom Eliot was re-reading at the time of writing *Felix Holt*, again provides a significant link. See *Letters*, iv, 208.

47. Eliot, *Felix Holt*, 45. Subsequent references will appear in the text.

48. An unusual nod to the ideals of the Young England and medievalist movements.

49. Note also the tradesmen in *Felix Holt*, who discuss politics and economics on election day (ch. 20). They represent embodiments of Adam Smith's butcher, baker and brewer described in *Wealth of Nations*, whose 'regard to their own interest' rather than benevolence underlies their social interaction (1, 27).

50. See Pamela Gilbert, *The Citizen's Body: Desire, Health, and the Social in Victorian England* (Columbus: Ohio State University Press, 2007). Gilbert perceptively addresses intoxication and addiction in *Felix Holt*, esp. 156–72.

51. *Essays*, 31.

52. See Gilbert, *The Citizen's Body*, on the high incidence of calculation in the novel, indicative of 'mathematical imagination' (167).
53. Mill, 'Utilitarianism', *Collected Works*, x, 212. Mill makes specific reference to a natural human awareness 'that health is the greater good', which Christian contradicts. He regards his health as merely a means to an end with no intrinsic worth.
54. See Elaine Freedgood, *Victorian Writing About Risk: Imagining a Safe England in a Dangerous World* (Cambridge University Press, 2000), esp. ch. 1, which examines the popular writings of Harriet Martineau and J. R. McCulloch. Freedgood concludes that 'the theories of political economy ... were quite precisely an attempt to eliminate the possibility that things might go wrong. What classical political economy attempted to do, particularly in its popularizations, was to cleanse the economic realm of contingency and uncertainty, to make it predictable' (16).
55. Eliot, *Adam Bede*, 161.
56. Dodd makes this central to her interpretation of Eliot's intellectual and artistic development. In rejecting philosophy for the novel, she 'ratified its conclusions about the inadequacies of the merely rational process as a way of contemplating the mysterious phenomena of mind and life' (*An Intellectual Life*, 315).
57. *Essays*, 148.
58. For marriage and the market and women as 'property', see Nunokawa, *The Afterlife of Property*, and Chapter 6 below.
59. Eliot frequently uses commercial language and imagery in emotional contexts to similar effect. See my comments on *The Mill on the Floss* and *Daniel Deronda* in Chapter 6, below. Note also Casaubon in *Middlemarch*, ch. 10: in his contemplation of marriage, he expects a 'compound interest of happiness' and a 'large draft' to be issued.
60. Arthur is 'a handsome generous young fellow ... who, if he should unfortunately break a man's legs in his rash driving, will be able to pension him handsomely' (*Adam Bede*, 118).
61. Note also that Lydgate doesn't manage calculations. He wants 'to live aloof from such abject calculations, such self-interested anxiety about the inclinations and pockets of men' (*Middlemarch*, 650).
62. See p. 42 above.
63. Eliot, *Felix Holt*, 222. Compare John Maynard Keynes, *A Tract on Monetary Reform* (London: Macmillan, 1924): 'The long-run is a misleading guide to current affairs. In the long-run we are all dead.'
64. Mill, 'Utilitarianism', *Collected Works*, x, 218.
65. Money is more than once associated with restraint or imprisonment, particularly at Transome Court. Thus, Mrs Transome, surrounded with luxuries by her son: 'The finest threads, such as no eye sees ... may make a worse bondage than any fetters' (99); and later Esther, imagining married life in the same location, 'saw herself in a silken bondage that arrested all motive, and was nothing better than a well-cushioned despair' (390).
66. '"I have sold some of the books to make money ... and I have looked into the shops where they sell caps and bonnets and pretty things, and I can do all that,

and get more money to keep us" '(Eliot, *Felix Holt*, 79). For Dorothea and the material, see Chapter 5 below.

67. Gallagher, *Industrial Reformation*, talks of the otherness of Felix's 'pure value' (244). See also Guy, *The Victorian Social-Problem Novel*: 'Felix's moral goodness is a negation of ... materialism' (199).

5 TESTING THE KANTIAN PILLARS: DEBT OBLIGATIONS AND FINANCIAL IMPERATIVES IN *MIDDLEMARCH*

1. *Letters*, IX, 217. Eliot's insistence on the 'moral motive', however, was essentially in line with Mill. See, for example, the discussion of 'Utilitarianism' in Chapter 4 above.
2. *Ibid.*, VI, 216.
3. Mark Pattison, 'Philosophy at Oxford', *Mind*, I, I (Jan. 1876), 82–97, and Henry Sidgwick, 'Philosophy at Cambridge', *Mind*, I, 2 (Apr. 1876), 235–46. Eliot received Pattison's article the month before publication and on 27 December 1875 Lewes wrote to him: 'Last night Mrs Lewes read aloud your remarkable paper on Philosophy at Oxford and I must scribble you a line to say how delighted and gratified we were with it' (*Letters*, IV, 202).
4. While best known for his moral philosophical writings, most notably *The Methods of Ethics* (1874), in 1883 Sidgwick produced *The Principles of Political Economy*. In the *Mind* article, he describes the Moral Sciences Tripos 'where exceptional stress is laid on Logic (including Methodology) and Political Economy, which are made departments co-ordinate with the larger but vaguer subjects of Mental Philosophy (Psychology and Metaphysics), and Moral and Political Philosophy' (245).
5. Sidgwick, 'Philosophy at Cambridge', 245.
6. Pattison, 'Philosophy at Oxford', 95.
7. See 'Sedgwick's Discourse' (1835), and 'Whewell on Moral Philosophy' (1852), in Mill, *Collected Works*, X, 'Essays on Ethics, Religion and Society', 165–201, 31–74. By the 1870s, the influence of Mill at the very university where many of these adversaries had earlier held sway is noted by Sidgwick: 'I should be disposed to think that no indigenous thinker, for 150 years, has had an influence in Cambridge at all equal to that recently exercised from a distance, by John Stuart Mill' ('Philosophy at Cambridge', 244).
8. Pattison, 'Philosophy at Oxford', 96.
9. See Rick Rylance, *Victorian Psychology and British Culture 1850–1880* (Oxford University Press, 2000), 311–18, for an account of the confrontation between Lewes and Green.
10. *Letters*, III, 318. In response to Sir Edward Bulwer-Lytton's criticism of Maggie Tulliver, she writes: 'If the ethics of art do not admit the truthful presentation of a character essentially noble but liable to great error – error that is anguish to its own nobleness – *then*, it seems to me, the ethics of art are too narrow, and must be widened to correspond with a widening psychology.'

11. If *The Methods of Ethics* does not attempt a full synthesis of the competing ethical schools, Sidgwick is anxious to examine different principles and methods 'from a neutral position'. See Schneewind, *Sidgwick's Ethics*, esp. part 2, ch. 6, 'The Aims and Scope of *The Method of Ethics*'. Sidgwick opens his posthumously published lecture on Green by locating himself in relation to two opposing positions: 'Spencer and Green represent two lines of thought divergent from my own in opposite directions, but agreeing in that they do not treat Ethics as a subject that can stand alone. Spencer bases it on Science, Green on Metaphysics.' Henry Sidgwick, *Lectures on the Ethics of T. H. Green, Mr. Herbert Spencer, and J. Martineau* (London: Macmillan, 1902), 1.

12. *Letters*, IX, 217.

13. *Essays*, 148–53. Eliot praises the subject of her review, Otto Friedrich Gruppe, who 'renounces the attempt to climb to heaven by the rainbow bridge of "the high *priori* road", and is content humbly to use his muscles in treading the uphill *a posteriori* path' (153).

14. As noted later in this chapter, scientific empiricism and ethics are frequently directly and metaphorically linked in the novels. In *Middlemarch*, Lydgate's realisation of the wider implications of his part in the events leading to Raffles's death represents a tainting of the scientific objectivity which was the bedrock of his ethics: 'the scientific conscience had got into the debasing company of money obligation and selfish respects' (729). Lydgate's rational error was not to locate and accommodate financial obligations and responsibilities within that ethical framework.

15. Immanuel Kant, *Groundwork of the Metaphysics of Morals*, trans. and ed. Mary Gregor (Cambridge University Press, 1998), IV, 389. Following standard method, all references are to the pagination of the standard German edition of Kant's works by the German Academy. Subsequent references will be parenthesised in the text.

16. *Essays*, 126. The reference to the 'optical instrument' reminds us of the constant references to and questioning of the optical in the novels and most notably *Middlemarch*.

17. G. H. Lewes, *A Biographical History of Philosophy* (1845) (London: Routledge, 1892), 561.

18. *Essays*, 387–8.

19. Rosemary Ashton, *The German Idea: Four English Writers and the Reception of German Thought, 1800–1860* (Cambridge University Press, 1980). Strauss's criticism, she writes, 'follows Kant's great critical method' (151). However, Ashton argues that the greatly more pervasive influence of Feuerbach was at least in part because his 'welcome religion of humanity was built on an empirical base' (159).

20. See, however, Carroll, *Conflict of Interpretations*, in relation to Eliot's partial reassessment of Lewes's position in the Utilitarianism versus intuitionism debate: 'Eliot clearly felt that Lewes had misrepresented the situation by coming down too firmly on the side of the former, underestimating the "a priori" principles that make moral experience intelligible in the first place' (22).

K. M. Newton's most recent work on Eliot also includes a chapter on Kantian influences in *The Mill on the Floss*. K. M. Newton, *Modernizing George Eliot: The Writer as Artist, Intellectual, Proto-Modernist, Cultural Critic* (London: Bloomsbury Academic, 2011), ch. 3.

21. Ashton makes a similar point with regard to Eliot's ambivalence over Strauss: 'Strauss's clinging to … [Christianity] … did not have her full approval. Nevertheless, she was aware of Strauss's immense importance for the progress of historical research, and was wise enough to see that if German transcendental philosophy and its heirs had some shortcomings, what was nonetheless needed in England was a fair welcome to such works as Strauss's, which were far in advance of British notions' (*The German Idea*, 153).

22. *Essays*, 134–5. This passage has a particularly Kantian tone. Note also that Kant contrasts prudence and duty (IV, 402), and later stresses prudence is 'always hypothetical' (IV, 416). It is significant, therefore, that in *Middlemarch* when Dorothea's family is discussing her decision to marry Ladislaw, Cadwallader admits that she may have acted 'imprudently', but not that she committed a 'wrong action' (875).

23. See note 35 below for Kant's financially informed value system in the 'kingdom of ends'. He distinguishes between 'market price', 'fancy price' and 'inner worth'.

24. See the perceptive 'Introduction' in John Clark Pratt and Victor A. Neufeldt (eds.), *George Eliot's Middlemarch Notebooks* (Berkeley: University of California Press, 1979).

25. William Edward Hartpole Lecky, *History of European Morals from Augustus to Charlemagne* (1869) (London: Longman, Green 1892).

26. Eliot's analysis of the material concerns of many of the novel's characters perceptively anticipates aspects of modern adaptation and aspiration-level theory. See Bruno S. Frey and Alois Stutzer, 'Testing Theories of Happiness', in Luigino Bruni and Pier Luigi Porta (eds.), *Economics and Happiness: Framing the Analysis* (Oxford University Press, 2005), 116–146.

27. 'But as Warren Hastings looked at gold and thought of buying Daylesford, so Joshua Rigg looked at Stone Court and thought of buying gold' (Eliot, *Middlemarch*, 509). Subsequent references will appear in the text.

28. Robert Audi, 'A Kantian Intuitionism', *Mind*, 110, 439 (2001), 601–33 (630).

29. As such, Eliot shared the ethical precision she attributed to Goethe's writing: 'his mode of treatment seems to us precisely that which is really moral in its influence. It is without exaggeration; he is in no haste to alarm readers into virtue by melodramatic consequences; he quietly follows the stream of fact and life; and waits patiently for the moral processes of nature as we all do for her material processes' (*Essays*, 146–7).

30. Iris Murdoch, 'Against Dryness: A Polemical Sketch', *Encounter*, 16, 1 (1961), quoted in Jane Adamson, 'Against Tidiness: Literature and/versus Moral Philosophy' in Adamson *et al.*, *Renegotiating Ethics in Literature, Philosophy, and Theory*, 84–110 (85).

31. The scenarios presented are often so far removed from everyday contemporary life that they sometimes go beyond parable to fairy tale; for example, Mill's consideration, in 'Utilitarianism', of the case of the motive and intention of an evil tyrant rescuing his enemy from drowning (Mill, *Collected Works*, x, 219).
32. Appiah, *Experiments in Ethics*, 100.
33. Eliot, *Middlemarch*, ch. 68.
34. Kant, Section II.
35. Compare Kant in the *Groundwork*, IV, 434: 'In the kingdom of ends everything has either a price or a dignity. What has a price can be replaced by something else as its equivalent; what on the other hand is raised above all price and therefore admits of no equivalent has a dignity.'
36. Note, however, Ladislaw is conscious of his financial obligations, while Garth's determination to make good the creditors of his failed building business while continuing a virtuous, observant life is in stark contrast to Mr Tulliver's tortured road out of insolvency.
37. 'What could he do? He could not see a man sink close to him for want of help. He rose and gave his arm to Bulstrode, and in that way led him out of the room; yet this act, which might have been one of gentle duty and pure compassion, was at this moment unspeakably bitter to him' (718).
38. This power structure is of course inverted and taken to a criminal extreme by Raffles who, lacking money, uses secret knowledge to extort it from Bulstrode. See Welsh, *George Eliot and Blackmail*, 243–55. Note also that Lydgate's awareness of his dwindling power in his marriage finds focus and becomes apparent in financial disagreements: 'There was gathering within him an amazed sense of his powerlessness over Rosamond' (631).
39. In Kant's example, the maxim 'when I believe myself to be in need of money I shall borrow money and promise to repay it, even though I know it will never happen' is shown to be logically incapable of being universalised (IV, 422).
40. '[Fred] suddenly saw himself as a pitiful rascal who was robbing two women of their savings' (244).
41. Note also his hope that material and transcendent values might be reconciled in a kind of formulaic equation: 'The secret hope that after some years he might come back with the sense that he had at least a personal value equal to her wealth' (613).
42. Valerie Wainwright, *Ethics and the English Novel from Austen to Forster* (Aldershot: Ashgate, 2007), includes a Kantian reading of Dorothea's struggle to reconcile duty and well-being and draws some similar conclusions, esp. 130–4.
43. Freedgood, *The Ideas in Things*, 118, 127.
44. Miller, *Novels Behind Glass*, 196, 197.
45. *Ibid.*, 192–214. Nicholas Shrimpton has calculated that the 'seven hundred a-year' on which Dorothea makes her spending calculations had a current-money value (as at 2007) of £52,000 in 1831: '"Even these metallic problems have their melodramatic side": Money in Victorian Literature', in Francis

O'Gorman, (ed.), *Victorian Literature and Finance* (Oxford University Press, 2007), 17–38 (33).

46. "'Young ladies don't understand political economy, you know," said Mr Brooke, smiling towards Mr Casaubon' (17).

47. And is accordingly teased by her sister:

> "'Oh, all the troubles of all people on the face of the earth," said Dorothea, lifting her arms to the back of her head.
>
> "Dear me, Dodo, are you going to have a scheme for them?" said Celia, a little uneasy at this Hamlet-like raving' (765).

48. Later on: 'She yearned towards the perfect Right, that it might make a throne within her, and rule her errant will' (777). Significantly, the epigraph heading this chapter (80) is from Wordsworth's *Ode to Duty*.

49. See David O. Brink, *Perfectionism and the Common Good: Themes in the Philosophy of T. H. Green* (Oxford University Press, 2003). Brink makes the same point in relation to Green's philosophy and the 'distributionally sensitive' nature of Kantianism: 'Utilitarianism is an agent-neutral form of consequentialism, because it says that an agent has the same reason to be concerned about anyone independently of the relationship in which he stands to that person. By contrast, both Green's ethics of self-realization and self-referential altruism are agent-relative in so far as they claim that an agent's reasons to be concerned about someone depend essentially on the nature of the relationship that exists between the agent and that person' (77).

50. *Essays*, 184, 186.

51. Again foreshadowed by the Dr Cumming essay. He too subjugates autonomous reason under 'a formula of imprisoning the intellect, depriving it of its proper function – the free search for truth – and making it the mere servant-of-all-work to a foregone conclusion' (*Essays*, 167).

52. Another natural scientific image in relation to moral motive.

53. All commerce in *Middlemarch*, from Vincy's exploitative dyeing business (funded by Bulstrode) down to 'that greater social power, the retail trader' (490) is tainted. Mr Mawmsey, in failing to understand Lydgate's reluctance to prescribe and take payment for useless or inappropriate medicines, expresses the need of the 'age of capital' to quantify and measure all service in cash-equivalent terms, 'so that for every half-crown and eighteen pence he was certain something measurable had been delivered' (436).

54. Mind and body connections, including physical manifestations of heightened emotional states, recur in *Middlemarch* and Eliot's understanding was undoubtedly informed by Lewes's physiological work and reading. In *The Physiology of Common Life* (Edinburgh: Blackwood, 1859–60), he wrote:

> Mental agitation will suddenly arrest or increase the secretions; imperfect, or too abundant secretion will depress or confuse the mind. An idea will agitate the heart and disturb the liver . . . So indissolubly is our mental life bound up with our bodily life. (II, 106–7)

55. Compulsive gambling is, of course, but one manifestation of how financially related actions can represent the abandonment of reason, an increasingly researched field in experimental psychology and experimental (behavioural) economics.

56. Dorothea's anti-utilitarianism is emphasised by her opposition to 'calculation' in human affairs: 'She disliked this cautious weighing of consequences, instead of an ardent faith in efforts of justice and mercy, which would conquer by their emotional force' (723). The novel's final sentence appropriately describes the 'effect of her being on those around her' as 'incalculably diffusive' (825).

57. See Brink, *Perfectionism*: 'In this respect, Green's form of perfectionism fits within the Greek eudaimonistic tradition of which Kant is so critical' (100).

58. T. H. Green, *Prolegomena to Ethics*, ed. David O. Brink (Oxford: Clarendon Press, 2003), 445. Green's intention to include the quotation is asserted by A. C. Bradley, who arranged for the posthumous publication of the work in 1883.

6 BEING GOOD AND DOING GOOD WITH MONEY: INCORPORATING THE BOURGEOIS VIRTUES

1. Emily Davies to Annie Crow, 24 September 1876, reprinted in *Letters*, VI, 284.
2. Eliot, *Impressions of Theophrastus Such*, 130.
3. Deirdre N. McCloskey, *The Bourgeois Virtues: Ethics for an Age of Commerce* (University of Chicago Press, 2006).
4. The literature relating to virtue ethics, much of which has an Aristotelian grounding, is extensive. In addition to those works directly referenced, my understanding owes much to the following: Philippa Foot, *Virtues and Vices and Other Essays in Moral Philosophy* (Oxford: Clarendon Press, 2002), and *Natural Goodness* (Oxford: Clarendon Press, 2001); Alasdair MacIntyre, *After Virtue: A Study in Moral Theory* (London: Duckworth, 1981); Roger Crisp, *How Should One Live? Essays on the Virtues* (Oxford: Clarendon Press, 1996); and Christine Swanton, *Virtue Ethics: A Pluralistic View* (Oxford University Press, 2003). Note also the explicit connection between the turn to ethics in literary studies, most prominently in the work of Martha Nussbaum, and Aristotle's theory of the virtues.
5. *Letters*, II, 26. The link between *Impressions of Theophrastus Such* and Aristotle is explicit: the historical Theophrastus was an important student of Aristotle. His *Characters* comprises 'thirty sketches of "types" observed in the city of Athens'. Nancy Henry, 'Introduction', in Eliot, *Impressions of Theophrastus Such*, xii.
6. Robert Audi, *Moral Knowledge and Ethical Character* (Oxford University Press, 1997), 174.
7. Gary Watson, 'On the Primacy of Character', in Owen Flanagan and Amélie Oksenberg Rorty (eds.), *Identity, Character, and Morality: Essays in Moral Psychology* (Cambridge, Mass.: MIT Press, 1990), 451.

8. *Ibid.*, 450.
9. Audi, *Moral Knowledge*, elaborates: 'Practical wisdom is not a specifically moral virtue but a higher order one applicable to reflections and decisions concerning moral and other kinds of virtues' (186).
10. McCloskey, *Bourgeois Virtues*, 485.
11. *Ibid.*, 306.
12. *Ibid.*, 350. My claims relate to the incorporation of commercial virtues within a wider moral philosophy. Eliot was not uncritical of the more purely economic arguments of *The Wealth of Nations*, particularly as they were adopted, shorn of that wider moral context, by the political economists of her own century.
13. Adam Smith, *Lectures on Jurisprudence*, ed. R. L. Meek, D. D. Raphael and P. G. Stein (Oxford: Clarendon Press, 1978), 538.
14. Smith, *The Theory of Moral Sentiments*, 235–7, 294.
15. This is one of Courtemanche's key arguments.
16. Stephen Darwall, 'Sympathetic Liberalism: Recent Work on Adam Smith', *Philosophy and Public Affairs* 28, 2 (1999), 139–64 (160).
17. See Chapter 2 above.
18. See Gallagher, *Body Economic*, 118–55. She relates Eliot's concern that she was merely adding to the 'heap of literature' when she wrote the novel to her portrayal of Gwendolen Harleth's fear of personal marginalisation or redundancy. Creator and creation, she argues, are influenced by Jevons's recently formulated theories of marginal utility.
19. Eliot, *Impressions of Theophrastus Such*, ch. 10, 'Debasing the Moral Currency'.
20. *Journals*, 108.
21. For a good summary, see Appiah, *Experiments in Ethics*, esp. ch. 2, 'The Case Against Character'.
22. *Essays*, 147. E. S. Dallas, in his review of *The Mill on the Floss* for *The Times* (19 May 1860), recognises a similar blurring. He praises Eliot's delineation of 'the sort of life which thousands of our countrymen lead – a life that outwardly is most respectable, but inherently is most degraded – so degraded, indeed, that the very virtues which adorn it are scarcely to be distinguished from vices'. Reprinted in Laurence Lerner and John Holmstrom (eds.), *George Eliot and Her Readers: A Selection of Contemporary Reviews* (London: Bodley Head, 1966), 36.
23. Eliot, *The Mill on the Floss*, 106. Subsequent references will appear in the text.
24. An extreme later century contrast to Mrs Glegg, in her need for the tangible and intimate presence of her wealth, is Ferdinand Lopez, who asks 'What's the use of money you can see? How are you to make money out of money by looking at it?' Anthony Trollope, *The Prime Minister*, ed. Jennifer Uglow (Oxford University Press, 1999), ii, 58.
25. *Essays*, 134.
26. Blake, *Pleasures of Bethamism*, 111.
27. *Essays*, 166.
28. *Ibid.*
29. Martha Nussbaum, *The Fragility of Goodness: Luck and Ethics in Greek Tragedy and Philosophy* (Cambridge University Press, 1986), 14.

30. See p. 41 above.
31. Eliot, *Adam Bede*, 476.
32. Later on, when Maggie rediscovers Thomas à Kempis, the narrator comments: 'I suppose that is the reason why the small old-fashioned book, for which you need only pay sixpence at a book-stall, works miracles to this day, turning bitter waters into sweetness' (254). Elsewhere in the novels, Daniel Deronda is surprised at Mordecai's inability to give him a price for the book he wants to buy from him: '"Don't you know how much it is worth?"' '"Not its market-price"' (Eliot, *Daniel Deronda*, 326).
33. 'It was always an incident Mr Tulliver liked, in his gloomy life, to fetch the tin box and count the money' (307).
34. Eliot, *Impressions of Theophrastus Such*, 'Only Temper', 56.
35. Eliot, *Daniel Deronda*, 43. Subsequent references will appear in the text.
36. Even her less than worldly wise mother comments, 'You never did learn anything about income and expenses' (197).
37. *Daniel Deronda* represents three of the very few occupations available to educated women needing to earn money: governess, book illustrator (Kate Meyrick) and singer. While only the third has the transcendent potential of art, the Meyricks's 'habitual industry' represents the value of skilful and virtuous application to even relatively mundane work. Governesses are generally treated unsympathetically in the novels, although this is reflective of Eliot's wider criticism against the inadequacy of education for girls. Both Gwendolen and Janet Dempster opt to become wives rather than governesses, decisions they later come to regret.
38. I use 'uncertain' to indicate that people gamble for different reasons, as is apparent in *Daniel Deronda*.
39. Lush twice offers (121, 243) to 'take odds' that the marriage between Grandcourt and Gwendolen will not happen. He is more successful in his prediction that Grandcourt would eventually sell his interest in Diplow to Sir Hugo – a subject he addresses in a letter that includes numerous gambling and betting references (270).
40. Meditations on probability recur throughout the book – for example, 'a great deal of what passes for likelihood in the world is simply the reflex of a wish' (82); 'In this way it happens that the truth seems highly improbable' (203); 'those endless things called probabilities' (320). See also p. 47 above.
41. For Gwendolen and the narrowing possibilities for action, see Markovits, *Crisis of Action*, 108–18.
42. Deronda's influence on her moral aspirations is extensive, symbolised by the image of him as a 'redeemer' figure.
43. Michael Slote, 'Some Advantages of Virtue Ethics', in Flanagan and Oksenberg Rorty, *Identity, Character, and Morality*, 429–48 (437).
44. Eliot, *Impressions of Theophrastus Such*, 129–30. Mrs Davilow's understanding of the collapse of Grapnell & Co bears relation to Sir Gavial's schemes: 'There were great speculations: he meant to gain. It was all about mines and things of that sort' (199).

45. *Letters*, I, 246–7. The letter was written in February 1848.
46. Hack, *Material Interests*, 163. Hack notes the recurrent narratorial critique of the pervasiveness of the market in contemporary society and perceptively concludes that 'even as the narrator continues to treat market exchange as vulgar, materialistic, unfair and dishonest, the novel has been charting several forms of traffic between prophet and merchant' (167–8). In this context, it is interesting to note that Daniel's first conversation with Mordecai takes place in a bookshop, in an exchange that hovers around the practice of market exchange (Eliot, *Daniel Deronda*, 325–7).
47. In Mr Bult's defence, it is not clear that Klesmer's outburst fully captures Bult's political views.
48. See Nunokawa, *The Afterlife of Property*, ch. 4, '*Daniel Deronda* and the Afterlife of Ownership', 77–99 (70).
49. 'And in considering the relation of means to ends ... Mr Gascoigne's calculations were of the kind called rational' (30).
50. Significantly, Klesmer's ability to maintain his wife (which ultimately is not tested as she retains her fortune) is supported by the supplementing of his artistic excellence with prudence. During his frank appraisal of Gwendolen's chances of building a sufficiently remunerative career on the stage, he shows a strong grasp of the business side of his profession and the relative wages of working women in other fields. He reaches his final judgement only after 'measuring probabilities' (221).
51. '"The boy will get them engraved within him," thought Mordecai; "it is a way of printing" '(408). For *Daniel Deronda* and concepts of inheritance that, by fusing 'separateness with communication', point to aspects of Eliot's social and political vision (which I discuss in the following two chapters), see Hao Li, *Memory and History in George Eliot: Transfiguring the Past* (Basingstoke: Macmillan, 2000), ch. 6; Lisabeth During, 'The Concept of Dread: Sympathy and Ethics in *Daniel Deronda*', in Adamson *et al.*, *Renegotiating Ethics in Literature, Philosophy, and Theory*, 65–83; and Amanda Anderson, *The Powers of Distance: Cosmopolitanism and the Cultivation of Detachment* (Princeton University Press, 2001), 119–46. Anderson persuasively describes Eliot's 'complex attempt to construct an ideal modern relation between identity and cultural heritage' (124).

7 THE INDIVIDUAL AND THE STATE: ECONOMIC SOCIOLOGY IN *ROMOLA*

1. Emile Durkheim, *The Rules of Sociological Method*, trans. W. D. Halls, ed. Steven Lukes (New York: Free Press, 1982), 64.
2. Letter to Richard Holt Hutton, 8 August 1863. *Letters*, IV, 97.
3. Alexander Bain, '*The Principles of Sociology* by Herbert Spencer', *Mind*, I, 1 (1876), 128–31 (128).
4. Wolf Lepenies, *Between Literature and Science: The Rise of Sociology*, trans. R. J. Hollingdale (Cambridge University Press, 1988), 1. While tracing the roots of

the discipline back much further, Lepenies identifies the mid-nineteenth century onwards as the crucial period for his study, when 'literature and sociology contested with one another the claim to offer the key orientation for modern civilization and the guide to living appropriate to industrial society'.

5. *Essays*, 28.
6. See Peel, *Evolution of a Sociologist*: '[Spencer] began at George Eliot's instigation to read the *Politique Positive*, disagreed with Comte's classification of the sciences, was glad to drop it, and then, like any self-improving mechanic, proceeded to pick up the outlines of Comte's system from a popular summary by Lewes in *The Leader*' (27–8). As Peel notes, Spencer consistently distanced himself from Comte and positivism generally.
7. Haight, 'Introduction', *Letters*, I, xliv: 'In 1852 Herbert Spencer ... published in *The Leader* "The Development Hypothesis," which contains the germ of his whole system of philosophy, and in the *Westminster Review* "A Theory of Population," in which for the first time the development of species is linked with the survival of the fittest.'
8. Letter to George Combe, 22 April 1852. *Letters*, VIII, 44.
9. Bain, 'The Principles of Sociology', 128.
10. Eliot mentions the *Logic* several times in her letters and journals. In 1875, she writes that she had studied the book 'with much benefit' (Letters, VI, 163).
11. J. W. Cross, *George Eliot's Life As Related in Her Letters and Journals*, 3 vols. (Edinburgh: William Blackwood, 1885), 620.
12. *Letters*, III, 438.
13. *Ibid.*, III, 320. The letter, to Sara Hennell, is predominantly by Lewes, although Eliot does conclude it with a few light-hearted lines. Lewes is both animated and critical of what he perceives as Sara's misinterpretation of Comte: 'it is obvious you cannot have read Comte or you would not commit such a glaring mistake as to accuse him of not taking the element of History into account'.
14. *Essays*, 153.
15. Cross, *George Eliot's Life*, 620.
16. *Letters*, IV, 287, 300. See, however, J. B. Bullen, 'George Eliot's *Romola* as a Positivist Allegory', *The Review of English Studies* 26, 104 (1975), 425–35. Bullen argues that the structure of the novel and the heroine's progression to liberation and enlightenment have strong affinities with Comte's interpretation of history.
17. *Letters*, VI, 426.
18. Nancy L. Paxton, *George Eliot and Herbert Spencer: Feminism, Evolution and the Reconstruction of Gender* (Princeton University Press, 1991).
19. Quoted in *ibid.*, 5.
20. Durkheim, *Rules of Sociological Method*, 179.
21. *Ibid.*, 176, 182, 176.
22. Mazlish, *New Science*, 138.
23. *Essays*, 271, 287. Subsequent references to the essay will appear in the text.
24. See both Lepenies, *Between Literature and Science*, and Mazlish, *New Science*, for detailed analysis of the literary origins of sociological writing and the relationship between the two disciplines as the latter developed.

25. Lepenies claims success along these lines for Balzac: 'for what sociologist of the mid-nineteenth century could compete with the analytical insight of this novelist and his *'science sociale'* ... ?' (*Between Literature and Science*, 5). Balzac was greatly admired by Eliot and Lewes.

26. This passage is discussed further in Chapter 8 below.

27. The link is extensively explored in Suzanne Graver, *George Eliot and Community: A Study in Social Theory and Fictional Form* (Berkeley: University of California Press, 1984), esp. ch. 2, 28–80.

28. See Mazlish, *New Science*, 161–78.

29. *Ibid.*, 169–70, describes a moderation of Tonnies's enthusiasm for Marx later in his life.

30. Eliot, *Romola*, 207. Subsequent references will appear in the text.

31. *Letters*, III, 320, discussed on p. 125 above. See also Collini *et al.*, *That Noble Science*, ch. 7, for the importance of Sir Henry Maine and the Comparative Method in the early 1860s, which influenced Eliot's historical thought.

32. *Essays*, 28.

33. *Letters*, IV, 58.

34. Max Weber, *Economy and Society: An Outline of Interpretive Sociology*, ed. Guenther Roth and Claus Wittich (Berkeley: University of California Press, 1978), I, 164–6. See also Richard Swedberg, 'Max Weber's Economic Sociology: The Centerpiece of *Economy and Society?*', in Charles Camic, Philip S. Gorski and David M. Trubek (eds.), *Max Weber's Economy and Society: A Critical Companion* (Stanford University Press, 2005), esp. 131–2.

35. Richard A. Goldthwaite, *The Economy of Renaissance Florence* (Baltimore: Johns Hopkins University Press, 2009), 588.

36. *Ibid.*, 590.

37. It is also significant that, in the previous century, the Bardi family were among several equally prominent firms, before being brought down by their exposure to the English crown, an episode Eliot accurately describes in *Romola*, 45–6.

38. Reprinted in Lerner and Holmstrom, *George Eliot and Her Readers*, 57.

39. *Westminster Review*, 80 (Oct. 1863), 347.

40. See notes 13 and 31 above.

41. *Letters*, IV, 97.

42. Carlo Trigilia, *Economic Sociology: State, Market, and Society in Modern Capitalism* (Oxford: Blackwell, 1998), 4.

43. Including the 'market' itself as a social institution not only shaping, but also shaped by the decisions of its participants and wider cultural influences.

44. Most famously in Max Weber, *The Protestant Ethic and the Spirit of Capitalism*, trans. Talcott Parsons (London: George Allen & Unwin, 1930); and *Economy and Society*.

45. See p. 28, below.

46. Mazlish, *New Science*, 218.

47. Weber, *The Protestant Ethic*, 39.

48. The reference is to the notes to *The Protestant Ethic*, where Weber describes the attitude of English Puritans to Jewish commerce: 'Jewish capitalism was

speculative pariah-capitalism, while the Puritan was bourgeois organization of labour' (271).

49. '[B]ut now that belief meant an immediate blow to their commerce, the shaking of their position among the Italian States, and an interdict on their city, there inevitably came the question, "What miracle showest thou?"' (Eliot, *Romola*, 514).

50. For earmarking in modern sociological thought, see Viviana A. Zelizer, *The Social Meaning of Money* (New York: Basic Books, 1994), 18–25. Romola regards the money left to her by Tito as unclean and gifts it to the State.

51. For a modern, and controversial, theory of this form of capital, see Catherine Hakim, 'Erotic Capital', *European Sociological Review*, 26, 5 (2010), 499–518.

52. Tito had earlier told the barber he had received a recommendation that 'Florence is the best market in Italy for commodities such as yours' (29).

53. Goldthwaite, *Economy of Renaissance Florence*, 591.

54. Swedberg summarises and distinguishes Weber's concept of economic social action: 'Economic action, the key unit in economic theory, is … constituted by the action of an individual, to which meaning is attached. Unlike social action, however, economic action can only be rational, and it is always rational; also its aim is utility. Economic social action, in contrast, is explicitly oriented to others and very rarely, if ever, rational; it also has utility as its aim' (129). For Durkheim's criticism of Utilitarian method, see Emile Durkheim, *The Division of Labor in Society*, in Dobbin, 242.

55. *Ibid.*, 237.

56. One of Durkheim's many points of dispute with Spencer was on the latter's suggestion that the absorption of the individual into a common social conscience is characteristic of a militant phase of society: 'according to him, this absorption of the individual into the group would be the result of force and of an artificial organization necessitated by the state of war in which lower societies chronically live'. *Ibid.*, 235.

57. *Ibid.*, 235.

8 THE POLITICS OF WEALTH: NEW LIBERALISM AND THE PATHOLOGIES OF ECONOMIC INDIVIDUALISM

1. J. S. Mill, *On Liberty*, in *Collected Works*, XVIII, 276.

2. Eliot, *Impressions of Theophrastus Such*, 63.

3. L. T. Hobhouse, *The World in Conflict* (London: T. Fisher Unwin, 1915), 35.

4. Cross, *George Eliot's Life*, 623.

5. Gladstone entered parliament in 1832 as a Tory but became progressively liberal serving under Peel, who he supported in the economic debates that split the Conservatives in the mid-1840s. From 1859 he served as chancellor in Palmerston's administration and later succeeded Russell as leader of the Liberal Party, serving four terms as prime minister between 1868 and 1894.

6. The few references to political events and personalities in her personal papers include some criticism of Gladstone, although these relate more to his foreign policy and personal style than his domestic liberal politics. The resolutely Tory John Blackwood often criticised Gladstone in correspondence and I do not believe too much should be read into his belief that Felix Holt was a flag-bearer for old-school Toryism: 'I had nearly forgot to say how good your politics are. As far as I see yet, I suspect I am a radical of the Felix Holt breed, and so was my father before me' (*Letters*, iv, 246).

7. See Gilbert, *The Citizen's Body*, 156, for how economics (embracing capitalism, self-interest and aspiration) links the individual to the social body.

8. *Letters*, iv, 208.

9. Mill, *Collected Works*, xviii, 219.

10. The distinction is crucial and provides an important link from Mill to new liberalism. See, for example, Avital Simhony and David Weinstein (eds.), 'Introduction', *The New Liberalism: Reconciling Liberty and Community* (Cambridge University Press, 2001), 16: 'Reconciling individuality and sociability rests on the distinction new liberals drew between individualism and individuality.' J. P. Parry, however, warns against reliance on 'the simplistic equation between political Liberalism and classical economic liberalism', arguing that the former had neither a monopoly on the free-trade rhetoric of the latter nor an exclusive policy focus on narrow economic issues. J. P. Parry, 'Liberalism and Liberty', in Peter Mandler (ed.), *Liberty and Authority in Victorian Britain* (Oxford University Press, 2006), 71. See also Daniel Cottom's added nuance on the distinction, which posits an elevated rank of 'liberal intellectual', transcending the concerns of both political and economic liberalism: 'Although these intellectuals were generally in sympathy with those interests of the middle classes represented by Liberalism, they would take liberal intellectual values to be more comprehensive than – and thus a corrective to – Liberal political goals. It was precisely from this appeal to values transcending politics that they defined their intellectual liberalism' (*Social Figures*, 21).

11. *Economist*, 10 December 1853, quoted in Peel, *Evolution of a Sociologist*, 71.

12. Peel, *Evolution of a Sociologist*, 71. See also the analysis of morals and the market in Chapter 2 above.

13. Herbert Spencer, author's 'Preface', *The Man Versus the State* (1884) (Indianapolis: Liberty Fund, 1982), 3–4.

14. The prominent new liberal and opponent of Spencer, D. G. Ritchie, recognised the importance of *The Man Versus the State*, describing it as 'the most conspicuous work of recent years in defence of Individualism and in opposition to the growing tendency of state intervention.' *The Principles of State Interference* (London: Sawn Sonnenschein, 1891), quoted in Stefan Collini, *Liberalism and Sociology: L. T. Hobhouse and Political Argument in England 1880–1914* (Cambridge University Press, 1979), 154.

15. Spencer, *The Man Versus the State*, 10. Spencer's argument is that the success of earlier liberal policy to promote individual freedom by the repeal of restrictive

laws had gradually given way to an expectation of positive legislation so that 'the welfare of the many came to be conceived alike by Liberal statesmen and Liberal voters as the aim of Liberalism' (14). While his argument is much wider than a complaint against specific legislation (some of which he would have been in favour of), it is notable that a number of 'coercive' laws that Spencer highlights in his post-1860 legislative history include those aimed at correcting harmful abuses of unregulated commercial practices, which Eliot herself had specifically criticised. For example, the 1860 extension of the restrictions of the Factories Act to bleaching and dyeing works (17): Eliot is critical of the harmful abuses of the dyeing industry in *Middlemarch*, 667, and 'Leaves from a Note-Book', *Essays*, 439–40.

16. Further references to 'old liberalism' in the text should be taken as a broadly characterised individualistic form of liberalism epitomised by Spencer, rather than, for example, Mill.
17. Eliot, *Impressions of Theophrastus Such*, 63. Subsequent references will appear in the text.
18. *Essays*, 287.
19. *Letters*, VII, 47. See Evan Horowitz, 'George Eliot: The Conservative', *Victorian Studies*, 49, 1 (2006), 7–32.Feminist critics, such as Deirdre David, have also criticised Eliot's conservatism, both in *Felix Holt*, in which 'Eliot ends up subversively rejecting political action through the agency of her own sexual politics' (*Intellectual Women*, 197), and, more generally, in her female characters 'who often become metaphors for nostalgic conservatism, emblems of Eliot's residual desire ... to affiliate herself with the land-owning classes' (167). Dorothea Barrett, however, resists such generalization, describing her as, simultaneously both 'radical and conservative' (*Vocation and Desire*, 13).
20. Winch, *Wealth and Life*, 19.
21. A. Toynbee, 'Are Radicals Socialists?' *Industrial Revolution* (London, 1884), quoted in Andrew Vincent and Raymond Plant, *Philosophy, Politics and Citizenship: The Life and Thought of the British Idealists* (Oxford: Basil Blackwell, 1984), 35.
22. Spencer, *The Man Versus the State*, 30.
23. Collini, *Liberalism and Sociology*, 20.
24. Gagnier, *Individualism*, 9.
25. Collini, *Liberalism and Sociology*, 154. See also Gagnier, *Individualism*: 'Herbert Spencer biologized the division of labor calling it the law of organic progress' (30).
26. Michael Freeden, quoted in Gagnier, *Individualism*, 18. See also Collini, *Liberalism and Sociology*, 154–70.
27. Again, Spencer's individualism was less simplistic than this might suggest: see p. 25 above describing his land nationalisation proposals in *Social Statics*.
28. *Essays*, 197.
29. *Ibid.*, 402.
30. As Graver explains, 'Lewes and Mill had also been attracted to socialism, but they brought to it many more reservations. While they favored voluntarily

arranged cooperative associations, they did not propose, as did Tonnies, "a new kind of *Gemeinschaft* based upon an organically developed combination of state and cooperative socialism." . . . Lewes, though he looked favourably upon the "*doctrine*" of communism, rejected "socialist *systems* as premature"' (*George Eliot and Community*, 16–17). Tonnies was, of course, greatly influenced by Riehl.

31. *Essays*, 289. Subsequent references to the essay will appear in the text.
32. Graver, *George Eliot and Community*, 17.
33. Collini, *Liberalism and Sociology*, identifies four types of individualist arguments against state-intervention: 'the political, the economic, the scientific and the moral' (22).
34. In 'The Natural History of German Life', Eliot acknowledges the social coherence custom supports, while demonstrating its limitations: 'The peasant never questions the obligation of family ties – he questions *no custom* – but tender affection, as it exists amongst the refined part of mankind, is almost as foreign to him as white hands and filbert-shaped nails' (*Essays*, 280). See also Hao Li, *Memory and History in George Eliot*, for a discussion of 'Communal memory', and Elizabeth Deeds Ermath, *George Eliot*, for how Eliot's concept of culture is rooted in tradition: 'Tradition is its element, its determining and material condition' (30).
35. *Essays*, 263.
36. *Ibid.*, 265.
37. Graver, *George Eliot and Community*, 21.
38. Graver, *ibid.*, cites works by Raymond Williams, Ian Milner, William Myers and Graham Martin.
39. A good summary of the debate is provided in Simhony and Weinstein, *The New Liberalism*, 1–20. Anthony Kwame Appiah, *The Ethics of Identity* (Princeton University Press, 2005) locates the philosophical reconciliation of communitarianism and liberalism some years earlier than the new liberals, within the writings of Mill.
40. It is not the only link. As a sixth-form student at Marlborough College in 1882, he wrote a complementary essay titled '"George Eliot" as a Novelist' (*Marlburian*, xvii). As discussed on p. 102 above, Green was also much affected by Eliot as a novelist.
41. L. T. Hobhouse, *Liberalism* (London: Thornton Butterworth, 1911), 60.
42. Collini, *Liberalism and Sociology*, 128. My italics.
43. See Chapter 5 above.
44. Avital Simhony, 'T. H. Green's Complex Common Good: Between Liberalism and Communitarianism', in Simhony and Weinstein, *The New Liberalism*, 74.
45. *Ibid.*
46. *Essays*, 290.
47. Green, *Prolegomena*, 218 (sect. 190).

48. The most prominent exception is Dunstan Cass's theft of Silas Marner's gold, an event, of course, on which the entire plot hinges.
49. See *Middlemarch*, ch. 61 for Bulstrode's meeting with Ladislaw: "'you have a claim on me, Mr Ladislaw ... not a legal claim'" (609); and *Romola*, ch. 32, for Tito's sale of Bardo's library, which Bernardo had legally secured against creditors, but not against a treacherous husband.
50. George Eliot, 'Brother Jacob' in *'The Lifted Veil and Brother Jacob'*, 51. Subsequent references will appear in the text.
51. '[T]he only good in the pursuit of which there can be no competition of interests, the only good which is really common to all who may pursue it, is that which consists in the universal will to be good – in the settled disposition on each man's part to make the most and best of humanity in his own person and in the persons of others' (*Prolegomena*, 288 (sect. 244)).
52. Mill's early economic writings included arguments against the under-consumptionist theories of Malthus and Sismondi; see Winch, *Wealth and Life*, 56–7. See also Kreisel, *Economic Woman*, esp. 30–6.
53. In particular, ch. 3, 'Of Individuality, as One of the Elements of Well-Being'.
54. Eliot, *Silas Marner*, 15. Subsequent references will appear in the text.
55. T. H. Green, 'Lectures on the Principles of Political Obligation', in T. H. Green, *Lectures on the Principles of Political Obligation and Other Writings*, ed. Paul Harris and John Morrow (Cambridge University Press, 1986), 174–5.
56. The imperfect state of affairs, he contends, 'is really due to the arbitrary and violent manner in which rights over land have been acquired and exercised, and to the failure of the state to fulfil those functions which under a system of unlimited private ownership are necessary to maintain the conditions of a full life' (Green, 'Lectures', 176).
57. *Ibid.*, 178.
58. *Ibid.*, 173.
59. Graver, *George Eliot and Community*, 95. The description is of the village of Hayslope community in which Adam Bede's 'inheritance of affections' were nurtured. Eliot, *Adam Bede*, 200.
60. Graver, *George Eliot and Community*, 96, referring to traditional, communal ceremonies.
61. *Ibid.*, 97.
62. As William Myers summarises Esther Lyon's final renunciation of her legal inheritance: 'The radicalism of *Felix Holt* ... whatever its precise content, has to encompass George Eliot's endorsement of a way of life which the novel's heroine finally repudiates' (*The Teaching of George Eliot*, 78).
63. 'To the proposal that "unearned increment" in the value of the soil, as distinct from value produced by expenditure of labour and capital, should be appropriated by the state ... the great objection is that the relation between earned and unearned increment is so complicated, that a system of appropriating the latter to the state could scarcely be established without

lessening the stimulus to the individual to make the most of the land'
(Green, *Lectures*, 178).

64. John Morrow, 'Private Property, Liberal Subjects, and the State', in Simhony
and Weinstein, *The New Liberalism*, 112.

65. Hobhouse, *Liberalism*, 136.

66. Green, 'Lectures', 164.

67. *Ibid.*, 172.

68. See Chapter 6 above. In behavioural economic terms, the Dodsons' prudence
actually inverts the theory of hyperbolic discounting, which states that individuals discount distant rewards in favour of lesser rewards in the near-term.
By contrast, Eliot's Utilitarian 'calculators' do hyperbolically discount; for
example, Tito who 'follows the impulse of the moment'.

69. Eliot, *Silas Marner*, 162.

70. 'Adam thought that he and Seth might carry on a little business for
themselves ... by buying a small stock of superior wood and making articles
of household furniture ... The money gained in this way, with the good
wages he received as foreman, would soon enable them to get beforehand
with the world, so sparingly as they would all live now' (Eliot, *Adam
Bede*, 198).

71. For Sidgwick's position, see Collini *et al.*, *That Noble Science*: 'by including,
as part of [*The Principles of Political Economy*] a detailed account of the very
limited role for state action in economic matters which was derivable from
the premises of classical political economy, Sidgwick was deliberately
attempting to confer (or rather restore) the authority of science on a view
of politics which remained, for all the qualifications, essentially
Individualistic' (283).

72. Green, 'Lectures', 202.

73. See pp. 23–4 above.

74. See John Morrow, 'Private Property'; also Gerald Gaus, 'Bosanquet's
Communitarian Defense of Economic Individualism: A Lesson in the
Complexities of Political Theory', in Simhony and Weinstein, *The New
Liberalism*, 137–58.

75. Eliot, *Scenes of Clerical Life*, 293.

76. *Letters*, VI, 46.

77. See Hardy, *A Critic's Biography*, 118–130 for a perceptive analysis of Eliot's
relationship with Senior and its possible influence on the novels.

78. *Letters*, VI, 87.

79. *Parliamentary Reports*: 'Education', 25 (1874).

80. For an extensive review of Eliot's thoughts on the subject and its incorporation
as an important theme in the novels, see Linda K. Robertson, *The Power of
Knowledge: George Eliot and Education* (New York: Peter Lang, 1997). See also
Cottom, *Social Figures*; and Gillian Beer, *George Eliot*, 174–180: 'the campaigns
for education, work and independent property rights are very closely and

coherently connected' (171). Spencer collected four periodical reviews, written between 1854 and 1859, into *Herbert Spencer on Education* (1861), ed. F. A. Cavenagh (Cambridge University Press, 1932).

81. *Letters*, vi, 202.
82. Eliot and Lewes stayed as guests of both men at the colleges they headed, Lincoln and Balliol, during the 1870s. For Pattison's educational importance, see H. S. Jones, *Intellect and Character in Victorian England: Mark Pattison and the Invention of the Don* (Cambridge University Press, 2007).
83. Eliot, *Daniel Deronda*, 152; Eliot, *Middlemarch*, 142.
84. Eliot supported the establishment of Girton College, although probably not to the extent that her friends Barbara Bodichon and Emily Davies, the co-founders, might have ideally wished for. In January 1878, she wrote to Elma Stuart, 'no doubt you are rejoicing too that London University has opened all its degrees to women' (*Letters*, vii, 6).
85. The heavy defeat of the Liberal government in the 1874 General Election was, in part, due to the alienation of many urban middle-class voters over educational reform. See Lawrence Goldman, 'The Defection of the Middle Class: The Endowed Schools Act, the Liberal Party, and the 1874 Election', in Peter Ghosh and Lawrence Goldman (eds.), *Politics and Culture in Victorian Britain: Essays in Memory of Colin Matthew* (Oxford University Press, 2006), 118–35.
86. Gillian Sutherland, 'Education', in F. M. L. Thompson (ed.), *The Cambridge Social History of Britain, 1750–1950*, 3 vols. (Cambridge University Press, 1990), iii, 'Social Agencies and Institutions', 144.
87. Smith, *Wealth of Nations*, bk. 5, ch. 1, pt. 3, 'Of the Expence of Publick Works and Publick Institutions', 760. Smith's broader argument throughout 'Article II: Of the Expence of the Institutions for the Education of Youth' is, not surprisingly, subtle and far-reaching.
88. Mill, *Collected Works*, xviii, 302.
89. *Ibid.*, xviii, 302.
90. *Essays*, 428.
91. *Ibid.*, 426.
92. *Ibid.*, 419.
93. See, for example, Andrew Vincent, 'The New Liberalism and Citizenship', in Simhony and Weinstein, *The New Liberalism*: 'the market continued to play an ambiguous role in new liberal thought. The new liberal perspective on social rights reveals the paradoxical need both for the redistribution to satisfy the requirements of social citizenship and consequently for productive markets to fund such rights' (220).
94. Michael J. Sandel, 'What Money Can't Buy: The Moral Limits of Markets', The Tanner Lectures on Human Values (Brasenose College, Oxford; May 11–12, 1998), 101.
95. *Journals*, 145 (13 January 1875).
96. Vincent, 'The New Liberalism and Citizenship', 220.

APPENDIX B: WAS EDWARD TULLIVER
MADE BANKRUPT? AN ANALYSIS OF HIS
FINANCIAL DOWNFALL

1. Mary Poovey, 'Writing about Finance in Victorian England: Disclosure and Secrecy in the Culture of Investment', in Nancy Henry and Cannon Schmitt (eds.), *Victorian Investments: New Perspectives on Finance and Culture* (Bloomington: Indiana University Press, 2009), 39–57 (52).
2. This part of the novel is set in the late 1820s, a few years after Lord Eldon's 1825 Bankruptcy Act, which V. Markham Lester describes as introducing 'many concepts on which all future legislation was based'. Of particular relevance here is the formalisation of creditor composition agreements: 'Under a composition or a deed of arrangement, bankruptcy law now formally recognized that the debtor and his creditors could settle their affairs and avoid the filing of a formal bankruptcy.' (*Victorian Insolvency: Bankruptcy, Imprisonment for Debt, and Company Winding-up in Nineteenth-Century England*, Oxford: Clarendon Press, 1995, 36.)

Bibliography

ARCHIVES

Berg Collection, New York Public Library
George Eliot–G. H. Lewes Collection, Beinecke Rare Book and Manuscript Library, Yale University

PRIMARY AND SECONDARY

Adamson, Jane, 'Against Tidiness: Literature and/versus Moral Philosophy', in Adamson, Freadman and Parker, 84–110.

Adamson, Jane, Richard Freadman and David Parker (eds.), *Renegotiating Ethics in Literature, Philosophy, and Theory* (Cambridge University Press, 1998).

Akerlof, George A. and Robert J. Schiller, *Animal Spirits: How Human Psychology Drives The Economy, and Why It Matters For Global Capitalism* (Princeton University Press, 2009).

Alborn, Timothy L., *Conceiving Companies: Joint-Stock Politics in Victorian England* (London: Routledge, 1998).

Anderson, Amanda, *The Powers of Distance: Cosmopolitanism and the Cultivation of Detachment* (Princeton University Press, 2001).

Anderson, Elizabeth, *Value in Ethics and Economics* (Cambridge, Mass.: Harvard University Press, 1993).

Anger, Suzy, *Victorian Interpretation* (Ithaca: Cornell University Press, 2005).

Annan, Noel, *Leslie Stephen: The Godless Victorian* (London: Weidenfeld and Nicolson, 1984).

Appiah, Kwame Anthony, *The Ethics of Identity* (Princeton University Press, 2005).
   Experiments in Ethics (Cambridge, Mass.: Harvard University Press, 2008).

Aristotle, *The Nicomachean Ethics*, trans. David Ross, ed. J. L. Ackrill and J. O. Urmson (Oxford University Press, 1998).

Ashton, Rosemary, *142 Strand: A Radical Address in Victorian London* (London: Chatto & Windus, 2006).
   George Eliot: A Life (London: Hamish Hamilton, 1996).
   The German Idea: Four English Writers and the Reception of German Thought, 1800–1860 (Cambridge University Press, 1980).

Audi, Robert, 'A Kantian Intuitionism', *Mind*, 110, 439 (2001), 601–35.
   Moral Knowledge and Ethical Character (Oxford University Press, 1997).
Auerbach, Nina, 'Dorothea's Lost Dog', in Chase, 87–105.
Bagehot, Walter, *The Collected Works of Walter Bagehot*, ed. Norman St John-
   Stevas, 15 vols. (London: The Economist, 1965–86).
Bain, Alexander, 'The Principles of Sociology by Herbert Spencer', *Mind*, 1, 1
   (1876), 128–31.
Baker, William, *The George Eliot–George Henry Lewes Library: An Annotated
   Catalogue of Their Books at Dr. Williams's Library, London* (New York and
   London: Garland, 1977).
Barnes, James J., *Free Trade in Books: A Study of the London Book Trade Since 1800*
   (Oxford: Clarendon Press, 1964).
Barrett, Dorothea, *Vocation and Desire: George Eliot's Heroines* (London:
   Routledge, 1989).
Beaty, Jerome, *Middlemarch, From Notebook to Novel: A Study of George Eliot's
   Critical Method* (Urbana: University of Illinois Press, 1960).
Becker, Gary S., *Accounting for Tastes* (Cambridge, Mass.: Harvard University
   Press, 1996).
Beer, Gillian, *Darwin's Plots: Evolutionary Narrative in Darwin, George Eliot and
   Nineteenth-Century Fiction* (London: Routledge and Kegan Paul, 1983).
   George Eliot (Brighton: Harvester Press, 1986).
   'What's Not in Middlemarch', in Chase, 15–35.
Bellamy, Liz, *Commerce, Morality and the Eighteenth-Century Novel* (Cambridge
   University Press, 1998).
Berg, Maxine and Helen Clifford (eds.), *Consumers and Luxury: Consumer Culture
   in Europe 1650–1850* (Manchester University Press, 1999).
Bernstein, Peter L., *Against the Gods: The Remarkable Story of Risk* (New York: John
   Wiley, 1996).
Berry, Christopher J., *The Idea of Luxury: A Conceptual and Historical Investigation*
   (Cambridge University Press, 1994).
Bigelow, Gordon, *Fiction, Famine and the Rise of Economics in Victorian Britain and
   Ireland* (Cambridge University Press, 2003).
Blake, Kathleen, *Pleasures of Benthamism: Victorian Literature, Utility, Political
   Economy* (Oxford University Press, 2009).
Bodenheimer, Rosemary, *The Real Life of Mary Ann Evans: George Eliot, Her Letters
   and Fiction* (Ithaca: Cornell University Press, 1994).
Bourdieu, Pierre, *The Field of Cultural Production: Essays on Art and Literature*, ed.
   and intro. Randal Johnson (Cambridge: Polity Press, 1993).
Bowley, Marian, *Nassau Senior and Classical Economics* (New York: Octagon,
   1967).
Brady, Kristin, *George Eliot* (New York: St Martin's Press, 1992).
Brantlinger, Patrick, *Fictions of State: Culture and Credit in Britain, 1694–1994*
   (Ithaca: Cornell University Press, 1996).
   The Spirit of Reform: British Literature and Politics, 1832–67 (Cambridge, Mass.:
   Harvard University Press, 1977).

Bray, Charles, *The Philosophy of Necessity or, Natural Law as Applicable to Moral, Mental, and Social Science*, 2nd edn (London: Longman, Green, Longman & Roberts, 1863).

Brewer, John, *The Pleasures of the Imagination: English Culture in the Eighteenth Century* (London: HarperCollins, 1997).

Brink, David O., *Perfectionism and the Common Good: Themes in the Philosophy of T. H. Green* (Oxford University Press, 2003).

Brocas, Isabelle and Juan D. Carillo (eds.), *The Psychology of Economic Decisions*, 2 vols. (Oxford University Press, 2003–4).

Bronk, Richard, *The Romantic Economist: Imagination in Economics* (Cambridge University Press, 2009).

Broome, John, *Ethics out of Economics* (Cambridge University Press, 1999).
   'A Reply to Sen', *Economics and Philosophy*, 7 (1991), 285–7.
   'Utility', *Economics and Philosophy*, 7 (1991), 1–12.

Bruce, Susan and Valeria Wagner (eds.), *Fiction and Economy* (Basingstoke: Palgrave Macmillan, 2007).

Bruni, Luigino and Pier Luigi Porta (eds.), *Economics and Happiness: Framing the Analysis* (Oxford University Press, 2005).

Bullen, J. B., 'George Eliot's *Romola* as a Positivist Allegory', *The Review of English Studies*, 26, 104 (1975), 425–35.

Burrow, J. W., *Whigs and Liberals: Continuity and Change in English Political Thought* (Oxford: Clarendon Press, 1988).

Cairnes, J. E., *Some Leading Principles of Political Economy Newly Expounded* (London: Macmillan, 1874).

Carpenter, Mary Wilson, *George Eliot and the Landscape of Time: Narrative Form and Protestant Apocalyptic History* (Chapel Hill: The University of North Carolina Press, 1986).

Carlyle, Thomas, *The Works of Thomas Carlyle*, Centenary Edition, 30 vols. (London: Chapman and Hall, 1898).

Carroll, David (ed.), *George Eliot: The Critical Heritage* (London: Routledge & Kegan Paul, 1971).
   George Eliot and the Conflict of Interpretations: A Reading of the Novels (Cambridge University Press, 1992).

[Chapman, John], 'The Commerce of Literature', *Westminster Review*, 57 (Apr. 1852), 511–54.

Chapman, Stanley, *The Rise of Merchant Banking* (London: Allen & Unwin, 1984).

Chase, Karen (ed.), *Middlemarch in the 21st Century* (Oxford University Press, 2006).

Christianson, Frank, *Philanthropy in British and American Fiction: Dickens, Hawthorne, Eliot and Howells* (Edinburgh University Press, 2007).

Cockram, Gill G., *Ruskin and Social Reform: Ethics and Economics in the Victorian Age* (London: Tauris Academic Studies, 2007).

Cohen, Deborah, *Household Gods: The British and Their Possessions* (New Haven: Yale University Press, 2006).

Cohen, Derek, and Deborah Heller (eds.), *Jewish Presences in English Literature* (Montreal and Kingston: McGill-Queen's University Press, 1990).

Coleman, Dermot, 'Money', in Margaret Harris (ed.), *George Eliot in Context* (Cambridge University Press, 2013), 197–205.

Collini, Stefan, *Liberalism and Sociology: L. T. Hobhouse and Political Argument in England 1880–1914* (Cambridge University Press, 1979).

Public Moralists: Political Thought and Intellectual Life in Britain 1850–1930 (Oxford: Clarendon Press, 1991).

Collini, Stefan, Donald Winch and John Burrow, *That Noble Science of Politics: A Study in Nineteenth-Century Intellectual History* (Cambridge University Press, 1983).

Colón, Susan E., *The Professional Ideal in the Victorian Novel: The Works of Disraeli, Trollope, Gaskell, and Eliot* (Basingstoke: Palgrave Macmillan, 2007).

Cottom, Daniel, *Social Figures: George Eliot, Social History, and Literary Representation* (Minneapolis: University of Minnesota Press, 1987).

Courtemanche, Eleanor, *The 'Invisible Hand' and British Fiction, 1818–1860: Adam Smith, Political Economy, and the Genre of Realism* (Basingstoke: Palgrave Macmillan, 2011).

Coyle, Diane, *The Soulful Science: What Economists Really Do and Why It Matters* (Princeton University Press, 2007).

Craig, David M., *John Ruskin and the Ethics of Consumption* (Charlottesville: University of Virginia Press, 2006).

Crisp, Roger, *How Should One Live? Essays on the Virtues* (Oxford: Clarendon Press, 1996).

Cross, J. W., *George Eliot's Life as Related in Her Letters and Journals*, 3 vols. (Edinburgh: William Blackwood, 1885).

Cudd, Anne E., 'Game Theory and the History of Ideas about Rationality', *Economics and Philosophy*, 9 (1993), 101–33.

Darnton, Robert, *The Kiss of Lamourette: Reflections in Cultural History* (New York: W. W. Norton, 1990).

Darwall, Stephen, 'Sympathetic Liberalism: Recent Work on Adam Smith', *Philosophy and Public Affairs*, 28, 2 (1999), 139–64.

Daunton, Martin, *Wealth and Welfare: An Economic and Social History of Britain, 1851–1951* (Oxford University Press, 2007).

David, Deirdre, *Intellectual Women and Victorian Patriarchy: Harriet Martineau, Elizabeth Barrett Browning, George Eliot* (Ithaca: Cornell University Press, 1987).

Davies, Glyn, *A History of Money from Ancient Times to the Present Day* (Cardiff: University of Wales Press, 1994).

Davis, Lance E. and Robert A. Huttenback, *Mammon and the Pursuit of Empire: The Economics of British Imperialism* (Cambridge University Press, 1988).

Davis, Lance E. and Robert E. Gallman, *Evolving Financial Markets and International Capital Flows: Britain, the Americas, and Australia, 1865–1914* (Cambridge University Press, 2001).

Delany, Paul, *Literature, Money and the Market: From Trollope to Amis* (Basingstoke: Palgrave, 2002).

Diamond, Cora, 'Martha Nussbaum and the Need for Novels', in Adamson, Freadman and Parker, 39–64.

Dixon, Thomas, *The Invention of Altruism: Making Moral Meanings in Victorian Britain* (London: British Academy, 2008).

Dobb, Maurice, *Theories of Value and Distribution Since Adam Smith: Ideology and Economic Theory* (Cambridge University Press, 1973).

Dobbin, Frank (ed.), *The New Economic Sociology: A Reader* (Princeton University Press, 2004).

Dodd, Nigel, *The Sociology of Money: Economics, Reason and Contemporary Society* (New York: Continuum, 1994).

Dodd, Valerie A., *George Eliot: An Intellectual Life* (Basingstoke: Macmillan, 1990).

Dolin, Tim, *Mistress of the House: Women of Property in the Victorian Novel* (Aldershot: Ashgate, 1997).

Dudley Edwards, Ruth, *The Pursuit of Reason: The Economist 1843–1993* (London: Hamish Hamilton, 1993).

During, Lisabeth, 'The Concept of Dread: Sympathy and Ethics in Daniel Deronda', in Adamson, Freadman and Parker, 65–83.

Durkheim, Emile, *The Rules of Sociological Method*, trans. W. D. Halls, ed. Steven Lukes (New York: The Free Press, 1982).

Eatwell, John (ed.), *Money: The New Palgrave* (New York: W. W. Norton, 1989).

Eliot, George, *Adam Bede*, ed. Carol A. Martin (Oxford: Clarendon Press, 2001).

Daniel Deronda, ed. Graham Handley (Oxford University Press, 1984).

Essays of George Eliot, ed. Thomas Pinney (London: Routledge & Kegan Paul, 1963).

Felix Holt, The Radical, ed. Fred C. Thomson (Oxford: Clarendon Press, 1980).

The George Eliot Letters, ed. Gordon S. Haight, 9 vols. (New Haven: Yale University Press, 1954–78).

Impressions of Theophrastus Such, ed. Nancy Henry (London: William Pickering, 1994).

The Journals of George Eliot, ed. Margaret Harris and Judith Johnston (Cambridge University Press, 1998).

'The Lifted Veil' and 'Brother Jacob', ed. Helen Small (Oxford University Press, 1999).

Middlemarch, ed. David Carroll (Oxford: Clarendon Press, 1986).

The Mill on the Floss, ed. Gordon S. Haight (Oxford: Clarendon Press, 1980).

Romola, ed. Andrew Brown (Oxford: Clarendon Press, 1993).

Scenes of Clerical Life, ed. Thomas A. Noble (Oxford University Press, 2000).

Silas Marner, ed. Terence Cave (Oxford University Press, 2008).

Ermath, Elizabeth Deeds, *George Eliot* (Boston: Twayne, 1985).

'Negotiating Middlemarch', in Chase, 107–31.

Evans, D. Morier, *Speculative Notes and Notes on Speculation, Ideal and Real* (London: Groombridge, 1864).

The History of the Commercial Crisis 1857–1858, and the Stock Exchange Panic of 1859 (London: Groombridge, 1859).

Evensky, Jerry, 'The Evolution of Adam Smith's Views on Political Economy', *History of Political Economy*, 21, 1 (1989), 123–45.

Farina, Francesco, Frank Hahn and Stefano Vannucci (eds.), *Ethics, Rationality and Economic Behaviour* (Oxford: Clarendon Press, 1996).

Fawcett, Henry, *The Economic Position of the British Labourer* (London: Macmillan, 1865).

Manual of Political Economy, 4th edn (London: Macmillan, 1874).

Feltes, N. N., *Modes of Production of Victorian Novels* (University of Chicago Press, 1986).

Ferguson, Niall, *The Cash Nexus: Money and Power in the Modern World, 1700–2000* (London: Allen Lane, 2001).

Fetter, Frank W., 'Economic Articles in the Westminster Review and Their Authors, 1824–51', *Journal of Political Economy*, 70, 6 (1962), 570–96.

Finkelstein, David, *The House of Blackwood: Author-Publisher Relations in the Victorian Era* (University Park, Pa.: The Pennsylvania State University Press, 2002).

Finn, Margot C., *The Character of Credit: Personal Debt in English Culture, 1740–1914* (Cambridge University Press, 2003).

Flanagan, Owen and Amélie Oksenberg Rorty (eds.), *Identity, Character, and Morality: Essays in Moral Psychology* (Cambridge, Mass.: The MIT Press, 1990).

Fleishman, Avrom, *George Eliot's Intellectual Life* (Cambridge University Press, 2010).

Folbre, Nancy, *Greed, Lust & Gender: A History of Economic Ideas* (Oxford University Press, 2009).

Foley, Duncan K., *Adam's Fallacy: A Guide to Economic Theology* (Cambridge, Mass.: Harvard University Press, 2006).

Foot, Philippa, *Natural Goodness* (Oxford: Clarendon Press, 2001).

Virtues and Vices and Other Essays in Moral Philosophy (Oxford: Clarendon Press, 2002).

Fowkes Tobin, Beth, *Superintending the Poor: Charitable Ladies and Paternal Landlords in British Fiction, 1770–1860* (New Haven: Yale University Press, 1993).

Freedgood, Elaine, *The Ideas in Things: Fugitive Meaning in the Victorian Novel* (University of Chicago Press, 2006).

Victorian Writing About Risk: Imagining a Safe England in a Dangerous World (Cambridge University Press, 2000).

Francis, Mark, *Herbert Spencer and the Invention of Modern Life* (Stocksfield: Acumen, 2007).

Frey, Bruno S. and Alois Stutzer, 'Testing Theories of Happiness', in Bruni and Porta, 116–46.

Frost, Simon R., *The Business of the Novel: Economics, Aesthetics and the Case of Middlemarch* (London: Pickering and Chatto, 2012).

Gagnier, Regenia, *Individualism, Decadence and Globalization: On the Relationship of Part to Whole, 1859–1920* (Basingstoke: Palgrave Macmillan, 2010).

The Insatiability of Human Wants: Economics and Aesthetics in Market Society (University of Chicago Press, 2000).

Gallagher, Catherine, *The Body Economic: Life, Death, and Sensation in Political Economy and the Victorian Novel* (Princeton University Press, 2006).

The Industrial Reformation of English Fiction: Social Discourse and Narrative Form 1832–67 (University of Chicago Press, 1985).

Gaus, Gerald, 'Bosanquet's Communitarian Defence of Economic Individualism: A Lesson in the Complexities of Political Theory', in Simhony and Weinstein, 137–58.

Gilbert, Pamela, *The Citizen's Body: Desire, Health, and the Social in Victorian England* (Columbus: Ohio State University Press, 2007).

Gissing, George, *New Grub Street*, ed. John Goode (Oxford University Press, 1993).

Goldman, Lawrence, 'The Defection of the Middle Class: The Endowed Schools Act, the Liberal Party, and the 1874 Election', in Peter Ghosh and Lawrence Goldman (eds.), *Politics and Culture in Victorian Britain: Essays in Memory of Colin Matthew* (Oxford University Press, 2006), 118–35.

Goldthwaite, Richard A., *The Economy of Renaissance Florence* (Baltimore: Johns Hopkins University Press, 2009).

Graver, Suzanne, *George Eliot and Community: A Study in Social Theory and Fictional Form* (Berkeley: University of California Press, 1984).

Green, David R. and Alastair Owens, 'Gentlewomanly Capitalism? Spinsters, Widows, and Wealth Holding in England and Wales, c. 1800–1860', *Economic History Review*, LVI (2003).

Green, David R., Alastair Owens, Josephine Maltby and Janette Rutterford (eds.), *Men, Women, and Money: Perspectives on Gender, Wealth, and Investment, 1850–1930* (Oxford University Press, 2011).

Green, T. H., *Prolegomena to Ethics*, ed. David O. Brink (Oxford: Clarendon Press, 2003).

Lectures on the Principles of Political Obligation and Other Writings, ed. Paul Harris and John Morrow (Cambridge University Press, 1986).

[Greg, W. R.], 'Charity, Noxious and Beneficient', *Westminster Review*, 59 (Jan. 1853), 62–88.

'Political Economy', *Westminster Review*, 84 (Jan. 1865), 106–33.

'The Relation Between Employers and Employed', *Westminster Review*, 57 (Jan. 1852), 61–95.

Guillory, John, *Cultural Capital: The Problem of Literary Canon Formation* (University of Chicago Press, 1993).

Guy, Josephine M., *The Victorian Social-Problem Novel: The Market, the Individual and Communal Life* (Basingstoke: Macmillan, 1996).

Hack, Daniel, *The Material Interests of the Victorian Novel* (Charlottesville: University of Virginia Press, 2005).

Hadas, Edward, *Human Goods, Economic Evils: A Moral Approach to the Dismal Science* (Wilmington, Del.: ISI Books, 2007).

Hadley, Elaine, *Living Liberalism: Practical Citizenship in Mid-Victorian Britain* (University of Chicago Press, 2010).

Haight, Gordon S., *George Eliot: A Biography* (Oxford: Clarendon Press, 1968).
Hakim, Catherine, 'Erotic Capital', *European Sociological Review*, 26.5 (2010), 499–518.
Hardy, Barbara, *George Eliot: A Critic's Biography* (London: Continuum, 2006).
Harford, Tim, *The Undercover Economist* (Oxford University Press, 2006).
Haskell, Thomas L. and Richard F. Teichgraeber III (eds.), *The Culture of the Market: Historical Essays* (Cambridge University Press, 1993).
Hausman, Daniel M. (ed.), *The Philosophy of Economics: An Anthology*, 2nd edn (Cambridge University Press, 1994).
Henry, Nancy, *George Eliot and the British Empire* (Cambridge University Press, 2002).
The Life of George Eliot (Chichester: Wiley-Blackwell, 2012).
Henry, Nancy and Cannon Schmitt (eds.), *Victorian Investments: New Perspectives on Finance and Culture* (Bloomington: Indiana University Press, 2009).
Heyne, Paul, *'Are Economists Basically Immoral?' and Other Essays on Economics, Ethics, and Religion*, ed. Geoffrey Brennan and A. M. C. Waterman (Indianapolis: Liberty Fund, 2008).
Hilton, Boyd, *The Age of Atonement: The Influence of Evangelicalism on Social and Economic Thought 1785–1865* (Oxford: Clarendon Press, 1988).
The New Oxford History of England: A Mad, Bad, and Dangerous People? England 1783–1846 (Oxford: Clarendon Press, 2006).
Himmelfarb, Gertrude, *Poverty and Compassion: The Moral Imagination of the Late Victorians* (New York: Alfred A. Knopf, 1991).
Hobhouse, L. T., *Liberalism* (London: Thornton Butterworth, 1911).
The World in Conflict (London: T. Fisher Unwin, 1915).
Hollander, Samuel, *The Economics of John Stuart Mill*, 2 vols. (University of Toronto Press, 1985).
Hont, Istvan and Michael Ignatieff (eds.), *Wealth & Virtue: The Shaping of Political Economy in the Scottish Enlightenment* (Cambridge University Press, 1983).
Horowitz, Evan, 'George Eliot: The Conservative', *Victorian Studies*, 49.1 (2006), 7–32.
Ingham, Geoffrey, *The Nature of Money* (Cambridge: Polity Press, 2004).
Itzkowitz, David C., 'Fair Enterprise or Extravagant Speculation: Investment, Speculation, and Gambling in Victorian England', *Victorian Studies*, 45, 1 (2002), Special Issue, 'Victorian Investments', 121–47.
Jarvis, Adrian, *Samuel Smiles and the Construction of Victorian Values* (Stroud: Sutton Publishing, 1997).
Jay, Elizabeth and Richard Jay (eds.), *Critics of Capitalism: Victorian Reactions to 'Political Economy'* (Cambridge University Press, 1986).
Jevons, W. Stanley, *The Theory of Political Economy*, ed. R. D. Collison Black (Harmondsworth: Penguin, 1970).
Jones, H. S., *Intellect and Character in Victorian England: Mark Pattison and the Invention of the Don* (Cambridge University Press, 2007).
Kant, Immanuel, *Groundwork of the Metaphysics of Morals*, trans. and ed. Mary Gregor (Cambridge University Press, 1998).

Keynes, John Maynard, *A Tract on Monetary Reform* (London: Macmillan, 1924)

Klamer, Arjo, Donald N. McCloskey and Robert M. Solow (eds.), *The Consequences of Economic Rhetoric* (Cambridge University Press, 1988).

Kreisel, Deanna, *Economic Woman: Demand, Gender, and Narrative Closure in Eliot and Hardy* (University of Toronto Press, 2012).

Kynaston, David, *The City of London. Volume 1: A World of its Own, 1815–90* (London: Chatto & Windus, 1994).

Lal, Deepak, *Reviving the Invisible Hand: The Case for Classical Liberalism in the Twenty-First Century* (Princeton University Press, 2006).

Lalor, John, *Money and Morals, A Book for the Times* (London: John Chapman, 1852).

Lecky, William Edward Hartpole, *History of European Morals from Augustus to Charlemagne* (1869) (London: Longman, Green, 1892).

Lepenies, Wolf, *Between Literature and Science: The Rise of Sociology*, ed. R. J. Hollingdale (Cambridge University Press, 1988).

Lerner, Laurence and John Holmstrom (eds.), *George Eliot and Her Readers: A Selection of Contemporary Reviews* (London: Bodley Head, 1966).

Levine, George, *Darwin and the Novelists: Patterns of Science in Victorian Fiction* (University of Chicago Press, 1991).

Levitt, Steven D. and Stephen J. Dubner, *Freakonomics: A Rogue Economist Explores the Hidden Side of Everything* (London: Allen Lane, 2005).

Lewes, G. H., *A Biographical History of Philosophy* (1845) (London: Routledge, 1892).

   The Physiology of Common Life (Edinburgh: Blackwood, 1859–60).

Li, Hao, *Memory and History in George Eliot: Transfiguring the Past* (Basingstoke: Macmillan, 2000).

Lightman, Bernard (ed.), *Victorian Science in Context* (University of Chicago Press, 1997).

Loewenstein, George, *Exotic Preferences: Behavioural Economics and Human Motivation* (Oxford University Press, 2007).

Loftus, Donna, 'Capital and Community: Limited Liability and Attempts to Democratize the Market in Mid-Nineteenth-Century England', *Victorian Studies*, 45, 1 (2002), Special Issue, 'Victorian Investments', 93–120.

Lynch, Deirdre Shauna, *The Economy of Character: Novels, Market Culture, and the Business of Inner Meaning* (University of Chicago Press, 1998).

Lysack, Krista, *Come Buy, Come Buy: Shopping and the Culture of Consumption in Victorian Women's Writing* (Athens: Ohio University Press, 2008).

MacIntyre, Alasdair, *After Virtue: A Study in Moral Theory* (London: Duckworth, 1981).

   The Tasks of Philosophy: Selected Essays, Volume 1 (Cambridge University Press, 2006).

Mackay, Charles, *Memoirs of Extraordinary Popular Delusions* (London: Richard Bentley, 1841).

Malchow, H. L., *Gentlemen Capitalists: The Social and Political World of the Victorian Businessman* (Stanford University Press, 1992).

Maloney, John, *Marshall, Orthodoxy and the Professionalisation of Economics* (Cambridge University Press, 1985).

Malthus, T. R., *An Essay on the Principle of Population*, 1798 edn, ed. Geoffrey Gilbert (Oxford University Press, 2004).

Mandler, Peter (ed.) *The English National Character: The History of an Idea from Edmund Burke to Tony Blair* (New Haven: Yale University Press, 2006).

Markham Lester, V., *Victorian Insolvency: Bankruptcy, Imprisonment for Debt, and Company Winding-up in Nineteenth-Century England* (Oxford: Clarendon Press, 1995).

Markovits, Stefanie, *The Crisis of Action in Nineteenth-Century English Literature* (Columbus: Ohio State University Press, 2006).

Marshall, Alfred, *Principles of Economics*, 8th edn (1920) (New York: Prometheus, 1997).

Martineau, Harriet, *Illustrations of Political Economy: Selected Tales*, ed. Deborah Anna Logan (Ontario: Broadview, 2004).

Mazlish, Bruce, *A New Science: The Breakdown of Connections and the Birth of Sociology* (University Park, Pa.: The Pennsylvania State University Press, 1989).

McCaw, Neil, *George Eliot and Victorian Historiography: Imagining the National Past* (Basingstoke: Palgrave Macmillan, 2000).

McCloskey, Deirdre N., *The Bourgeois Virtues: Ethics for an Age of Commerce* (University of Chicago Press, 2006).

The Rhetoric of Economics (Madison: University of Wisconsin Press, 1995).

McCulloch, J. R., *Considerations on Partnerships with Limited Liability* (London: Longman, Brown, Green & Longmans, 1856).

McDonagh, Josephine, *De Quincey's Disciplines* (Oxford: Clarendon Press, 1994).

McKelvy, William R., *The English Cult of Literature: Devoted Readers, 1774–1880* (Charlottesville: University of Virginia Press, 2007).

McVeagh, John, *Tradefull Merchants: The Portrayal of the Capitalist in Literature* (London: Routledge & Kegan Paul), 1981.

Michie, R. C., *The London and New York Stock Exchanges 1850–1914* (London: Allen & Unwin, 1987).

Mill, John Stuart, *Collected Works of John Stuart Mill*, gen. ed. John M. Robson, 33 vols. (University of Toronto Press, 1963–91).

Utilitarianism, ed. Mary Warnock (Glasgow: William Collins, 1962).

Miller, Andrew H., *The Burdens of Perfection: On Ethics and Reading in Nineteenth-Century British Literature* (Ithaca: Cornell University Press, 2008).

Novels Behind Glass: Commodity Culture and Victorian Narrative (Cambridge University Press, 1995).

Mintz, Alan, *George Eliot and the Novel of Vocation* (Cambridge, Mass.: Harvard University Press, 1978).

Mirowski, Philip (ed.), *Natural Images in Economic Thought: 'Markets Read in Tooth and Claw'* (Cambridge University Press, 1994).

Morrow, John, 'Private Property, Liberal Subjects, and the State', in Simhony and Weinstein, 92–114.

Mulgan, Tim, *The Demands of Consequentialism* (Oxford: Clarendon Press, 2001).

Myers, William, *The Teaching of George Eliot* (New Jersey: Barnes & Noble, 1984).

Nelson, Julie A., *Economics for Humans* (University of Chicago Press, 2006).

Newton, K. M., *George Eliot: Romantic Humanist* (London: Macmillan, 1981).

Modernizing George Eliot: The Writer as Artist, Intellectual, Proto-Modernist, Cultural Critic (London: Bloomsbury Academic, 2011).

Nunokawa, Jeff, *The Afterlife of Property: Domestic Security and the Victorian Novel* (Princeton University Press, 1994).

Nussbaum, Martha, *The Fragility of Goodness: Luck and Ethics in Greek Tragedy and Philosophy* (Cambridge University Press, 1986).

Love's Knowledge: Essays on Philosophy and Literature (Oxford University Press, 1990).

O'Brien, D. P., *The Classical Economists Revisited* (Princeton University Press, 2004).

O'Gorman, Francis (ed.), *Victorian Literature and Finance* (Oxford University Press, 2007).

Owen, W. C., *The Economics of Herbert Spencer*, 1891 edn (Honolulu: University Press of the Pacific, 2002).

Paris, Bernard J., *Experiments in Life: George Eliot's Quest for Values* (Detroit: Wayne State University Press, 1965).

Parry, J. P., 'Liberalism and Liberty' in Peter Mandler (ed.), *Liberty and Authority in Victorian Britain* (Oxford University Press, 2006), 71–100.

The Rise and Fall of Liberal Government in Victorian Britain (New Haven: Yale University Press, 1993).

Pattison, Mark, 'Philosophy at Oxford', *Mind*, 1, 1 (1876), 82–97.

Paxton, Nancy L., *George Eliot and Herbert Spencer: Feminism, Evolutionism and the Reconstruction of Gender* (Princeton University Press, 1991).

Payne, David, *The Reenchantment of Nineteenth-Century Fiction: Dickens, Thackeray, George Eliot, and Serialization* (Basingstoke: Palgrave Macmillan, 2005).

Peart, Sandra, *The Economics of W. S. Jevons* (London: Routledge, 1996).

Peel, J. D. Y., *Herbert Spencer: The Evolution of a Sociologist* (London: Heinemann, 1971).

Perkin, Harold, *The Origins of Modern English Society, 1780–1880* (London: Routledge & Kegan Paul, 1969).

Pettitt, Clare, *Patent Inventions: Intellectual Property and the Victorian Novel* (Oxford University Press, 2004).

Pigou, A. C. (ed.), *Memorials of Alfred Marshall* (London: Macmillan, 1925).

Plotz, John, *Portable Property: Victorian Culture on the Move* (Princeton University Press, 2008).

Poovey, Mary, *Genres of the Credit Economy: Mediating Value in Eighteenth- and Nineteenth-Century Britain* (University of Chicago Press, 2008).

A History of the Modern Fact: Problems of Knowledge in the Sciences of Wealth and Society (University of Chicago Press, 1998).

Making a Social Body: British Cultural Formation, 1830–1864 (University of Chicago Press, 1995).

'Writing about Finance in Victorian England: Disclosure and Secrecy in the Culture of Investment', in Henry and Schmitt, 39–57.

Pratt, John Clark and Victor A. Neufeldt (eds.), *George Eliot's Middlemarch Notebooks* (Berkeley: University of California Press, 1979).

[Procter, R. A.], 'Gambling Superstitions', *Cornhill Magazine*, 25 (June 1872), 704–17.

Raphael, D. D., *The Impartial Spectator: Adam Smith's Moral Philosophy* (Oxford: Clarendon Press, 2007).

Ratcliffe, Sophie, *On Sympathy* (Oxford: Clarendon Press, 2008).

Redinger, Ruby V., *George Eliot: The Emergent Self* (New York: Alfred A. Knopf, 1975).

Redman, Deborah A., *The Rise of Political Economy as a Science: Methodology and the Classical Economists* (Cambridge, Mass.: MIT Press, 1997).

Reed, John R., 'A Friend to Mammon: Speculation in Victorian Literature', *Victorian Studies*, 27 (1983–4), 179–202.

Ricardo, David, *On the Principles of Political Economy and Taxation*, Vol. 1 of *The Works and Correspondence of David Ricardo*, ed. Piero Sraffa, with the collaboration of M. H. Dobb, 11 vols. (Indianapolis: Liberty Fund, 2004).

Ritchie, D. G., *The Principles of State Interference: Four Essays on the Political Philosophy of Mr. Herbert Spencer, J. S. Mill, and T. H. Green* (London: Swan Sonnenschein, 1891).

Robertson, Linda K., *The Power of Knowledge: George Eliot and Education* (New York: Peter Lang, 1997).

Rothschild, Emma, *Economic Sentiments: Adam Smith, Condorcet, and the Enlightenment* (Cambridge, Mass.: Harvard University Press, 2001).

Ruskin, John, *'Unto this Last': Four Essays on the First Principles of Political Economy* (London: George Allen, 1907).

Ruth, Jennifer, *Novel Professions: Interested Disinterest and the Making of the Professional in the Victorian Novel* (Columbus: The Ohio State University Press, 2006).

Rylance, Rick, *Victorian Psychology and British Culture 1850–1880* (Oxford University Press, 2000).

Sachs, Jeffrey, *The Price of Civilization: Economics and Ethics After the Fall* (London: Bodley Head, 2011).

Saint-Amour, Paul K., *The Copywrights: Intellectual Property and the Literary Imagination* (Ithaca: Cornell University Press, 2003).

Sandel, Michael J., 'What Money Can't Buy: The Moral Limits of Markets', the Tanner Lectures on Human Values (Brasenose College, Oxford; 11–12 May 1998).

What Money Can't Buy: The Moral Limits of Markets (London: Allen Lane, 2012).

Schabas, Margaret, *The Natural Origin of Economics* (University of Chicago Press, 2005).

Schneewind, J. B., *Sidgwick's Ethics and Victorian Moral Philosophy* (Oxford: Clarendon Press, 1977).

Scitovsky, Tibor, *The Joyless Economy: The Psychology of Human Satisfaction*, revised edn (Oxford University Press, 1992).

Searle, G. R., *Morality and the Market in Victorian Britain* (Oxford: Clarendon Press, 1998).

Searle, John R., *Making the Social World: The Structure of Human Civilization* (Oxford University Press, 2010).

Sen, Amartya, 'On the Foundations of Welfare Economics: Utility, Capability and Practical Reason', in Farina, Hahn and Vannucci, 50–65.

Senior, Nassau W., *Selected Writings on Economics 1827–1852* (Honolulu: University Press of the Pacific, 1996).

Shell, Marc, *The Economy of Literature* (Baltimore: Johns Hopkins University Press, 1978).

  Money, Language, and Thought: Literary and Philosophical Economies from the Medieval to the Modern Era (Berkeley: University of California Press, 1982).

Shiller, Robert J., *Finance and the Good Society* (Princeton University Press, 2012).

Shrimpton, Nicholas, '"Even These Metallic Problems have Their Melodramatic Side": Money in Victorian Literature', in O'Gorman, 17–38.

Shuttleworth, Sally, *George Eliot and Nineteenth-Century Science: The Make-Believe of a Beginning* (Cambridge University Press, 1984).

Sidgwick, Henry, *Lectures on the Ethics of T. H. Green, Mr. Herbert Spencer, and J. Martineau* (London: Macmillan, 1902).

  The Methods of Ethics (London: Macmillan, 1874).

  'Philosophy at Cambridge', *Mind*, 1, 2 (1876), 235–46.

  The Principles of Political Economy (London: Macmillan, 1883).

Simmel, Georg, *Philosophy of Money*, 3rd enlarged edn, trans. Tom Bottomore and David Frisby, ed. David Frisby (London: Routledge, 1978).

Simhony, Avital, 'T. H. Green's Complex Common Good: Between Liberalism and Communitarianism', in Simhony and Weinstein, 69–91.

Simhony, Avital, and David Weinstein (eds.), *The New Liberalism: Reconciling Liberty and Community* (Cambridge University Press, 2001).

Skidelsky, Robert, *Keynes: The Return of the Master* (London: Allen Lane, 2009).

Skidelsky, Robert and Edward Skidelsky, *How Much is Enough? The Love of Money, and the Case for the Good Life* (London: Allen Lane, 2012).

Slote, Michael, 'Some Advantages of Virtue Ethics', in Flanagan and Oksenberg Rorty, 429–48.

Small, Helen, 'Chances Are: Henry Buckle, Thomas Hardy, and the Individual at Risk', in Helen Small and Trudi Tate (eds.), *Literature, Science, Psychoanalysis, 1830–1970: Essays in Honour of Gillian Beer* (Oxford University Press, 2003), 64–85.

Smart, J. J. C. and Bernard Williams, *Utilitarianism: For and Against* (Cambridge University Press, 1973).

Smiles, Samuel, *Self Help: With illustrations of Character, Conduct, and Perseverance*, ed. Peter W. Sinnema (Oxford University Press, 2002).

Smith, Adam, *An Inquiry into the Nature and Causes of the Wealth of Nations*, ed. R. H. Campbell and A. S. Skinner, textual ed. W. B. Todd, 2 vols. (Oxford: Clarendon Press, 1976).

   Lectures on Jurisprudence, ed. R. L. Meek, D. D. Raphael and P. G. Stein (Oxford: Clarendon Press, 1978).

   The Theory of Moral Sentiments, ed. D. D. Raphael and A. L. Macfie (Oxford: Clarendon Press, 1976).

Spencer, Herbert, *Herbert Spencer on Education*, ed. F. A. Cavenagh (Cambridge University Press, 1932).

   The Man Versus the State (1884) (Indianapolis: Liberty Fund, 1982).

   'The Morals of Trade', *Westminster Review*, 71 (Apr. 1859), 357–90.

   'Parliamentary Reform: The Dangers, and the Safeguards, *Westminster Review*, 17, 2 (1860), 486–507.

Spiegel, Henry William, *The Growth of Economic Thought*, 3rd edn (Durham: Duke University Press, 1991).

Stephen, Leslie, *Life of Henry Fawcett* (London: Smith, Elder, 1885).

   The English Utilitarians, 3 vols. (London: Duckworth, 1900).

Sugden, Robert, 'Beyond Sympathy and Empathy: Adam Smith's Concept of Fellow-Feeling', *Economics and Philosophy*, 18, 1 (2002), 63–87.

Sutherland, Gillian, 'Education', in F. M. L. Thompson (ed.), *The Cambridge Social History of Britain, 1750–1950*, 3 vols. (Cambridge University Press, 1990), 1, 119–69.

Swanton, Christine, *Virtue Ethics: A Pluralistic View* (Oxford University Press, 2003).

Swedberg, Richard, 'Max Weber's Economic Sociology: The Centerpiece of Economy and Society?' in Charles Camic, Philip S. Gorski and David M. Trubek (eds.), *Max Weber's Economy and Society: A Critical Companion* (Stanford University Press, 2005), 127–42.

Taylor, James, *Creating Capitalism: Joint-Stock Enterprise in British Politics and Culture, 1800–1870* (Woodbridge: The Boydell Press, 2006).

Tett, Gillian, *Fool's Gold: How Unrestrained Greed Corrupted a Dream, Shattered Global Markets and Unleashed Catastrophe* (London: Little Brown, 2009).

Thompson, James, *Models of Value: Eighteenth-Century Political Economy and the Novel* (Durham: Duke University Press, 1996).

Trigilia, Carlo, *Economic Sociology: State, Market, and Society in Modern Capitalism* (Oxford: Blackwell, 1998).

Trollope, Anthony, *An Autobiography*, ed. Michael Sadlier and Frederick Page (Oxford University Press, 1998).

   The Prime Minister, ed. Jennifer Uglow (Oxford University Press, 1999).

Vermeule, Blakey, *Why Do We Care About Literary Characters?* (Baltimore: The Johns Hopkins University Press, 2010).

Vernon, John, *Money and Fiction: Literary Realism in the Nineteenth and Early Twentieth Centuries* (Ithaca: Cornell University Press, 1984).

Vincent, Andrew, 'The New Liberalism and Citizenship', in Simhony and Weinstein, 205–27.

Vincent, Andrew and Raymond Plant, *Philosophy, Politics and Citizenship: The Life and Thought of the British Idealists* (Oxford: Basil Blackwell, 1984).

Wagner, Tamara S., *Financial Speculation in Victorian Fiction: Plotting Money and the Novel Genre, 1815–1901* (Columbus: Ohio State University Press, 2010).

Wainwright, Valerie, *Ethics and the English Novel from Austen to Forster* (Aldershot: Ashgate, 2007).

Waterman, A. M. C., *Revolution, Economics and Religion: Christian Political Economy, 1798–1833* (Cambridge University Press, 1991).

Watson, Gary, 'On the Primacy of Character', in Flanagan and Oksenberg Rorty, 449–69.

Weber, Max, *Economy and Society: An Outline of Interpretive Sociology*, ed. Guenther Roth and Claus Wittich (Berkeley: University of California Press, 1978).

The Protestant Ethic and the Spirit of Capitalism, trans. Talcott Parsons (London: George Allen & Unwin, 1930).

Weinstein D., *Equal Freedom and Utility: Herbert Spencer's Liberal Utilitarianism* (Cambridge University Press, 2006).

Weiss, Barbara, *The Hell of the English: Bankruptcy and the Victorian Novel* (Lewisburg: Bucknell University Press, 1986).

Welsh, Alexander, *George Eliot and Blackmail* (Cambridge, Mass.: Harvard University Press, 1985).

Winch, Donald, *Riches and Poverty: An Intellectual History of Political Economy in Britain, 1750–1834* (Cambridge University Press, 1996).

Wealth and Life: Essays on the Intellectual History of Political Economy in Britain, 1848–1914 (Cambridge University Press, 2009).

Woodmansee, Martha, *The Author, Art, and the Market: Rereading the History of Aesthetics* (New York: Columbia University Press, 1994).

Woodmansee, Martha and Mark Osteen (eds.), *The New Economic Criticism: Studies at the Intersection of Literature and Economics* (London and New York: Routledge, 1999).

Wright, T. R., *The Religion of Humanity: The Impact of Comtean Positivism on Victorian Britain* (Cambridge University Press, 1986).

Wrigley, E. A., *Poverty, Progress, and Population* (Cambridge University Press, 2004).

Wynne, Deborah, *Women and Personal Property in the Victorian Novel* (Farnham: Ashgate, 2010).

Zelizer, Viviana A., *The Purchase of Intimacy* (Princeton University Press, 2005).

The Social Meaning of Money (New York: Basic Books, 1994).

Index

CAMBRIDGE STUDIES IN NINETEENTH-CENTURY
LITERATURE AND CULTURE

General editor

Gillian Beer, *University of Cambridge*

Titles published